Doing
Social

Studies
IN
Morning Meeting

150 Quick Activities
THAT
Connect TO Your Curriculum

Leah Carson ■ Jane Cofie

All net proceeds from the sale of this book support the work of Center for Responsive Schools, a not-for-profit educational organization and the developer of the *Responsive Classroom*® approach to teaching.

ISBN: 978-1-892989-88-8
Library of Congress Control Number: 2017938218

Book design by Helen Merena
Illustrations for cover and introduction © Lynn Zimmerman, Lucky Dog Design. All rights reserved.

Center for Responsive Schools, Inc.
85 Avenue A, P.O. Box 718
Turners Falls, MA 01376-0718

800-360-6332
www.responsiveclassroom.org

Third printing 2021

Printed on recycled paper

Contents

Social Studies Belongs in Morning Meeting

The advancement of "liberty and justice for all" . . . requires that citizens have the knowledge, attitudes and values to both guard and endorse the principles of a constitutional democracy. . . . If the young learners of this nation are to become effective participants in a democratic society, then social studies must be an essential part of the curriculum in each of the elementary years.

—Task Force on Early Childhood/Elementary Studies
and members of the NCSS Board of Directors

Picture the children you teach. At recess, are they playing games and following a set of rules they all agree on? During lunch, are they listening to and talking respectfully with their tablemates? In the classroom, are they working cooperatively on assignments and taking care of the room, classroom supplies, and each other?

As students interact in everyday school activities, they're developing key social-emotional skills. They're also participating in experiences that are fundamental to social studies—the study of how human societies work. The more of these types of experiences we provide students throughout the school day, the more we foster the academic, social, emotional, and civic growth that paves the way to their becoming contributing, active members of a civil society.

The *Responsive Classroom®* practice of Morning Meeting offers an ideal opportunity to keep social studies alive and present beyond its often tightly scheduled block of instructional time. Morning Meeting gives students more opportunities to think about the social studies content they've been learning; to explore concepts, issues, and skills in new and engaging ways; and to investigate and propose solutions to fun, interesting challenges that connect to their personal lives, school, and community.

In a very real sense, Morning Meeting *is* social studies. According to the National Council for the Social Studies, "the primary purpose of social studies is to help young people make informed and reasoned decisions for the public good as citizens of a culturally diverse, democratic society in an interdependent world" (NCSS, 1994). During Morning Meeting, students are actively participating in authentic experiences that embody many key social studies concepts. They're learning to interact with peers in respectful ways, to appreciate differences, and to build empathy through commonalities.

With its lively interactivity, Morning Meeting offers numerous opportunities for making challenging social studies concepts such as map skills, economic principles, and models of government more tangible and thus more easily grasped. Students learn better—and remember more of what they learn—when they can link social studies concepts with things they care about in their own lives: making and maintaining friendships, feeling a sense of belonging and significance, and meeting academic and social-emotional challenges in a safe and cooperative environment.

The four-component structure of Morning Meeting (greeting, sharing, group activity, and morning message) offers a perfect context in which to use meaningful social interactions as a way to deepen students' understanding of core social studies concepts, content, and issues in safe, engaging ways.

- During **greeting**, students welcome everyone to the classroom (and the day) as equal and valued participants in a social group dedicated to learning.

- For **sharing**, students hear one another's thoughts and ideas about various aspects of their current learning and discover respectful ways to respond to multiple perspectives.

- With **group activity**, students interact with one another in fun and lively ways while also stretching their social skills and deepening their understanding of academic content.

- A social-studies-oriented **morning message** (linked to previous or upcoming learning) gives students the opportunity to reflect on and interact with social studies concepts, content, or skills and build confidence, competence, and curiosity.

The social studies activities in this book are easy to prepare for and straightforward to teach, and they're engaging for students. Because every state's social studies curriculum standards vary, we based our choice of topics and activities on the

National Curriculum Standards for Social Studies—The Themes of Social Studies and the *College, Career, & Civic Life C3 Framework for Social Studies State Standards.**

With this firm foundation, we designed activities that cover a broad range of social studies topics and skills—activities that you can use "as is" to support and bolster your teaching. Besides embodying many essential social studies concepts and skills, these activities are also flexible in terms of content, so you can easily adapt them to better target your specific curriculum needs.

In addition, the activities have been selected to get students more engaged in learning history, geography, civics, economics, and other fundamental areas of social studies curriculum. You'll soon see how easy it can be to do social studies in Morning Meeting and to teach students to become active, compassionate, and enlightened participants in our communities, our country, and the world. This book will help your students become enthusiastic learners of all things social studies and carry that knowledge and skill set with them throughout school and into their adult lives.

Morning Meetings and Social Studies

Responsive Classroom Morning Meeting offers teachers a structured, purposeful, and fun way to start each day on a positive note and build a strong sense of classroom community. Beginning the day in such a powerful way sets students up for success for the day and enables them to approach learning with an open mind and a willingness to take academic risks. Morning Meeting:

- Typically occurs at the beginning of the school day and lasts about 20 to 30 minutes

- Takes place in a circle in which everyone can see and be seen by everyone else, and follows a predictable structure that students come to rely on

- Gives teachers and students a chance to explore academics in playful, interesting, and intriguing ways while simultaneously building community and social skills

In a world filled with academic pressure and high-stakes testing, the opportunity Morning Meeting offers for exploring academic concepts and skills in such an engaging and supportive way makes it a fruitful and essential part of each classroom day.

*Note: Because this book is not intended as a curriculum, but as a supplement to whatever curriculum you're using, it does not address every C3 Framework or Common Core standard.

Social Studies in Each Component of Morning Meeting

Morning Meeting has four components: greeting, sharing, group activity, and morning message. Each component has a specific purpose and offers different, but equally powerful, ways to explore social studies content.

GREETING

At the start of each Morning Meeting, students greet each other by name.

PURPOSES

- Set a positive tone for the day

- Provide a sense of recognition and belonging

- Help students learn each other's names and foster friendships

- Build friendly social skills that enable students to learn together

EXAMPLES

- Students go around the circle and greet each other with a simple "Good morning, _____."

- Students mix and mingle, greeting as many classmates as possible in a minute.

- For variety, students can add a high-five or special handshake, or chant each student's name to a certain rhythm.

BRINGING SOCIAL STUDIES INTO GREETINGS

- Students greet each other with a friendly "Hello" and then add a fact about an institution they've been studying: "Hello, Mallory! A bank is an institution that keeps people's money safe."

- Students mingle to greet a few classmates by sharing a quote from a Supreme Court justice.

- As students toss a ball around the circle, they recall facts about or make connections to the terms, ideas, or places listed on the ball.

SHARING

During sharing, students present news or information that helps the class get to know them and their ideas.

PURPOSES

- Practice speaking and listening skills (especially speaking in a group and careful listening)

- Develop vocabulary and language skills

- Get to know classmates

EXAMPLES

- **Around-the-circle sharing**—Each student briefly shares in response to the same prompt from the teacher.

- **Partner sharing**—Students talk about a specified topic with a partner (or small group).

- **Dialogue sharing**—Each day, a few students share in greater detail about an assigned or open topic and take a few questions or comments from classmates about what they shared.

BRINGING SOCIAL STUDIES INTO SHARING

- Students take turns, going around the circle, sharing about a place they'd like to explore and one reason why.

- With a partner or small group, students talk about how a historical event might have looked to people representing two different perspectives, such as patriots and loyalists during the American Revolutionary War.

- As students share their design for a postage stamp commemorating a personal hero, the class discusses ideas about identity and the importance of ordinary people within a community.

GROUP ACTIVITY

Group activities give students a variety of ways to interact, cooperate, and have fun together.

PURPOSES

- Foster active, engaged participation

- Develop a shared repertoire of activities, including energizers, chants, and songs

EXAMPLES

- **Whole class**—While a poem is read aloud, students perform movements (chosen ahead of time) for specific words or stanzas.

- **Pairs**—Two students work together on a challenge, such as sequencing a timeline of events.

- **Small groups (or whole class)**—One student chooses a specific topic and classmates ask that student questions before guessing the answer.

BRINGING SOCIAL STUDIES INTO GROUP ACTIVITIES

- Students chant or sing a song (set to a familiar tune) about social studies content—for example, methods of modern transportation or the names of the seven continents.

- Students create a chronological sequence of events that an immigrant would have experienced traveling to Ellis Island during the late 19th and early 20th centuries.

- One student chooses a social studies event, idea, or historic change and classmates ask that student questions before guessing the answer.

MORNING MESSAGE

Before students arrive, the teacher writes a brief, academically related message to welcome them. Students read the message individually as they enter the classroom and then read it again in a designated way (for example, chorally) to work with the message during Morning Meeting.

PURPOSES

- Reinforce reading and other academic skills

- Engage children in exploring social and academic topics

- Generate interest and excitement for the day's learning

EXAMPLE

Dear Thoughtful Observers,

Artifacts can yield clues about how people in a particular culture lived and what they thought was important. What do you notice or wonder about the artifact below that might tell you something about the people who made or used it? Write your thoughts on a sticky note and post it below.

BRINGING SOCIAL STUDIES INTO MORNING MESSAGES

- A message like the one shown above helps students stretch their thinking about a culture they've been studying by reflecting on an everyday object that people used.

- Students review what they've been learning about maps with the help of a message that invites them to decide what features they would add to a simple school map to make it more helpful.

- A message about significant women in history helps students look forward to a lesson later that day or week and gives them a chance to make connections to other events, people, and technology based on their prior knowledge.

What's Special About the Activities in This Book?

The activities in this book combine the community- and confidence-building goals of Morning Meeting with the goal of giving students meaningful experiences and practice with social studies. These activities also address the practical considerations that are at the heart of every teacher's busy days and are designed to:

Take little time—Activities are intentionally designed to be quick to do so they fit easily into the Morning Meeting structure. Most take only five to ten minutes.

Require few materials—Many activities require no materials at all. When materials are required, they're simple objects or supplies that are most often readily available to teachers, familiar to students, and easy to care for.

Be easy to manage—Activities are structured with a limited number of easy-to-learn steps and clear, detailed instructions.

Offer variety—This collection covers a broad variety of social studies topics and skills, so no matter which curriculum or standards you're using, you'll find activities to complement and support your teaching.

Include everyone—The activities in this book are designed to focus on cooperation rather than competition and to build a sense of community and foster each student's sense of belonging, key goals of Morning Meeting.

Cross subjects—Although the primary academic focus of each activity is social studies, many activities touch on other curriculum areas as well. For example, most activities give students practice with the speaking and listening skills addressed in the Common Core State Standards for English Language Arts. These connections to standards are listed in the side columns for easy reference.

Why Morning Meeting is a Great Time to Do Social Studies

- Provides engaging ways to capitalize on children's natural curiosity about the world and its people, places, and environments

- Is a safe time for positive risk-taking

- Brings social studies content to life through active (hands-on) and interactive (social) learning

- Enables students to practice communicating their social studies thinking

- Links social studies with fun

- Shows students that social studies content and ideas are an essential part of everyday life—all day long, inside and outside the classroom

Getting the Most From This Book

You can use this book in many ways:

- **Browse the activities for your grade level.** Look for those that are specifically designed for the grade you teach.

- **Use the tables starting on page 177.** Look for activities that address the social studies content and standards on which your curriculum focuses.

- **Skim the whole book.** Choose activities that appeal to you and adapt them, if necessary, to fit your class's grade and skill level.

Regardless of which approach you use, keep in mind the following tips for getting the most out of this book.

Stick to the Morning Meeting basics
Be sure you and your class have developed strong
Morning Meeting routines:

- **Have a supportive physical environment.** You'll need a large enough space for the whole class to gather in a circle. (In some smaller classrooms, students can learn how to safely and efficiently move furniture to clear a space if necessary.) You'll also need a display space that enables all students to easily read and access the message, whether on chart paper or a whiteboard.

- **Share with students why Morning Meetings matter.** All of us do best when we understand the goals of what we're doing. At the beginning of the year and periodically throughout the year, explain to students why Morning Meetings are important to them and the classroom community.

- **Teach the behaviors necessary for Morning Meetings** to run smoothly and feel safe for all. Among other things, teach students how to:

  - ➤ Move to and from the circle, and where and how to sit in the circle

  - ➤ Respond to a signal for quiet attention

  - ➤ Greet others in a safe and friendly way

  - ➤ Share information, ask questions, and make comments

Use Interactive Modeling (see next page) to teach and frequently revisit these behaviors. As students practice and grow in their skill level, be sure to reinforce their efforts to do routines as taught and help them quickly get back on track if they forget to do so.

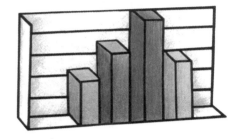

Introduce activities carefully

To get the most out of these activities:

- **Gather any required materials** ahead of time.

- **Consider what skills students may need to review** before beginning an activity. For instance, for greetings, you may want to quickly remind students about the characteristics of a friendly greeting.

- **Model key aspects of the activity as needed** and consider doing a practice round before starting "officially." Interactive Modeling starts with the teacher naming and then modeling a desired action or behavior. Then it actively involves students in noticing, naming, and practicing aspects of the modeled action or behavior. These extra steps help students better grasp and remember new routines. In the following example, the teacher follows the steps of Interactive Modeling to show students how to respond to a signal for quiet attention. (Note that in this example, the teacher has asked two students ahead of time to assist with the modeling.)

   1. **Say what you will model and why:** "There will be times during Morning Meeting when I will need to get your attention quickly. The way I'll signal for you to stop and listen is to ring this chime. I'm going to show you what to do when you hear it. Watch me and see what you notice."

   2. **Model the behavior:** Teacher pretends to be involved in a partner share with student 1, Brandon. When student 2, Lena, rings the chime, Teacher and Brandon quickly wrap up their conversation, put their hands in their laps, and look at Lena.

   3. **Ask students what they noticed.** Possible student answers: "You stopped talking." "You both looked at Lena."

   4. **Invite one or more students to model:** "Who would like to show us how to respond to the chime the same way Brandon and I did?" Teacher chooses two volunteers.

   5. **Again, ask students what they noticed:** Teacher leads the class in a discussion of what they noticed about the two volunteers modeling.

   6. **Have all students practice:** "Now everyone will practice. Your job is to respond to the chime just the way you saw us do it. This time I'll do the watching and noticing."

   7. **Provide feedback:** "That was so fast! You ended your conversations and turned toward me, and your quiet faces tell me you're ready to listen to what comes next."

As students become familiar with the Morning Meeting format and desired actions and behaviors, you may find that abbreviated Interactive Modeling (steps 4–7) is all you need to review expectations.

- **Scaffold.** It's essential to break down Morning Meeting skills and routines based on students' developmental needs and abilities and then gradually put the pieces together. For instance, teach a complex activity in small chunks over a couple of days. Use the following guidelines to help you adjust the complexity of an idea so that it's appropriate for students at any given point in the school year.

  - **Phase in Morning Meeting** by teaching one component at a time. (The best order of introduction is greeting, group activity, morning message, and sharing, even though this isn't their eventual order in Morning Meeting.)

  - **Break down routines into bite-sized pieces.** For example, before introducing a greeting that involves saying a classmate's name, asking and answering a question, and doing a handshake, be sure you've taught—and students have a solid command of—each of these elements.

  - **Use reinforcing language and open-ended questions** to help students build and expand their skills. Use the examples in individual activities for reference. Be sure to give some think time after posing a question before signaling students to start the next step.

  - **Spread out an activity over a few days or a week.** For example, with the Time Capsule sharing (see page 20), you might scaffold it so that students first bring in their three pictures, work on their three sentences another day, and then share about their pictures at a future Morning Meeting.

  - **Know that it's OK to repeat an idea multiple times.** As students gain expertise, introduce variations one at a time. To keep students engaged, try to balance repetition, variety, and challenge.

  - **Write out chants, songs, poems, and other helpful texts.** Also consider using anchor charts, such as for timelines and cardinal directions.

  - **Keep it simple.** Doing so helps students stay focused and keeps them from getting overwhelmed.

- **Preview activities when appropriate.** For instance, if you know you're going to ask students to share on a specific social studies topic, give them a heads-up a day or two before the sharing so that they'll have time to think about what they want to say.

Vary and modify activities

All the activities in this book can be adapted to a variety of situations. Here are some things to consider when modifying activities:

- **Choose activities according to your teaching purposes.** With a little modification, activities might be used to activate students' prior knowledge at the start of a new unit, enable students to practice skills they're learning or deepen their understanding of content, or help students make connections or review information they've already learned.

- **Adapt activities to current content.** For instance, some of the greetings in this book involve using a set of matching content-based cards (for example, historical events and their key participants). Each student receives a card, finds a person with the matching card, and then greets that person. This type of greeting is easily adaptable to a wide variety of social studies topics and terms.

- **Consider your school's policies** or students' needs in regard to touching. If your school prohibits student contact or you feel that students aren't developmentally ready for it, adjust activities accordingly. For instance, instead of shaking hands during a greeting, students can simply look at each other, smile, and speak their greeting words.

- **Support English language learners and emerging readers.** The activities in this book can give all students, including English language learners, a chance to successfully engage with rich social studies content. If your students need additional support, use sentence frames for some of the greeting and sharing ideas, add picture clues to morning messages, let students write out what they're going to say for certain sharing topics, or have students pair up to do certain greetings or group activities.

- **Adjust the reading level of messages as needed.** Throughout the book, we provide sample social studies messages for each of the grade levels (K–6), but you may want to adapt particular messages to meet your students' specific needs.

- **Adjust for any time constraints.** For example, if you want to spend more time on a group activity or are trying one that may be a bit challenging for your class, use a shorter and simpler greeting, sharing, and morning message that day.

Look beyond your grade level

With some adaptation, most of the activities in this book
can be used in any grade.

■ **If you teach younger grades,** you may be able to use an older grade activity after simplifying some of the vocabulary or content.

■ **If you teach older grades,** your students will likely enjoy some of the games and activities from the younger sections, especially by doing more challenging variations.

Branching out beyond your grade level and adjusting activities as needed will open up many more learning opportunities for your students.

Consider students' needs, interests, and abilities

Morning Meetings are designed to set a positive tone for the day
and to help students make a successful start.

■ **Choose activities** that allow students to practice or apply social studies skills or concepts you've already presented to them, rather than introducing new content.

■ **Avoid playing it too safe,** or students will lose interest. Aim for activities challenging enough to engage every child, yet not so challenging as to be discouraging.

Use, Adapt, Invent, Enjoy!

The activities in this book will inspire both you and your students to think like historians, geographers, economists, and engaged citizens of a participatory democracy. As you probe questions, explore social studies concepts, and help students extend their understanding out into the world, remember to have fun, embrace mistakes as opportunities for learning, and keep a curious and open mind.

References

National Council for Social Studies, *Expectations of Excellence: Curriculum Standards for Social Studies* (Washington, D.C.: NCSS, 1994): 3.

Task Force on Early Childhood/Elementary Studies and Members of the NCSS Board of Directors (2009). *Powerful and Purposeful Teaching and Learning in Elementary School Social Studies*. National Council for the Social Studies (NCSS).

Visit us online to download sample materials and handouts.

Some activities (where indicated) include sample cards, facts, or other materials you can download to help you prepare for the activity. You'll find the complete list of available materials to download here:

www.responsiveclassroom.org/product/doing-social-studies-in-morning-meeting/

Grade Level
K
Greeting

Address Match

Social Studies Content
Address

NCSS Standards Theme
People, Places, and Environments

C3 Framework
D2.Geo.2.K–2 Use maps, graphs, photographs, and other representations to describe places and the relationships and interactions that shape them.

Common Core Standards
SL.K.1 Participate in collaborative conversations with diverse partners about kindergarten topics and texts with peers and adults in small and larger groups.

SL.K.6 Speak audibly and express thoughts, feelings, and ideas clearly.

Materials Needed
Matching sets of index cards or slips of paper with 1- and 2-digit numbers written on them

Vocabulary
Address

How to do it:

1 Hand out one card to each student. Then introduce the greeting: "The buildings we live in have numbers on them that help us tell which building is which. The number of your building is part of your address."

2 Explain how to do the greeting: "Today, we'll do a mix-and-mingle greeting. Each of you will find one classmate with an address number that matches yours. When you find that person, shake hands and say 'Good morning, _____. We have the same address!' Then return to your circle spot."

3 Remind students of safe movement: "What are some ways we can move around safely during our greeting?"

4 Start the greeting. When all students have returned to their spots, reinforce their efforts: "You paid careful attention to the addresses on your cards!"

VARIATION

■ Have students stay in pairs when they return to the circle. When all students are in place, have each pair hold up their cards and say together: "Our address number is _____."

EXTENDING THE SOCIAL STUDIES LEARNING BEYOND MORNING MEETING

■ Display a photograph of one or more buildings with the address numbers clearly visible. Talk about why it's helpful to be able to tell which building is which (for example, so the postal carrier knows where to deliver mail).

Greeting Now and Long Ago

Social Studies Content

Past and present

NCSS Standards Theme

Individual Development and Identity

C3 Framework

D2.His.2.K–2 Compare life in the past to life today.

Common Core Standards

RI.K.10 Actively engage in group reading activities with purpose and understanding. (Extending the learning)

SL.K.1 Participate in collaborative conversations with diverse partners about kindergarten topics and texts with peers and adults in small and larger groups.

SL.K.6 Speak audibly and express thoughts, feelings, and ideas clearly.

Materials Needed

None

Vocabulary

Long ago
Now

How to do it:

1 Introduce the greeting: "We're going to compare how we greet each other now to a way that people greeted each other long ago. What are some ways we greet each other now?"

2 Agree on one modern greeting, such as "Hello, _____, what's up?" or "Hi there, _____!" Model and practice a friendly way to do this "now" greeting.

3 Explain how to do a greeting from the past: "Long ago, many people greeted each other by shaking hands and saying 'Good day, sir' or 'Good day, ma'am.' People responded by saying 'Good day to you, too.'" Model and practice this greeting.

4 Pass the "long ago" greeting around the circle. Then reverse direction and have students greet each other with the "now" greeting.

5 Reinforce students' efforts: "I saw lots of smiles and heard friendly voices!"

VARIATION

■ Have students brainstorm how people might greet each other in the future (with words and gestures).

EXTENDING THE SOCIAL STUDIES LEARNING BEYOND MORNING MEETING

■ Read a book about long ago, such as one from the list below. Have students discuss the similarities and differences between the book's time period and now.

➤ *Grandfather's Journey* by Allen Say

➤ *A Medieval Feast* by Aliki

➤ *Twenty-One Elephants and Still Standing* by April Jones Prince, illustrated by François Roca

Kind Kids Greeting

Social Studies Content

Kindness

NCSS Standards Theme

Culture and Cultural Diversity

C3 Framework

D2.Civ.7.K–2 Apply civic
virtues when participating
in school settings.

D2.Civ.8.K–2 Describe
democratic principles such as
equality, fairness, and respect
for legitimate authority
and rules.

Common Core Standards

L.K.5 With guidance and
support from adults, explore
word relationships and
nuances in word meanings.

Materials Needed

None

Vocabulary

Caring
Generous
Kind
Respectful

How to do it:

1 Introduce the greeting: "When we get along with each other, it's easier to learn and play together. Being kind helps us get along. What are some ways we can show kindness to other people in our classroom?" Take a few responses. Then expand the discussion: "What are some ways we can show kindness to people in our families?"

2 Explain how to do the greeting: "We know lots of ways to show kindness. For today's greeting, we're going to sing a song about kindness, and it's going to include all your names! When you hear your name, wave to the class."

3 Teach the song (to the tune of *Twinkle, Twinkle, Little Star*) by having students repeat each line after you:

FIRST STANZA:

> *We are kind kids, yes we are!*
> *We help others near and far.*

SECOND STANZA (INSERT STUDENTS' NAMES):

> *Kiera, Luke, Tamika, and Sam*
> *Nural, José, Sienna, and Tim . . .*
> *[continue until all students have been named]*

THIRD STANZA:

> *We show kindness every day*
> *When we work and when we play!*

VARIATION

■ Adapt the song for other character traits, such as *generosity, respectfulness,* and *caring.* Have students brainstorm ways they can show these traits in what they say and do.

**EXTENDING THE SOCIAL STUDIES LEARNING
BEYOND MORNING MEETING**

■ Find one or more news articles about children in other parts of the world who help others. Share and discuss these stories with students.

Red, White, and Blue: Good Morning to You!

How to do it:

In advance, make sure you have two more cubes of each color than the number of students in your class. For example, for 19 students, have 21 red, 21 white, and 21 blue cubes. Each student should start out with three cubes of the same color.

1 Introduce the greeting: "We've been learning about symbols that represent our country. One American symbol is our flag. The colors in our flag are red, white, and blue. Today we're going to do a red, white, and blue greeting."

2 Explain how to do the greeting: "You'll start with three cubes, either all red, all white, or all blue. When you greet someone, say 'Red, white, and blue! Good morning to you!' If they have a different color cube than you, trade one of your cubes for one of theirs. When you have one cube of each color, go back to your circle seat."

3 Reinforce students' efforts: "Everyone is remembering to give a friendly greeting before trading cubes." When all students are seated back in the circle, have students hold up their three cubes and say in unison: "Red, white, and blue! Good morning to you!"

VARIATION

- Vary the cube colors by using school colors or the flag colors of another country you're studying.

EXTENDING THE SOCIAL STUDIES LEARNING BEYOND MORNING MEETING

- Have students brainstorm symbols that can be used to represent their classroom community.

Social Studies Content

American symbols/patriotism

NCSS Standards Theme

Culture and Cultural Diversity

C3 Framework

D2.Civ.11.K–2 Explain how people can work together to make decisions in the classroom.

Common Core Standards

SL.K.1 Participate in collaborative conversations with diverse partners about kindergarten topics and texts with peers and adults in small and larger groups.

SL.K.6 Speak audibly and express thoughts, feelings, and ideas clearly.

Materials Needed

Red, white, and blue connecting cubes (2 more of each color than the number of students)

Vocabulary

Flag
Symbol

Artifacts Around the World

Social Studies Content

Cultural artifacts

NCSS Standards Theme

Culture and Cultural Diversity

C3 Framework

D2.Geo.6.K–2 Identify some cultural and environmental characteristics of specific places.

Common Core Standards

SL.K.6 Speak audibly and express thoughts, feelings, and ideas clearly.

Materials Needed

Artifacts or pictures of artifacts from other countries

Vocabulary

Artifact
Culture

How to do it:

In advance, have students bring in an artifact—a human-made object or a picture of one—from another country. For example, they might bring in a coin from Spain, a photo of a sari from India, or a set of Russian nesting dolls. Ask parents to help students find an appropriate item, and encourage them to send something related to their family's culture. (A sample letter you might send to parents is available to download; see page 12.)

1 Explain and model how to do the sharing: "When it's your turn, you'll walk around the circle, showing your artifact. Then you'll return to your circle spot and share two or three brief sentences about your artifact, including its country of origin. For example, my artifact is a soup spoon. It's from China. The flower on it is called a peony."

2 Have several students share each day. Add their artifacts and pictures to a class display of "Artifacts From Around the World." Label each item with its country of origin.

EXTENDING THE SOCIAL STUDIES LEARNING BEYOND MORNING MEETING

■ Display artifacts from a "mystery" place. Have students examine the artifacts throughout the week and discuss where they might be from. At the end of the week, have students guess the place before you reveal it.

Classroom Citizens

Social Studies Content

Classroom citizenship

NCSS Standards Theme

Individuals, Groups, and
Institutions

C3 Framework

D2.Civ.7.K–2 Apply civic
virtues when participating
in school settings.

Common Core Standards

W.K.2 Use a combination
of drawing, dictating, and
writing to compose
informative/explanatory
texts in which they name
what they are writing
about and supply some
information about the topic.
(Extending the learning)

SL.K.4 Describe familiar
people, places, things, and
events and, with prompting
and support, provide
additional detail.

SL.K.6 Speak audibly and
express thoughts, feelings,
and ideas clearly.

Materials Needed

Chart paper or whiteboard

Vocabulary

Citizen
Responsible

How to do it:

1 Introduce the sharing: "A citizen is a member of a community, like our classroom. One of the ways we show we are responsible classroom citizens is by following our class rules. Today we're going to talk about how we follow our rule to 'Take care of each other.'"

2 Explain how to do the sharing: "We're going to go around the circle, and each of you will say one way that we show we are classroom citizens by taking care of each other. I'll go first: 'Classroom citizens work quietly so their classmates can do their work, too.'"

3 Give a few moments of think time. Then have students share around the circle. List their ideas on chart paper or a whiteboard. Reinforce their thinking: "Look at all these ideas you have about how to be responsible classroom citizens!"

4 After everyone shares, ask: "Why do you think it's important to be a responsible classroom citizen?"

VARIATION

■ Have students share with a partner one example of being a responsible classroom citizen. Then, call on a few student volunteers to share one of their ideas with the class.

EXTENDING THE SOCIAL STUDIES LEARNING BEYOND MORNING MEETING

■ Have students illustrate their ideas about being classroom citizens. Post these where everyone can see them. Discuss with students how they can be responsible citizens outside the classroom, too. For example, they can use friendly words and speak respectfully to family and friends.

Family Foods

Social Studies Content

Family traditions

NCSS Standards Theme

Culture and Cultural Diversity

C3 Framework

D2.Geo.6.K–2 Identify some cultural and environmental characteristics of specific places.

Common Core Standards

RI.K.10 Actively engage in group reading activities with purpose and understanding. (Extending the learning)

W.K.2 Use a combination of drawing, dictating, and writing to compose informative/ explanatory texts in which they name what they are writing about and supply some information about the topic. (Extending the learning)

SL.K.4 Describe familiar people, places, things, and events and, with prompting and support, provide additional detail.

SL.K.6 Speak audibly and express thoughts, feelings, and ideas clearly.

Materials Needed

None

Vocabulary

Family
Food

How to do it:

1 Introduce the sharing: "Many families have special foods they like to eat. Today, you're going to share with a partner about one food that's special in your family." Model the sharing for students: "For our family picnics, my grandmother always makes her delicious barbecued chicken."

2 Remind students of the expectations for respectful listening. Have students sit face-to-face with a partner and share about their family food.

3 After a few minutes, say: "I'm going to make a statement. If my statement is true for the food you shared about, raise your hand." Choose statements that are most likely true for several students, such as:

➤ My family food is sweet.

➤ My family food has rice in it.

➤ My family food cooks in the oven.

4 Optional: Invite students to recall classmates' responses. For example, "Who remembers someone whose family food is sweet?"

VARIATION

■ Spread this sharing over a week by having a few students share each day. Invite students to bring in a photograph or drawing of their family food.

EXTENDING THE SOCIAL STUDIES LEARNING BEYOND MORNING MEETING

■ Have students read picture books about foods from different cultures, such as one from the list below. Students can draw pictures of the foods they learn about, add simple captions, and create a classroom display.

➤ *Bread, Bread, Bread* by Ann Morris, photographs by Ken Heyman

➤ *Hot, Hot Roti for Dada-ji* by F. Zia, illustrated by Ken Min

➤ *The Ugly Vegetables* by Grace Lin

Time Capsule

Social Studies Content
Personal identity

NCSS Standards Theme
Individual Development and
Identity

C3 Framework
D2.Civ.10.K–2 Compare
their own point of view
with others' perspectives.

Common Core Standards

RI.K.10 Actively engage in
group reading activities with
purpose and understanding.
(Extending the learning)

SL.K.1 Participate in
collaborative conversations
with diverse partners about
kindergarten topics and texts
with peers and adults in
small and larger groups.

SL.K.6 Speak audibly and
express thoughts, feelings,
and ideas clearly.

Materials Needed
Students' premade drawings
and photographs

Envelopes, one for each
student

Box (time capsule) to hold
students' envelopes

Vocabulary
Capsule
Time

How to do it:

This is a great activity to do early in the school year to help students get to know each other. In advance, have students draw or cut out three pictures that tell about a favorite activity, place, and person.

1 Introduce the sharing: "Today we're going to share about ourselves: things we like to do, places we like to be, and people we like to be with." Model the sharing: "I like playing guitar, so I found a picture of a guitar. I like going to the beach, so I cut out a picture of a seashell. I like spending time with my brother, Kenny, so I drew a picture of him."

2 Have several students share each day until everyone has had a turn. Post each student's drawings or pictures after their turn. Each day, have students note similarities and differences of what was shared: "Who else shared a drawing of their house as a place they like to be?"

3 At the end of the week, have students put their pictures in an envelope labeled with their name and then place their envelope in a "Time Capsule" box. The box can be brought out later in the year and used for a "then and now" activity to see how students' likes and interests have changed.

**EXTENDING THE SOCIAL STUDIES LEARNING
BEYOND MORNING MEETING**

■ As a class, read a short biography of a historical figure and make a list of "time capsule" facts for that figure.

Taking Care Everywhere

Social Studies Content

Responsibilities of citizens

NCSS Standards Theme

Civic Ideals and Practices

C3 Framework

D2.Civ.7.K–2 Apply civic virtues when participating in school settings.

D4.3.K–2 Present a summary of an argument using print, oral, and digital technologies. (Extending the learning)

Common Core Standards

SL.K.1 Participate in collaborative conversations with diverse partners about kindergarten topics and texts with peers and adults in small and larger groups.

SL.K.6 Speak audibly and express thoughts, feelings, and ideas clearly

Materials Needed

Three large pictures representing areas in a school

CD player or other way to play music

Vocabulary

Safe

Take care

How to do it:

In advance, select three pictures representing different areas of the school (for example, an art room, a playground, and a hallway). Post the pictures in different parts of the classroom.

1 Assign partners, or have students form pairs. Then introduce the sharing: "Today, we're going to share how we can take care of ourselves, our friends, and our spaces. You're going to walk around with your partner while the music plays. When the music stops, walk to the picture that's closest to you." Ask: "How can we be safe as we move around the room with our partners?"

2 Play music as partners walk around together. Reinforce safe movement: "I see students walking slowly and carefully."

3 After 15 seconds or so, stop the music and wait for students to move to one of the pictures. Then say: "Look at the picture you're near. Talk to your partner about one way you can take care of *others* in that place." Give a couple of examples: "In the art room, you might help someone with cleanup. On the playground, you might ask someone to play with you."

4 Give students a moment to chat about their ideas. Then restart the music, repeating the process with the following prompts (be sure to give examples for each):

➤ Talk about how you can take care of *yourself* in this place.

➤ Talk about ways we can take care of this *space*.

VARIATION

■ Post classroom or schoolwide rules instead of pictures. Have students chat with their partners about a way they can follow that rule.

EXTENDING THE SOCIAL STUDIES LEARNING BEYOND MORNING MEETING

■ Video-record students' ideas about taking care of themselves, others, and their space, and create a class movie using the video clips. Or, write students' ideas on chart paper and post them on a bulletin board for reference.

Choose Your Natural Resource

Social Studies Content

Natural resources

NCSS Standards Theme

Production, Distribution, and Consumption

C3 Framework

D2.Geo.8.K–2 Compare how people in different types of communities use local and distant environments to meet their daily needs.

Common Core Standards

W.K.8 With guidance and support from adults, recall information from experiences or gather information from provided sources to answer a question. (Extending the learning)

SL.K.1 Participate in collaborative conversations with diverse partners about kindergarten topics and texts with peers and adults in small and larger groups.

SL.K.3 Ask and answer questions in order to seek help, get information, or clarify something that is not understood.

Materials Needed

Pictures of various natural resources

Vocabulary

Natural resources

How to do it:

In advance, post pictures of natural resources from different locations.

1 Introduce the activity: "There are things all around us in the natural world that we use in everyday life. We call these things natural resources. For example, we use wood from forests and water from lakes and rivers."

2 Explain how to do the activity: "I'm going to name a place and two natural resources that come from that place. You'll walk to one side of the room or the other to show which natural resource you are interested in learning more about."

3 Point to the corresponding pictures. "The first place is a river. Walk to the left side of the room if you are interested in learning more about water. Walk to the right side of the room if you are interested in learning more about fish."

4 Once everyone has moved to a place, have students find a partner and share something they're interested in learning about their natural resource.

5 Repeat several more times using different pictures. For example:

➤ Forest: wood from trees on the left; maple syrup on the right

➤ Desert: Sun for solar power on the left; wind for wind power on the right

6 For reflection, ask: "What would you do if you lived in a place that did not have a natural resource you needed?" Guide students to understand that people trade with people in other areas to get the things they both need, or they find alternative resources or products.

EXTENDING THE SOCIAL STUDIES LEARNING BEYOND MORNING MEETING

■ Discuss ways to conserve natural resources to help protect the earth, such as recycling materials, using water and electricity efficiently, and so on. Then have the class create a "Protecting Our Natural Resources" poster or bulletin board that highlights their ideas.

Grade Level

K

Group Activity

Social Studies Content

Directional words

NCSS Standards Theme

People, Places, and Environments

C3 Framework

D2.Geo.2.K–2 Use maps, graphs, photographs, and other representations to describe places and the relationships and interactions that shape them.

Common Core Standards

L.K.5 With guidance and support from adults, explore word relationships and nuances in word meanings.

Materials Needed

A beanbag or ball of crumpled paper for each student

Vocabulary

Behind
In
In front of
Next to
On
Over
Under

Follow the Directions!

How to do it:

1 Introduce the activity: "For today's activity, we're going to practice some directional words. These are words that help us know where something is. For example, 'under' is a directional word."

2 Pass out the beanbags (or paper balls) and explain the activity: "We'll use these beanbags to practice our directional words. When I give you a beanbag, place it on the floor at your feet. When I give you a direction, repeat it back to me. Then move your beanbag wherever the direction tells you to move."

3 Say: "Over your head." Wait for students to repeat the direction and move their beanbags over their heads. Reinforce students' efforts: "You all moved your beanbags just the way the direction said! Now put your beanbags back at your feet." Repeat several times with different directions. For example:

➣ *Under* your chin

➣ *In front of* your feet

➣ *Behind* your left foot

➣ *On the back of* your left hand

➣ *In* your hands (cup palms together)

➣ *Next to* your right foot

VARIATION

■ Have students pair up. One student moves the beanbag from place to place and the other student uses directional words to describe its location.

EXTENDING THE SOCIAL STUDIES LEARNING BEYOND MORNING MEETING

■ Work together to make posters showing the meaning of each directional word you practiced. Display for reference.

It's Our Job!

Social Studies Content

Responsibility

NCSS Standards Theme

Civic Ideals and Practices

C3 Framework

D2.Civ.6.K–2 Describe how communities work to accomplish common tasks, establish responsibilities, and fulfill roles of authority.

Common Core Standards

SL.K.1 Participate in collaborative conversations with diverse partners about kindergarten topics and texts with peers and adults in small and larger groups.

L.K.5 With guidance and support from adults, explore word relationships and nuances in word meanings.

Materials Needed

Optional: Class jobs chart

Vocabulary

Community
Responsibility

How to do it:

Optional: Display the class jobs chart where everyone can see it.

1 Introduce the activity: "Our classroom is a community, and we all have a responsibility to work and play well together. Our class jobs help us take care of each other in our classroom community."

2 Explain how to do the activity: "Today, we're going to act out some of our class jobs. I'm going to name one of the jobs on our chart. You'll have a chance to make up a motion to go with that job, and then we will all do the same motion together."

3 Model and practice with students how to pantomime a class job. "I'm going to pretend to be the Handout Manager. Watch what I do." (Pretend to hold papers and make a motion as though you are handing them out.) "Now let's all make that motion."

4 Point to one of the jobs on the chart (or name a job) and call on a student volunteer to pantomime doing that job. Then have all students do the same motion. Repeat as time allows or until all students who would like to make up a motion have had a chance.

EXTENDING THE SOCIAL STUDIES LEARNING BEYOND MORNING MEETING

- Invite students to draw a picture of a job they would like to do when they're grown up and share one or two reasons why with the class.

Just Like My Family!

Social Studies Content

Families

NCSS Standards Theme

Individual Development and Identity

C3 Framework

D2.Civ.10.K–2 Compare their own point of view with others' perspectives.

Common Core Standards

RI.K.10 Actively engage in group reading activities with purpose and understanding. (Extending the learning)

SL.K.2 Confirm understanding of a text read aloud or information presented orally or through other media by asking and answering questions about key details and requesting clarification if something is not understood.

Materials Needed

None

Vocabulary

Family

How to do it:

When choosing statements, consider the variety of family situations so that all students have a chance to stand up and feel a sense of belonging.

1 Introduce the activity: "Today, we're going to learn more about each other and our families. I'll make a statement, and if it's true for your family, stand up and say together 'Just like my family!' Then sit back down and wait for the next statement."

2 Make a statement that could be true for one's family history or culture. For example:

➤ I have brothers or sisters.

➤ Some of my family lives in a big city [on a farm, near the ocean, etc.].

➤ My family speaks more than one language.

➤ Some of my family lives far away.

3 Reinforce students' efforts: "You're really listening, and that's helping us learn a lot about everyone's family!"

4 Repeat for several statements. Then ask students to reflect on what they noticed: "What's one thing you learned about our families?"

VARIATION

■ As students become familiar with the activity, invite them to create their own statements about families.

EXTENDING THE SOCIAL STUDIES LEARNING BEYOND MORNING MEETING

■ Read a book about families, such as one listed below. Have students bring in photos to share about their families and create a classroom display.

➤ *The Family Book* by Todd Parr

➤ *Who's In My Family? All About Our Families* by Robie H. Harris, illustrated by Nadine Bernard Westcott

Learning All Around

Social Studies Content

Neighborhoods

NCSS Standards Theme

People, Places, and
Environments

C3 Framework

D2.Geo.2.K–2 Use maps,
graphs, photographs, and
other representations to
describe places and the
relationships and interactions
that shape them.

Common Core Standards

W.K.2 Use a combination
of drawing, dictating, and
writing to compose
informative/explanatory texts
in which they name what
they are writing about and
supply some information
about the topic. (Extending
the learning)

L.K.4 Determine or clarify the
meaning of unknown and
multiple-meaning words
and phrases based on
kindergarten reading
and content.

Materials Needed

Optional: World map

Vocabulary

City
Country
State
Town
World

How to do it:

1 Introduce the activity: "Our school is in a town [or city]. Towns are part of states. These states make up our country, which is just one of the many countries in the world. Today, we're going to sing a song about these places." If possible, use a map to show how the world is the biggest area, followed by the country, and then the state, and then the town or city.

2 Teach students the following lyrics, to the tune of "And the Green Grass Grew All Around" (search online to hear the song):

FIRST STANZA (STUDENTS REPEAT EACH LINE AFTER YOU):

> *There is a state*
> *In a country*
> *With citizens*
> *Like you and me*

CHORUS (EVERYONE SINGS TOGETHER; NO REPEATING LINES):

> *The state's in the country*
> *And the country's in the world*
> *And the students learn all around, all around*
> *The students learn all around*

SECOND STANZA (STUDENTS REPEAT EACH LINE):

> *And in this state*
> *There is a town [city]*
> *With citizens*
> *Like you and me*

CHORUS (EVERYONE SINGS TOGETHER; NO REPEATING LINES):

> *The town's in a state*
> *And the state's in a country*
> *And the country's in the world*
> *And the students learn all around, all around*
> *The students learn all around*

THIRD STANZA (STUDENTS REPEAT EACH LINE):

> *And in this town*
> *There is a school*
> *With citizens*
> *Like you and me*

CHORUS (EVERYONE SINGS TOGETHER; NO REPEATING LINES):

The school's in a town
And the town's in a state
And the state's in a country
And the country's in the world
And the students learn all around, all around
The students learn all around

VARIATIONS

- Add additional verses to include continent, galaxy, universe.
- Split the class into two groups. Have one group lead and the other group repeat the lines; alternate stanzas so each group has a chance to lead.

EXTENDING THE SOCIAL STUDIES LEARNING
BEYOND MORNING MEETING

- Have students create flipbooks or maps showing how their school fits into the town or city, state, and country.

Let's Plant a Garden!

Social Studies Content

Trade

NCSS Standards Theme

Production, Distribution, and
Consumption

C3 Framework

D2.Eco.14.K–2 Describe why
people in one country trade
goods and services with
people in other countries.

Common Core Standards

RI.K.10 Actively engage in
group reading activities with
purpose and understanding.
(Extending the learning)

SL.K.1 Participate in
collaborative conversations
with diverse partners about
kindergarten topics and texts
with peers and adults in
small and larger groups.

L.K.6 Use words and phrases
acquired through
conversations, reading
and being read to, and
responding to texts.

Materials Needed

Index cards with "soil," "water,"
or "seeds" on them, in words or
pictures

Vocabulary

Seeds
Soil
Trade
Water

How to do it:

In advance, make a few more of each card than the number of students in
the class. Give each child three cards, all with the same word or picture on
them. Put the extra cards in the "Garden Shed" (a box or pile on a table) that
students can choose from if needed to complete their gardens. (A sample set
of cards is available to download; see page 12.)

1 Introduce the activity: "Today, each of you
will gather what you need to plant a garden.
You'll need soil, seeds, and water. To get all
three things, you'll trade cards with each
other." Model with a student how to trade
cards and how to politely decline a card
they already have.

2 Explain how to do the activity: "When I say
'Go,' begin trading. When you have all three
things you need for your garden, return to
your circle spot." Reinforce students' efforts:
"I hear friendly greetings. I hear people
politely saying 'No, thank you' if they don't
need to trade."

3 Introduce the Garden Shed when most of the class is seated: "If you still
need a card to finish your garden, come over to the Garden Shed and
trade for the card you need."

4 Finish with a brief reflection: "What made your trading successful? How
can trading help people?"

VARIATION

■ Have students "build a house" by trading "hammer," "nails," and "wood"
cards, and visiting the "Tool Shed" if they need a card.

**EXTENDING THE SOCIAL STUDIES LEARNING
BEYOND MORNING MEETING**

■ Read a book about trading, such as one listed below. Have students brainstorm other ways people from long ago (and today) might trade.

➤ *Erandi's Braids* by Antonio Hernández Madrigal, illustrated by Tomie
dePaola

➤ *Ox-Cart Man* by Donald Hall, illustrated by Barbara Cooney

➤ *Sheep in a Shop* by Nancy Shaw, illustrated by Margot Apple

Community Places

Social Studies Content

Community places

NCSS Standards Theme

Individuals, Groups, and Institutions

C3 Framework

D2.Civ.6.K–2 Describe how communities work to accomplish common tasks, establish responsibilities, and fulfill roles of authority.

Common Core Standards

W.K.8 With guidance and support from adults, recall information from experiences or gather information from provided sources to answer a question.

Materials Needed

None

Vocabulary

Building

Community

(Various community places, such as library, school, fire station, etc.)

How to do it:

1 Display a message like the one below:

> Hello, Neighbors!
>
> Yesterday, we talked about buildings in our community. Look at the buildings below. Put a check mark under the buildings you have visited.
>
> Fire Station   Grocery Store   Library   Post Office

2 Read the message aloud as you point to each word. Then say: "Wow! Looks like you have visited lots of places." Invite a few students to share out which buildings they have visited.

3 Ask why these buildings are important places in your community: "Why do you think we need a grocery store [or library] in our neighborhood?"

VARIATION

■ In addition to sharing which buildings they've visited, invite volunteers to share which is their favorite to visit, and why.

EXTENDING THE SOCIAL STUDIES LEARNING BEYOND MORNING MEETING

■ Have students create a class mural of all the community buildings they've visited, with brief captions or labels.

Put It to a Vote

Social Studies Content

Voting

NCSS Standards Theme

Civic Ideals and Practices

C3 Framework

D2.Civ.11.K–2 Explain how people can work together to make decisions in the classroom.

Common Core Standards

SL.K.1 Participate in collaborative conversations with diverse partners about kindergarten topics and texts with peers and adults in small and larger groups.

Materials Needed

None

Vocabulary

Represent
Vote

How to do it:

1 Display a message like the one below:

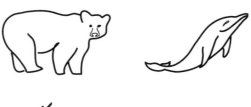

Good Morning, Voters,

Today is voting day! We are going to vote to choose an animal to represent our classroom. Vote once by putting a check mark below one of the animals.

2 Reinforce students' efforts: "I noticed people helping others read the message. I saw people taking time to think before making a check mark."

3 Read the message aloud as you point to each word. Then say: "When each person in a group votes, it helps the group make a choice in a fair way. This morning, we voted for one animal to represent our classroom. Let's count and see which animal got the most votes!"

4 Count the check marks together. Then celebrate the class choice with a simple cheer: "Hooray for dolphins!"

EXTENDING THE SOCIAL STUDIES LEARNING BEYOND MORNING MEETING

■ Have students vote for which recess game, class pet, or new class job they would prefer.

The First Thanksgiving

Social Studies Content

The first Thanksgiving

NCSS Standards Theme

Time, Continuity, and Change

C3 Framework

D2.His.2.K–2 Compare life in the past to life today.

Common Core Standards

RI.K.10 Actively engage in group reading activities with purpose and understanding. (Extending the learning)

W.K.2 Use a combination of drawing, dictating, and writing to compose informative/explanatory texts in which they name what they are writing about and supply some information about the topic. (Extending the learning)

SL.K.5 Add drawings or other visual displays to descriptions as desired to provide additional detail.

Materials Needed

Chart paper or whiteboard

Sticky notes

Vocabulary

Thanksgiving

How to do it:

1 Display a message like the one below:

Good Morning, Thankful Students,

Today, we are going to learn about the first Thanksgiving. What do you think people ate at the first Thanksgiving? Write or draw one idea on a sticky note. Place it below.

---

2 Have students read the message chorally. Then read the sticky notes out loud. Reinforce students' efforts: "You listed some interesting food ideas for the first Thanksgiving."

3 Ask: "What is something about the first Thanksgiving that you'd like to learn more about? Pair up with the person next to you and take turns sharing your ideas."

4 After two or three minutes, have each pair or each student share one of their ideas; list these on chart paper or a whiteboard.

VARIATION

■ Have students share one thing they are thankful for. Discuss what the people at the first Thanksgiving might have been thankful for.

EXTENDING THE SOCIAL STUDIES LEARNING BEYOND MORNING MEETING

■ Read a book or two with the class about the first Thanksgiving, such as those suggested below. Then have students write and draw what they learned about the first Thanksgiving. Display the finished drawings.

➤ *The Pilgrims' First Thanksgiving* by Anne McGovern, illustrated by Elroy Freem

➤ *Squanto's Journey: The Story of the First Thanksgiving* by Joseph Bruchac, illustrated by Greg Shed

Tools From the Past

Social Studies Content

Tools

NCSS Standards Theme

Science, Technology, and Society

C3 Framework

D2.His.2.K–2 Compare life in the past to life today.

Common Core Standards

W.K.8 With guidance and support from adults, recall information from experiences or gather information from provided sources to answer a question.

SL.K.6 Speak audibly and express thoughts, feelings, and ideas clearly.

Materials Needed

Picture of a tool from long ago

Vocabulary

Past
Tools

How to do it:

1 Display a message like the one below:

Good Morning, Kindergartners,

Tools make jobs easier. Look at this tool from long ago.

What do you think it was used for?

2 Read the morning message aloud, pointing to each word as you read.

3 Have volunteers share their ideas about the tool. Then explain to students what the tool is called and what it was used for.

EXTENDING THE SOCIAL STUDIES LEARNING BEYOND MORNING MEETING

- Brainstorm with students everyday tools we use today (toothbrushes, scissors, flashlights, etc.). Write these on chart paper or a whiteboard. Have students discuss why we need tools.

- Have students draw tools we might use in the future. Students can share their future tool ideas with the class at an upcoming Morning Meeting.

Where Do You Like to Work?

Social Studies Content

Maps

NCSS Standards Theme

People, Places, and
Environments

C3 Framework

D2.Geo.1.K–2 Construct
maps, graphs, and other
representations of
familiar places. (Extending
the learning)

D2.Geo.2.K–2 Use maps,
graphs, photographs, and
other representations to
describe places and the
relationships and interactions
that shape them.

Common Core Standards

SL.K.1 Participate in
collaborative conversations
with diverse partners about
kindergarten topics and texts
with peers and adults in small
and larger groups.

Materials Needed

None

Vocabulary

Map
Symbol

How to do it:

1 Display a message like the one below:

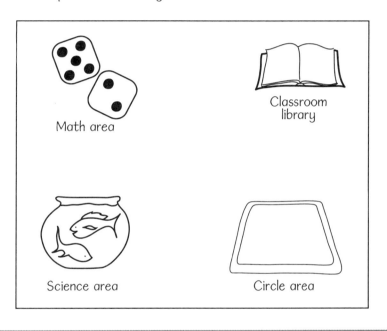

Hello, Workers!

A map is a drawing of a place. It uses symbols to show where things are. Below is a map of our classroom. Draw a happy face on the map to show where you like to work.

Math area

Classroom library

Science area

Circle area

2 Read the message aloud. Then summarize what you noticed about the happy faces on the chart. For example: "I see that some of you like to work inside our circle area. Many of you like to work near our classroom library."

3 Extend students' thinking: "What other sections of our classroom could we add by drawing them on the map? Where on the map should they go?"

**EXTENDING THE SOCIAL STUDIES LEARNING
BEYOND MORNING MEETING**

■ Work together to create a map of the playground (or another area of your school). Agree on symbols and colors to use for different structures and areas on the playground. Create a key for the map and give it a title.

Block Party Greeting

Social Studies Content

Neighbors

NCSS Standards Theme

People, Places, and
Environments

C3 Framework

D2.Civ.14.K–2 Describe how
people have tried to improve
their communities over time.

Common Core Standards

SL.1.1 Participate in
collaborative conversations
with diverse partners about
grade 1 topics and texts with
peers and adults in small
and larger groups.

Materials Needed

None

Vocabulary

Block party
Neighbor
Neighborhood
Next-door neighbor

How to do it:

1 Introduce the greeting: "The people who live near us are called our neighbors. Sometimes, people have an outdoor gathering called a block party to get to know everyone in the neighborhood. Today, we will practice greeting our neighbors and having a block party."

2 Explain and model how to do the greeting: "The people on either side of you will be your next-door neighbors. When I call out 'Next-door neighbor,' greet one of the classmates next to you with a wave and 'Hi, neighbor!' Then greet the classmate on your other side the same way. When I call out 'Block party!' mix and mingle with everyone and greet as many classmates as you can."

3 Reinforce students' efforts: "I see students using friendly words and faces as they greet their neighbors."

4 After the "block party," signal for students to return to their circle spots. If time allows, ask a reflective question: "Why might neighbors choose to have a block party?"

**EXTENDING THE SOCIAL STUDIES LEARNING
BEYOND MORNING MEETING**

■ Have students discuss other neighborhood events such as clothing swaps, yard sales, recreational sports, holiday celebrations, and neighborhood cleanups.

Jobs of the Future

Social Studies Content

Jobs and the common good

NCSS Standards Theme

Individual Development and Identity

C3 Framework

D2.Civ.2.K–2 Explain how all people, not just official leaders, play important roles in a community.

Common Core Standards

W.1.8 With guidance and support from adults, recall information from experiences or gather information from provided sources to answer a question.

SL.1.6 Produce complete sentences when appropriate to task and situation.

Materials Needed

Optional: Chart paper and marker

Vocabulary

Community helper
Job

How to do it:

1 Introduce the greeting: "Today, we're going to greet each other around the circle by naming a community helper job we might like to do when we grow up. What are some helper jobs we've been learning about?" (Possible jobs: firefighter, farmer, mayor, athletic coach, ambulance driver, nurse, weather forecaster, bank teller, cook, construction worker.) List jobs on chart paper or a whiteboard for reference.

2 Explain how to do the greeting: "When it's your turn, state which job you might like to do. The rest of us will greet you using the job you named. For example, when it's my turn, I might say 'In the future, I'd like to be a firefighter.' The class all together will say 'Good morning, future firefighter.'"

3 Remind students to be friendly greeters: "Remember to let the person finish speaking and use a friendly voice when you greet them."

4 Continue around the circle until everyone has been greeted.

VARIATION

■ Have students name a city, state, or country they'd like to visit in the future. For example, a student might say "In the future, I'd like to visit Japan." The class responds with "Good morning, future Japan visitor."

EXTENDING THE SOCIAL STUDIES LEARNING BEYOND MORNING MEETING

■ Invite students to read about the job they named, using classroom or library resources. They can draw pictures with captions to show what they learn or record facts in a graphic organizer.

Musical Meet and Greet

Social Studies Content

World music

NCSS Standards Theme

Culture and Cultural Diversity

C3 Framework

D2.Geo.6.K–2 Identify some cultural and environmental characteristics of specific places.

Common Core Standards

RI.1.10 With prompting and support, read informational texts appropriately complex for grade 1. (Extending the learning)

SL.1.5 Add drawings or other visual displays to descriptions when appropriate to clarify ideas, thoughts, and feelings. (Extending the learning)

SL.1.6 Produce complete sentences when appropriate to task and situation.

Materials Needed

Audio recording of a song from another country (search online)

World map or globe

Vocabulary

Artifacts

Music

How to do it:

1 Introduce the greeting: "People create music all over the world. Today we're going to do a mix-and-mingle greeting while we listen to a song from Ghana, a country in West Africa." Show students where West Africa and Ghana are on the map or globe.

2 Explain how to do the greeting: "When I start the music, you'll move around the room slowly and safely until the music stops. Then you'll greet someone near you with a friendly handshake, a 'Good morning,' and the person's name." Model walking carefully around the room and greeting a student.

3 Start and stop the music several times so that students can greet different classmates.

4 Signal for students to return to the circle. Ask: "What did you notice about the song? How is this music similar to music you listen to? How is it different?"

VARIATION

■ Post pictures around the room of artifacts from the same country as the music. While the music plays, have students walk around the room looking at the pictures. When the music stops, have students move to the closest picture and greet their classmates who have gathered there.

EXTENDING THE SOCIAL STUDIES LEARNING BEYOND MORNING MEETING

■ Guide students in exploring the artwork of the country or region using classroom, library, and online resources. Students can work in groups and present what they learn in a song, dance, skit, or piece of art.

Super Citizen Sharing

Social Studies Content

Citizenship

NCSS Standards Theme

Individual Development and Identity

C3 Framework

D2.Civ.2.K–2 Explain how all people, not just official leaders, play important roles in a community.

Common Core Standards

W.1.8 With guidance and support from adults, recall information from experiences or gather information from provided sources to answer a question.

SL.1.4 Describe people, places, things, and events with relevant details, expressing ideas and feelings clearly.

Materials Needed

None

Vocabulary

Citizen

How to do it:

1 Introduce the greeting: "Super Citizens are people who help make their community a better place by doing things like picking up litter or helping a neighbor. Think about how you can be a Super Citizen in our school community. What kinds of things could you do?" (If necessary, explain that "citizens" are the people who live in a particular community.)

2 After some think time, let students brainstorm ideas aloud, and list them on chart paper or a whiteboard.

3 Explain how to do the greeting and sharing: "You'll start by 'flying' around the room as Super Citizens. When I say 'Super Citizens unite,' stop flying and find a partner. Greet each other by saying 'Good morning, Super Citizen!' Then take turns sharing how you will be a Super Citizen in our school community." Model and practice these actions as needed, including how to 'fly' safely around the room (for example, by walking slowly with arms outstretched).

4 Ask students to reflect: "While sharing with your partners, what new ideas did you hear about being a Super Citizen?"

VARIATION

■ Vary the prompt by asking:
 ➤ What are ways we can be Super Classroom Citizens?
 ➤ What are ways we can be Super Digital Citizens?
 ➤ What are ways we can be Super Cafeteria Citizens?

EXTENDING THE SOCIAL STUDIES LEARNING BEYOND MORNING MEETING

■ Create a class book titled "Super Citizens in Our Community." Have students write and illustrate their ideas. Some students might also enjoy creating a Super Citizen comic or skit.

Fairness First

Social Studies Content

Fairness

NCSS Standards Theme

Individual Development and Identity

C3 Framework

D2.Civ.7.K–2 Apply civic virtues when participating in school settings.

D2.Civ.8.K–2 Describe democratic principles such as equality, fairness, and respect for legitimate authority and rules.

Common Core Standards

W.1.8 With guidance and support from adults, recall information from experiences or gather information from provided sources to answer a question. (Extending the learning)

SL.1.4 Describe people, places, things, and events with relevant details, expressing ideas and feelings clearly.

Materials Needed

None

Vocabulary

Compromise
Fair
Perspective
Unfair

How to do it:

1 Introduce the concept of "fairness" by briefly discussing with students what they think it means. Acknowledge that students are going to have different ideas about fairness.

2 Explain how to do the sharing: "I'm going to give you a situation that might happen here at school. Let's talk about fair ways to handle it. Let's say Yossef and Ariel are working on a project together. Ariel wants to type, but Yossef sits down at the computer first. What are some ways Ariel and Yossef could handle this situation?" Take some answers. (Possible answers: Ariel could ask Yossef for some computer time; they could agree to take turns.)

3 Have students partner up with someone near them. Say: "Now you'll talk about another situation with your parter. What are some things both people in the situation could do to make sure things are fair?" Possible scenarios for discussion:

➤ Jeff wants to trade snacks with Raj; Raj wants to keep his snack.

➤ Kimiko wants a turn on the swing; Natalie is already on the swing.

4 After students discuss the scenario with their partners, talk with them about how different people have different perspectives and that to create a situation that is fair for everyone, we may need to compromise.

VARIATION

■ Stretch students' thinking by discussing scenarios related to your community. For example: "Do you think our city should build a new skateboard park or a dog park? Give a reason for your choice."

EXTENDING THE SOCIAL STUDIES LEARNING BEYOND MORNING MEETING

■ As a class, write a letter to the principal about a situation at school that students feel is unfair, suggesting possible compromises.

Family Flags

How to do it:

In advance, have students create paper flags (at school or home) using colors and symbols to represent their family.

1 Introduce the sharing: "Each day this week, a few of you will share two or three sentences about your family flag." Model how to share by holding up your flag: "My flag is red and blue because my family likes strawberry picking and going to the lake. The black dog in the upper left corner represents our dog Midnight. The five hearts circling him represent how many people are in my family. I'm ready for comments and questions."

2 Remind students to be respectful of the sharer: "Remember to use kind words and a friendly tone when asking questions or making comments." Model how to respond to questions and comments from students.

3 Invite a few students to present their flags. Reinforce students' positive actions: "You showed you were listening as your classmates shared—your eyes were on the speaker and your mouths were quiet."

4 Display students' flags where everyone can see them.

VARIATION

- To build community within your classroom, have students create and share flags for their table teams or learning groups.

EXTENDING THE SOCIAL STUDIES LEARNING BEYOND MORNING MEETING

- Once all the family flags are displayed, have students do a Museum Walk to look for similarities and differences. (Museum Walk is an interactive learning structure in which small groups of students or partners examine and discuss a display as if in a museum.)

Social Studies Content

Family

NCSS Standards Theme

Individual Development and Identity

C3 Framework

D2.Civ.10.K–2 Compare their own point of view with others' perspectives.

Common Core Standards

SL.1.4 Describe people, places, things, and events with relevant details, expressing ideas and feelings clearly.

SL.1.5 Add drawings or other visual displays to descriptions when appropriate to clarify ideas, thoughts, and feelings.

Materials Needed

Students' premade paper flags

Vocabulary

Family
Flag
Represent
Symbol

Rules in the Round

Social Studies Content

Rules

NCSS Standards Theme

Civic Ideals and Practices

C3 Framework

D2.Civ.3.K–2 Explain the need for and purposes of rules in various settings inside and outside of school.

Common Core Standards

SL.1.1 Participate in collaborative conversations with diverse partners about grade 1 topics and texts with peers and adults in small and larger groups.

SL.1.2 Ask and answer questions about key details in a text read aloud or information presented orally or through other media.

Materials Needed

None

Vocabulary

Rules

How to do it:

Divide the class into two groups and have students form an inner circle facing out and an outer circle facing in, so each student faces a partner.

1 Introduce the sharing: "Today, we're going to talk about our classroom rules with inside-outside partners. I'll give you a question, and you and your partner will take turns sharing your ideas. For example, when we're in the cafeteria, how can we follow our classroom rule 'Keep our area clean'? You might say 'We can clean up our table after we eat.' When you hear the chime, stop talking and change partners for a new question."

2 Pose a question: "When we are in the school library, what is one way we can follow our rule 'Do your best work'?" Give some think time, then signal students to discuss for a minute or so.

3 If needed, model how students in the outside circle can move safely one person to their right. Once students are in position, pose another question: "How might we follow our rule 'Take care of each other' when we are on the playground?"

4 Continue posing questions for several rounds using these or similar questions:

➤ Why are rules important?

➤ What would happen if we didn't have rules?

5 To close the activity, have students make one circle. Call on a few pairs to share one of their ideas.

VARIATION

■ Give students a category, such as school, community, or country. Have students share one rule for that category that they think is important, and why.

EXTENDING THE SOCIAL STUDIES LEARNING BEYOND MORNING MEETING

■ Have students work in pairs or small groups to make posters about the importance of rules. Discuss similarities, differences, and common themes between the posters.

Shop Around

Social Studies Content

Products

NCSS Standards Theme

Production, Distribution, and
Consumption

C3 Framework

D2.Eco.2.K–2 Identify the
benefits and costs of making
various personal decisions.

Common Core Standards

W.1.2 Write informative/
explanatory texts in which
they name a topic, supply
some facts about the topic,
and provide some sense
of closure. (Extending the
learning)

SL.1.1 Participate in
collaborative conversations
with diverse partners about
grade 1 topics and texts with
peers and adults in small and
larger groups.

Materials Needed

None

Vocabulary

Choices
Products

How to do it:

1 Introduce the sharing: "When we go shopping, we make choices about which products to buy. Today, we're going to practice making these choices. I'll name two products, and you'll walk to the side of the room that represents the product you would choose. For example, if I say 'Apples or bananas,' everyone who chooses apples walks to the left [point to left side of room]. Everyone who chooses bananas walks to the right [point to right side]."

2 Pose the first set of choices: "A box of colored markers or a box of crayons?" Give students a moment to think, then signal for students to move to their choice.

3 Once everyone has moved to their side of the room, say: "Look around at who else has chosen your product. Chat with someone near you about why you made this choice." Give students a minute or so to discuss.

4 Continue posing new sets of choices as time allows, such as a book or a game; pizza or ice cream; stickers or face paint.

5 Ask a few volunteers to share with the whole class why they made one of their choices.

VARIATION

■ Once students become comfortable with two choices, add a third option (for example: colored markers, crayons, or colored pencils).

EXTENDING THE SOCIAL STUDIES LEARNING BEYOND MORNING MEETING

■ Have students draw a picture of one of their choices and write two to three sentences about why they chose it. Display students' drawings.

Whose Favorite Place?

Social Studies Content

Favorite places

NCSS Standards Theme

People, Places, and
Environments

C3 Framework

D2.Geo.6.K–2 Identify some
cultural and environmental
characteristics of specific
places.

Common Core Standards

W.1.8 With guidance and
support from adults, recall
information from experiences
or gather information from
provided sources to answer
a question.

SL.1.1 Participate in
collaborative conversations
with diverse partners about
grade 1 topics and texts with
peers and adults in small
and larger groups.

SL.1.4 Describe people,
places, things, and events with
relevant details, expressing
ideas and feelings clearly.

SL.1.5 Add drawings or other
visual displays to descriptions
when appropriate to clarify
ideas, thoughts, and feelings.
(Extending the learning)

Materials Needed

None

Vocabulary

Favorite
Place

How to do it:

1 Introduce the sharing: "We've been talking about how people all around
the world have places that are special to them. Today, we're going to share
one of our favorite places in our neighborhood, and why we like it so
much. For example, one of my favorite places is the bike trail because I
like to walk on it."

2 Remind students to listen carefully to remember what classmates share.
Then, going around the circle, have students share one favorite neighborhood place and one reason why it's their favorite.

3 After all students have shared, challenge the class with four or five
"Whose Favorite Place?" questions: "Whose favorite place is the soccer
field?" "Who remembers why?" "Whose favorite place is the science
museum?"

VARIATION

■ When students gain experience with this sharing, invite a few volunteers
to ask "Whose Favorite Place?" questions for Step 3.

**EXTENDING THE SOCIAL STUDIES LEARNING
BEYOND MORNING MEETING**

■ Have students make and display a collage of all the favorite places that
were mentioned. Throughout the following weeks, choose some of the
places to "explore" in more depth using school or online resources.

Everyone Has Needs and Wants

Social Studies Content

Needs and wants

NCSS Standards Theme

Production, Distribution, and Consumption

C3 Framework

D2.Eco.2.K–2 Identify the benefits and costs of making various personal decisions.

Common Core Standards

SL.1.5 Add drawings or other visual displays to descriptions when appropriate to clarify ideas, thoughts, and feelings. (Extending the learning)

L.1.5 With guidance and support from adults, demonstrate understanding of word relationships and nuances in word meanings.

Materials Needed

None

Vocabulary

Needs
Wants

How to do it:

1 Introduce the activity: "Today, we're going to sing a song about needs and wants. A 'need' is something we must have, such as water or food. A 'want' is something we would like to have, such as a toy or a game. In this song, you'll get to name a need or a want when I call out your name!"

2 Have students brainstorm some needs and wants. You may want to do this in small groups or as a whole group and list ideas.

3 Teach this song (to the tune of "Mary Had a Little Lamb") and sing it as a group, inserting a student's name into the last line:

> *Everyone has needs and wants*
> *Needs and wants*
> *Needs and wants*
>
> *Everyone has needs and wants*
> *Just like [Insert student's first name]*

4 The named student responds by saying a "need" or a "want." The class responds by:

➤ Crossing their arms over their chest if they think the item is a need

➤ Raising both hands in the air if they think the item is a want

5 Give each student a turn, or do the activity over a few days.

6 Ask students to reflect: "Did anyone hear an item that could be both a need and a want? For example, having shoes to wear is a need, but having a pair of fancy shoes is a want."

EXTENDING THE SOCIAL STUDIES LEARNING BEYOND MORNING MEETING

■ Have students create collages of needs and wants using pictures from magazines and catalogs.

Grade Level

1

Group Activity

Social Studies Content

Sequencing

NCSS Standards Theme

Time, Continuity, and Change

C3 Framework

D2.His.1.K–2 Create a chronological sequence of multiple events.

Common Core Standards

SL.1.4 Describe people, places, things, and events with relevant details, expressing ideas and feelings clearly.

Materials Needed

Premade sheets of paper or large index cards (enough for every pair of students)

Wall calendar

Vocabulary

Date
Day
Future
Past
Present

Human Calendar

How to do it:

In advance, write the names of special days and their dates (month and day only) on sheets of paper or index cards, one for every pair of students. Include one with today's date. See examples below.

> First Day of School
> September 5

> Today
> October 8

> Election Day
> November 3

1 Use a wall calendar to introduce the activity: "Lots of you wonder about what is coming up on our calendar, like holidays and school events. Today, we're going to make a Human Calendar by putting special days in order from the start of the school year in September to the end of the school year in June."

2 Show students where the line will start and where it will end. Ask: "What can we do to work together and get all the special days in order?"

3 Pair students up and give each pair a sheet. Give them time to think. Then signal when it's time to put the special days in order.

4 After everyone lines up, go down the line and have each pair read their special day and date aloud. As a whole group, make any needed corrections to the order.

5 Encourage further reflection about past, present, and future dates: "Who has a date that has already happened this school year? Who has a date that will happen next month?"

VARIATION

■ Use students' birthdays to create a Human Birthday Calendar.

EXTENDING THE SOCIAL STUDIES LEARNING BEYOND MORNING MEETING

■ Give students calendar templates (search online for free resources) and have them create family calendars. Invite students to talk about their calendars during a future Morning Meeting sharing.

44

Landform Match

Social Studies Content

Landforms

NCSS Standards Theme

People, Places, and
Environments

C3 Framework

D2.Geo.6.K–2 Identify some
cultural and environmental
characteristics of specific
places.

Common Core Standards

SL.1.1 Participate in
collaborative conversations
with diverse partners about
grade 1 topics and texts with
peers and adults in small
and larger groups.

L.1.5 With guidance and
support from adults,
demonstrate understanding
of word relationships and
nuances in word meanings.

Materials Needed

None

Vocabulary

Landform
Mountain
Plain
River

How to do it:

1 Introduce the activity: "Today, we're going to learn motions to represent different landforms." Model and practice the motions for each landform:

➤ **Mountain**—Make a triangle shape with two arms raised overhead

➤ **River**—Make a wavy motion with both hands

➤ **Plain**—Make a flat sweeping movement with one hand

Emphasize the importance of safe movements: "When you make your land-form, stay in your own space and pay attention to what's around you."

2 Pair students and explain how to do the activity: "Stand back to back with your partner. Both of you say, '1, 2, 3, go!' Then turn around and show one of the landform motions." Model and practice how to do this.

3 Signal to start. After everyone has made their motion, say: "If you and your partner showed the same landform—for example, both of you made the sign for mountain—you made a match! Celebrate with a high five. If you did not make a match, try again."

4 Repeat the activity for as many rounds as time allows. Reinforce students' efforts: "I see you staying in your own space and moving carefully. That makes this activity fun and safe for everyone."

VARIATION

■ Include additional landforms and motions, such as valley (make a V shape with hands), plateau (raised hand held flat), and peninsula (arm extended out from side of body).

**EXTENDING THE SOCIAL STUDIES LEARNING
BEYOND MORNING MEETING**

■ Have students work with partners to identify these landforms on maps.

North, East, South, West

Social Studies Content

Cardinal directions

NCSS Standards Theme

People, Places, and
Environments

C3 Framework

D2.Geo.2.K–2 Use maps,
graphs, photographs and
other representations to
describe places and the
relationships and interactions
that shape them.

Common Core Standards

L.1.5 With guidance and
support from adults,
demonstrate understanding
of word relationships and
nuances in word meanings.

Materials Needed

North, East, South, and
West signs

Vocabulary

Cardinal directions
East
North
South
West

How to do it:

In advance, make a sign for each cardinal direction and post it on the appropriate wall. (Note: You can download a free compass app for your smartphone or tablet to help you identify the directions of your classroom.)

1 Introduce the activity: "Today, we're going to learn more about cardinal directions—north, east, south, and west. Knowing these directions helps us find our way around. Now, look at the signs on each wall for the four directions."

2 Explain how to do the activity: "I'm going to call out a direction. You're all going to say the direction back to me and then turn toward that direction."

3 Call out a direction: "West." Wait for all students to echo "West" and turn to that direction. Continue with the other three directions. Reinforce students' efforts: "You are turning carefully. That helps us take care of ourselves and each other."

4 End the activity by reviewing the four cardinal directions (for example, by having students point and say the directions).

VARIATIONS

■ If your space allows for students to move safely, vary your instructions using different movements: "Walk to the east." "Hop to the north." "Skip to the west."

■ As your students become more familiar with the activity, add the intercardinal directions: northwest, northeast, southwest, and southeast.

**EXTENDING THE SOCIAL STUDIES LEARNING
BEYOND MORNING MEETING**

■ Have students work with partners to create silly sentences to act as mnemonic devices for remembering cardinal directions (for example, Nobody Eats Soapy Watermelon). Post these sentences near a classroom map or globe.

Our Leaders Song

Social Studies Content

Community leaders

NCSS Standards Theme

Civic Ideals and Practices

C3 Framework

D2.Civ.1.K–2 Describe roles and responsibilities of people in authority.

Common Core Standards

L.1.5 With guidance and support from adults, demonstrate understanding of word relationships and nuances in word meanings.

Materials Needed

None

Vocabulary

Mayor
Governor
President
Principal

How to do it:

1 Introduce the activity: "Today, we're going to learn a song to help us remember the names of different leaders and how they help our community. We'll start by singing about our principal."

2 Teach the words to the song (sing to the tune of "The Farmer in the Dell"):

The principal leads the school.
The principal leads the school.
Hi ho here we go,
The principal leads the school!

3 Continue the song using other school leaders. Some possible verses include: the teacher leads the class; the coach leads the team; the director leads the chorus [or band].

VARIATIONS

■ Add the names of school leaders to the chant:

Mrs. Yung leads the lunch servers.
Mrs. Yung leads the lunch servers.
Hi ho here we go,
Mrs. Yung leads the lunch servers!

■ Use the roles of other leaders, such as mayor, governor, or president.

■ Have students help you change the third line of the song to include specific responsibilities of the job. For example:

The governor leads the state.
The governor leads the state.
The governor signs bills into laws;
The governor leads the state!

**EXTENDING THE SOCIAL STUDIES LEARNING
BEYOND MORNING MEETING**

■ As a class, brainstorm questions and interview a school leader.

U.S. Symbol Refrain

Social Studies Content

Patriotism

NCSS Standards Theme

Civic Ideals and Practices

C3 Framework

D2.Civ.8.K–2 Describe democratic principles such as equality, fairness, and respect for legitimate authority and rules.

Common Core Standards

RF.1.4 Read with sufficient accuracy and fluency to support comprehension.

SL.1.5 Add drawings or other visual displays to descriptions when appropriate to clarify ideas, thoughts, and feelings. (Extending the learning)

Materials Needed

None

Vocabulary

Symbol

How to do it:

In advance, post a poem such as the one below so everyone can read it.

1 Introduce the activity: "We have learned about American symbols and how they represent our country. Today, we are going to do a call-and-response reading of a poem about the Statue of Liberty."

2 Have students count off by twos. Then ones go to one side of the room and twos go to the other side.

3 Review the words of the poem as a whole class. Then designate which side will recite which lines. For example, ones say each "Lady Liberty" line, and twos say the other lines.

4 When students finish reciting the poem, have them switch sides so that the twos say "Lady Liberty" and the ones recite the accompanying lines.

SAMPLE POEM: LADY LIBERTY

> *Lady Liberty*
> > *She's a gift from France*
> *Lady Liberty*
> > *She's made of copper*
> *Lady Liberty*
> > *She's more than one hundred feet tall*
> *Lady Liberty*
> > *She stands in the harbor*
> *Lady Liberty*
> > *She carries a torch*
> *Lady Liberty*
> > *She's a symbol of freedom*

VARIATION

- Use or adapt another poem about America or other themes for this activity, such as "Human Family" by Maya Angelou, "maggie and milly and molly and may" by E. E. Cummings, or "Dream Variations" by Langston Hughes.

EXTENDING THE SOCIAL STUDIES LEARNING
BEYOND MORNING MEETING

- Invite pairs to create a drawing or collage that represents the poem. Display and discuss the finished artwork.

Attention, Mapmakers!

Social Studies Content

Maps

NCSS Standards Theme

People, Places, and
Environments

C3 Framework

D2.Geo.1.K–2 Construct
maps, graphs, and other
representations of
familiar places.

Common Core Standards

RF.1.4 Read with sufficient
accuracy and fluency to
support comprehension.

SL.1.5 Add drawings or other
visual displays to descriptions
when appropriate to clarify
ideas, thoughts, and feelings.

Materials Needed

None

Vocabulary

Maps
Symbols

How to do it:

1 Display a message like the one below:

> Good Morning, Mapmakers!
>
> We have been learning how maps help people. We will learn more about maps this afternoon. Get ready to be a mapmaker! Draw a symbol that a mapmaker might use for one of these places:
>
> Lake   Mountain   River

2 Do a choral reading of the message with your students.

3 Ask: "What do you notice about the symbols we drew for a lake, mountain, and river?"

4 Point out that symbols are small, simple pictures that resemble real geographic features.

VARIATION

■ Have students create symbols for structures such as buildings and bridges.

EXTENDING THE SOCIAL STUDIES LEARNING BEYOND MORNING MEETING

■ Guide students in creating a simple map of the school that includes a few symbols they create and an accompanying key.

Invention Convention

How to do it:

1 Display a message like the one below:

Hello Inventors,

Here are pictures of two inventions. One is from long ago. The other is something people use today. What is one thing you know about one of these inventions? Bring your thoughts to Morning Meeting.

2 Read the message aloud, pointing to each word as you read it.

3 Going around the circle, invite students to share something they know about one of the inventions. List their statements on the message chart beneath the corresponding picture. Gently correct any misstatements.

4 Ask: "Are the statements about the 'long ago' invention also true for the one we use today? Let's look at a few of them."

5 Read a statement and invite responses from the class. If it's true for both inventions, circle it. Repeat with other statements as time allows.

VARIATION

■ Post a photo of an invention from the past in the message and have students guess what it was used for and what a comparable modern-day invention might be.

EXTENDING THE SOCIAL STUDIES LEARNING BEYOND MORNING MEETING

■ Let students imagine and either draw or create models of their own inventions.

Social Studies Content

Inventions

NCSS Standards Theme

Science, Technology, and Society

C3 Framework

D2.His.2.K–2 Compare life in the past to life today.

Common Core Standards

RI.1.7 Use the illustrations and details in a text to describe its key ideas.

SL.1.5 Add drawings or other visual displays to descriptions when appropriate to clarify ideas, thoughts, and feelings. (Extending the learning)

Materials Needed

Pictures of inventions from modern day and from long ago

Vocabulary

Inventions
Past (long ago)
Present (modern day)

Our Favorite Places

Social Studies Content

Places

NCSS Standards Theme

People, Places, and Environments

C3 Framework

D2.Geo.6.K–2 Identify some cultural and environmental characteristics of specific places.

Common Core Standards

W.1.2 Write informative/ explanatory texts in which they name a topic, supply some facts about the topic, and provide some sense of closure. (Extending the learning)

SL.1.1 Participate in collaborative conversations with diverse partners about grade 1 topics and texts with peers and adults in small and larger groups.

Materials Needed

Sticky notes

Vocabulary

Favorite
Geography

How to do it:

1 Display a message like the one below:

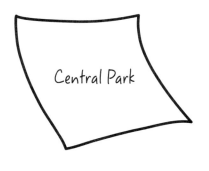

Happy Monday, First Graders!

Today, we begin our unit on geography. Geography is the study of places in our world. Which places have you visited? Write or draw one of your favorite places on a sticky note. Then put it below.

Central Park

2 Read each line of the message and have students echo-read it back.

3 Read aloud students' favorite places and group them according to similarities, pointing these out as you do.

4 Pair students with a person sitting next to them. Have partners take turns sharing the name of their favorite place and one reason they chose it.

5 Ask for a few volunteers to share out their partner's favorite place.

VARIATION

- Have students share places they have read about in social studies, places they would like to learn more about, or places they would like to visit in the future.

EXTENDING THE SOCIAL STUDIES LEARNING BEYOND MORNING MEETING

- Have students write a letter to a friend, giving some interesting facts about their favorite place.

Picture History

How to do it:

1 Display a message like the one below:

Dear Social Studies Students,

We have learned a lot about historical Americans this month! Here is a picture of someone we have been studying. Think of one fact you know about this person. Be prepared to share your thoughts.

Social Studies Content
Historical figures

NCSS Standards Theme
Time, Continuity, and Change

C3 Framework
D2.His.3.K–2 Generate questions about individuals and groups who have shaped a significant historical change.

Common Core Standards
W.1.7 Participate in shared research and writing projects (e.g., explore a number of "how-to" books on a given topic and use them to write a sequence of instructions). (Extending the learning)

SL.1.4 Describe people, places, things, and events with relevant details, expressing ideas and feelings clearly.

Materials Needed
Photograph of a historical person you are studying

Vocabulary
American
Historical

2 Read the morning message aloud to your students. Say: "Each person will have a chance to say one thing they know about Abraham Lincoln. If you hear something you already know, give a thumbs-up. If you hear a new fact, point to your head." Model and practice these motions, if needed.

3 Going around the circle, have each student share their fact. Gently correct any misstatements.

4 Invite deeper reflection: "Wow! We know a lot about Abraham Lincoln. What more would you like to learn about him?" Record students' responses.

VARIATION

■ Instead of a historical figure, use a picture of a place, landmark, or event that you are studying.

EXTENDING THE SOCIAL STUDIES LEARNING BEYOND MORNING MEETING

■ Have students research one thing from the list of questions they generated, using online research tools or the classroom or school library.

We've Got a Job to Do!

Social Studies Content

Responsibility

NCSS Standards Theme

Civic Ideals and Practices

C3 Framework

D2.Civ.2.K–2 Explain how all people, not just official leaders, play important roles in a community.

D2.Civ.6.K–2 Describe how communities work to accomplish common tasks, establish responsibilities, and fulfill roles of authority.

Common Core Standards

SL.1.1 Participate in collaborative conversations with diverse partners about grade 1 topics and texts with peers and adults in small and larger groups.

Materials Needed

None

Vocabulary

Responsibility

How to do it:

1 Display a message like the one below:

Hello, Responsible Students,

Everyone in our school has responsibilities. Responsibilities are tasks we are expected to do. Put a tally mark next to your favorite classroom responsibility:

Cleaning the paintbrushes |||| ||||

Organizing our supplies ///

Watering the plants |||| ///

Delivering notes to the office //

Passing out papers ||||

2 Read the message chorally with students.

3 Ask volunteers to lead the class in counting up the tallies on the chart.

4 Use the following questions for a class discussion about responsibilities:

➣ Why do we have responsibilities at school?

➣ How does it feel to do a job that is our responsibility?

VARIATION

▪ Instead of classroom responsibilities, adapt the message for responsibilities on the playground, in the cafeteria, and so on.

**EXTENDING THE SOCIAL STUDIES LEARNING
BEYOND MORNING MEETING**

▪ Talk about different positions at your school—custodian, cafeteria monitor, librarian, nurse, principal, teacher. Pair students to interview these individuals and report back to the class what they learned about the person's responsibilities.

Body of Water Greeting

How to do it:

Prior to this mix-and-mingle greeting, brainstorm with students different motions and voice tones to go along with different bodies of water. For example, if "brook" is called out, students could "meander" into the circle and greet each other in light, high voices.

1 Introduce the greeting: "Today, we're going to greet each other in the manner of different bodies of water."

2 Explain how to do the greeting: "I will call out a body of water, and you will come into the circle and greet each other using the motions and voices we just brainstormed. When I signal, you'll return to your circle spots."

3 Call out the first body of water: "Greet each other in the manner of a lake." Repeat with other bodies of water as time allows, such as river, pond, and ocean.

VARIATION

■ Name specific bodies of water students are studying, but without identifying the type (for example, "the Mississippi" or "the Pacific"). Have students do the motions and voice tones that match each body of water.

EXTENDING THE SOCIAL STUDIES LEARNING BEYOND MORNING MEETING

■ Create an illustrated class chart showing different bodies of water, from smallest to largest, with a brief description of each one.

Social Studies Content

Bodies of water

NCSS Standards Theme

People, Places, and Environments

C3 Framework

D2.Geo.6.K–2 Identify some cultural and environmental characteristics of specific places.

Common Core Standards

SL.2.1 Participate in collaborative conversations with diverse partners about grade 2 topics and texts with peers and adults in small and larger groups.

Materials Needed

None

Vocabulary

Body of water
Brook
Lake
Ocean
Pond
River

Global Good Mornings

Social Studies Content

Countries

NCSS Standards Theme

People, Places, and
Environments

C3 Framework

D2.Geo.2.K–2 Use maps,
graphs, photographs, and
other representations to
describe places and the
relationships and interactions
that shape them.

Common Core Standards

SL.2.1 Participate in
collaborative conversations
with diverse partners about
grade 2 topics and texts with
peers and adults in small and
larger groups.

Materials Needed

Inflatable globe (or a plain
beach ball on which you write
names of countries)

Vocabulary

Globe

How to do it:

1 Introduce the greeting: "We're going to pretend we're greeting each other from different countries around the globe!"

2 Explain how to do the greeting: "We'll toss this globe to each other. When you catch it, look to see which country is closest to your right thumb. You'll use that country's name in your greeting. For example, if the country is Mexico, you'll say 'Hello from Mexico!' Then toss the globe to someone else. After your turn, cross your arms so everyone knows you've been greeted."

3 Model and practice gently tossing the globe, and remind students to make eye contact before tossing it to someone. Ask: "How might we help someone if they have trouble reading the country closest to their thumb?" (Possible answers: The person next to them could quietly help them read it. They could just pick a country they like.)

4 Signal students to begin. Have the last student who receives the globe gently toss or hand it to you. Reinforce students' efforts: "You named lots of different countries in your greetings. That will help us recognize them later today when we continue our work with maps."

VARIATION

■ Students gently toss the globe to a classmate and ask them to find a country. For example: "Good morning, Sarah! Can you find Brazil?"

**EXTENDING THE SOCIAL STUDIES LEARNING
BEYOND MORNING MEETING**

■ Students can use classroom or library resources to find three interesting facts about a country named during the greeting. At future Morning Meetings, students can share their facts.

State Postcard Puzzles

Social Studies Content

States

NCSS Standards Theme

People, Places, and
Environments

C3 Framework

D2.Geo.6.K–2 Identify some
cultural and environmental
characteristics of specific
places.

Common Core Standards

SL.2.1 Participate in
collaborative conversations
with diverse partners about
grade 2 topics and texts with
peers and adults in small
and larger groups.

Materials Needed

State postcards

Vocabulary

Various state names

How to do it:

In advance, cut different state postcards (or printed images from a "state postcard" Internet search) into three to five pieces to create mini-puzzles. You'll need one piece for each student.

1 Mix up the postcard pieces and give one to each student. Then introduce the greeting: "When I say 'Start,' mix and mingle until you find the classmates with matching pieces to complete your postcard puzzle. Greet all your puzzle mates by naming the state on your postcard: 'Hello, Florida friends!'"

2 Reinforce students' efforts throughout the greeting: "I see people helping each other match up their puzzle pieces."

VARIATIONS

- Have students create their own postcard puzzles.
- Create other postcard puzzles related to different units of study (for example, famous landmarks, countries in Asia, or U.S. state capitals).

EXTENDING THE SOCIAL STUDIES LEARNING BEYOND MORNING MEETING

- Have each group research facts about the state on their postcard and share what they've learned during a Morning Meeting later in the week.

Bread, Meet Baker!

Social Studies Content

Goods and services

NCSS Standards Theme

Production, Distribution, and Consumption

C3 Framework

D2.Eco.4.K–2 Describe the goods and services that people in the local community produce and those that are produced in other communities.

Common Core Standards

W.2.2 Write informative/ explanatory texts in which they introduce a topic, use facts and definitions to develop points, and provide a concluding statement or section. (Extending the learning)

SL.2.1 Participate in collaborative conversations with diverse partners about grade 2 topics and texts with peers and adults in small and larger groups.

Materials Needed

Index cards prepared in advance (one per student)

Anchor chart with definitions of goods, services, producers

Vocabulary

Goods
Needs
Producers
Services
Wants

How to do it:

In advance, write a good or service on half the cards, and the producer who creates or provides it on the other cards. For example: bread/baker; haircut/ barber; vegetables/farmer; learning/teacher; health care/doctor; car repair/ mechanic. You may also want to include images on the cards.

1 Introduce the greeting: "Today, we're going to greet each other in a way that will help us review our unit on economics. You'll each get a card like one of these." Show one card of each type. Define any terms as needed (or post an anchor chart):

> **Goods**—things we use, eat, or drink (books, pizza, orange juice)
>
> **Services**—things people do for us (deliver mail, fix computers)
>
> **Producers**—people who make the goods or provide the services (factory worker, plumber)

2 Explain how to do the greeting: "Mix and mingle until you find your match. If your card has the name of a producer, look for someone who has the good or service you provide. If your card has the name of a good or service, look for the producer who provides that good or service. Greet your match with a friendly handshake, then return to the circle and sit together." Invite a student to model this with you, if needed.

3 Signal for students to begin. After everyone has found their match and returned to the circle, say: "Discuss with your partner whether your good or service is a 'need' (such as food) or a 'want' (such as a new game).

4 Give a minute or two for discussion. As time allows, go around the circle and have each pair share their match and whether it's a need or a want.

VARIATION

■ Have students create their own pairs of cards.

EXTENDING THE SOCIAL STUDIES LEARNING BEYOND MORNING MEETING

■ Create a class book of producers, goods, and services, with each pair of students contributing a page about their producer and good or service.

People of Interest

Social Studies Content

Historical figures

NCSS Standards Theme

Time, Continuity, and Change

C3 Framework

D2.His.3.K–2 Generate
questions about individuals
and groups who have shaped
a significant historical change.
(Extending the learning)

Common Core Standards

W.2.2 Write informative/
explanatory texts to examine
a topic and convey ideas and
information clearly. (Extending
the learning)

SL.2.2 Recount or describe
key ideas or details from a text
read aloud or information
presented orally or through
other media.

Materials Needed

None

Vocabulary

None

How to do it:

1 Introduce the greeting and sharing: "For this greeting, you'll share with different partners the person from our current unit of study who interests you most, and why."

2 Explain how to do the greeting: "When I say 'Go,' walk around the room until I say 'Stop.' Then greet the person closest to you with 'Hi, partner!' and a fist bump, and share your interesting person. For example, when it's my turn, I might say 'Hi, partner! I think Ben Franklin is the most interesting person we've learned about because he started America's first lending library.'"

3 Throughout the greeting and sharing, reinforce students' efforts: "You are all listening respectfully to your partners and sharing facts about a lot of interesting people!"

4 Signal for students to return to the meeting circle. Ask a few volunteers to share the name of their person with the whole group and why they find them most interesting.

VARIATIONS

■ Have students greet their partner by standing toe to toe or elbow to elbow, or by giving a high five.

■ Ask for volunteers to recall and share a classmate's interesting person.

**EXTENDING THE SOCIAL STUDIES LEARNING
BEYOND MORNING MEETING**

■ As a mini research project, have students list questions they have about their interesting person. Students can then research the answers to their questions and create illustrated charts listing their questions and answers.

Explore Galore

Social Studies Content

Exploration

NCSS Standards Theme

People, Places, and
Environments

C3 Framework

D2.Geo.6.K–2 Identify some
cultural and environmental
characteristics of specific
places.

Common Core Standards

W.2.6 With guidance and
support from adults, use a
variety of digital tools to
produce and publish writing,
including in collaboration with
peers. (Extending the learning)

SL.2.1 Participate in
collaborative conversations
with diverse partners about
grade 2 topics and texts with
peers and adults in small and
larger groups.

Materials Needed

None

Vocabulary

Explore

How to do it:

1 Introduce the sharing: "We've had such a good time learning about explorers and all the places they've gone. Today, we're going to share about a place *we'd* like to explore. It could be close to home or far away. For example, a place I'd like to explore is Guyana because that's where my grandmother grew up."

2 Explain how to do the sharing: "Think about the place you'd like to explore and one reason why. Give a thumbs-up when you're ready to share." When all thumbs are up, ask a volunteer to start, and then go around the circle.

3 Ask: "Who heard someone share a place that you'd also like to explore?" Take a few responses as time allows.

VARIATION

■ Have students share with a partner about a place (near or far) that they have already explored, giving at least two details about the place.

EXTENDING THE SOCIAL STUDIES LEARNING BEYOND MORNING MEETING

■ Have students use the computer to virtually explore a place they're interested in, or have students find books about the place in the library. They can present their findings during sharing at a future Morning Meeting.

If I Were Mayor

Social Studies Content

Government leaders

NCSS Standards Theme

Power, Authority, and Governance

C3 Framework

D2.Civ.1.K–2 Describe roles and responsibilities of people in authority.

Common Core Standards

W.2.1 Write opinion pieces in which they introduce the topic or book they are writing about, state an opinion, supply reasons that support the opinion, use linking words (e.g., because, and, also), and provide a concluding statement or section. (Extending the learning)

SL.2.6 Produce complete sentences when appropriate to task and situation in order to provide requested detail or clarification.

Materials Needed

Chart paper or whiteboard

Vocabulary

Elect
Leader
Local government
Mayor

How to do it:

1 Introduce the sharing: "In our city, we elect a mayor to lead our local government. The mayor is like the president, but just of our city. If you were mayor, what would you do to make our city a better place? Today, we'll each share one idea." (Note: Adjust the wording in this sharing to reflect your local government; for example, instead of mayor, use member of the town council, chairperson of the selectboard, etc.).

2 Post a sentence frame on chart paper or a whiteboard. For example: "If I were mayor, I would _____ so that _____." Model the sharing: "If I were mayor, I would create a public park with a swimming pool so that people could have fun outdoors."

3 As students share, list their ideas on the chart paper or whiteboard. Reinforce their thinking: "You are thinking of very specific ways to make our city a better place."

4 If time allows, ask one or two reflective questions: "Which ideas are alike?" "Who remembers why Tanya would add more construction workers if she were mayor?"

VARIATION

- Instead of local government leaders, use other leaders such as school principal or president of the United States.

EXTENDING THE SOCIAL STUDIES LEARNING BEYOND MORNING MEETING

- Have students write an essay that expands on the idea they shared, including two or more reasons for their idea and a concluding statement.

What's Your Animal?

Social Studies Content

Personal Identity

NCSS Standards Theme

Individual Development and Identity

C3 Framework

D2.Civ.10.K–2 Compare their own point of view with others' perspectives.

Common Core Standards

W.2.6 With guidance and support from adults, use a variety of digital tools to produce and publish writing, including in collaboration with peers. (Extending the learning)

SL.2.1 Participate in collaborative conversations with diverse partners about grade 2 topics and texts with peers and adults in small and larger groups.

Materials Needed

Pictures of national and state animals

Vocabulary

Various animal names

How to do it:

1 Introduce the sharing: "Some states and countries have one animal that is very special to them. For example, the state animal of Kansas is the American buffalo. The national animal of India is the Bengal tiger."

2 Explain how to do the sharing: "We're each going to choose an animal that we think is special and share one reason why. For example, I choose the wolf because wolves are loyal to their pack. What animal might you choose to be your personal animal? Give a thumbs-up when you're ready to share."

3 Remind students to be respectful of other students' responses: "Remember to keep your voice and body quiet when someone is sharing." Then, going around the circle, have each student share their personal animal and reason why.

4 Ask students to reflect: "Which reasons for choosing a personal animal were similar?"

VARIATION

■ Have students share with partners. Then go around the circle and have each student share which animal their partner chose and why.

EXTENDING THE SOCIAL STUDIES LEARNING BEYOND MORNING MEETING

■ Have students draw their own personal flag on a sheet of paper and use designs, colors, and symbols to show things that are meaningful to them, including their personal animal.

■ Have teams of students investigate different state and national animals and learn more about those animals. Invite students to create a classroom slideshow or collage to share what they have learned.

Cooperation Call-Out

Social Studies Content

Cooperation

NCSS Standards Theme

Civic Ideals and Practices

C3 Framework

D2.Civ.7.K–2 Apply civic
virtues when participating
in school settings.

Common Core Standards

SL.2.1 Participate in
collaborative conversations
with diverse partners about
grade 2 topics and texts with
peers and adults in small and
larger groups.

Materials Needed

None

Vocabulary

Cooperation

How to do it:

1 Introduce the sharing: "For today's sharing, we're going to think about times when we have cooperated, or worked together, so that we could get things done and learn a lot. For example, yesterday, I saw students helping each other clean up materials at their table after our word study."

2 Going around the circle, put students in groups of three. Explain how to do the sharing: "As a group, come up with one example of how you all cooperate. This cooperation can be from anywhere in school, such as during recess, in music class, or during Morning Meeting. Show that your team is ready to share with a thumbs-up."

3 Remind students about working respectfully with others: "Remember to make sure everyone in your group gets a chance to speak."

4 Choose one volunteer from each group to share their group's example of cooperation. To finish, have all students repeat each line of the following cheer after you:

2, 4, 6, 8
That's how we cooperate!
Yay, team!

VARIATION

■ Have each student think of one example of cooperation and share it one by one around the circle. Then have everyone repeat each line of the cheer after you.

EXTENDING THE SOCIAL STUDIES LEARNING BEYOND MORNING MEETING

■ Create a class "Cooperation Chain." Have students write instances of cooperation on paper strips and link them together. Add new ones as you and your students see additional acts of cooperation.

Grade Level

2

Group Activity

Social Studies Content

Black History Month

NCSS Standards Theme

Time, Continuity, and Change

C3 Framework

D2.His.3.K–2 Generate questions about individuals and groups who have shaped a significant historical change.

Common Core Standards

W.2.2 Write informative/ explanatory texts in which they introduce a topic, use facts and definitions to develop points, and provide a concluding statement or section. (Extending the learning)

SL.2.1 Participate in collaborative conversations with diverse partners about grade 2 topics and texts with peers and adults in small and larger groups.

Materials Needed

Black History Month facts on paper strips

Vocabulary

African American
Black History Month

Black History Month

How to do it:

In advance, prepare a set of facts about Black History Month so that you have one fact for each student. (A list of sample facts is available to download; see page 12.)

1 Introduce the activity: "In honor of Black History Month, we're going to share interesting facts about important African Americans in U.S. history."

2 Explain how to do the activity: "Everyone will get one fact. When I say 'Go,' mix and mingle until I say 'Stop.' Then pair up with someone close to you. The first person will say 'Did you know?' and read their fact. The other person will respond with 'I do now!' Then switch roles. After everyone has shared, you'll mix and mingle again to find a new partner."

3 After students have shared with three or four partners, have everyone return to the circle. Ask reflective questions: "What's one fact you were most surprised to learn?" "Which person would you like to learn more about, and why?"

VARIATION

■ Have students research their own facts to share about a figure of their choosing.

**EXTENDING THE SOCIAL STUDIES LEARNING
BEYOND MORNING MEETING**

■ Have students choose one person they learned about in this activity to research. They can find three or more new facts and write an essay, make a poster, or create a slideshow that highlights their discoveries.

Community Worker Riddles

Social Studies Content

Community workers

NCSS Standards Theme

Production, Distribution, and
Consumption

C3 Framework

D2.Civ.2.K–2 Explain how
all people, not just official
leaders, play important roles
in a community.

Common Core Standards

SL.2.3 Ask and answer
questions about what a
speaker says in order to clarify
comprehension, gather
additional information, or
deepen understanding of a
topic or issue.

Materials Needed

Chart paper or whiteboard

Community Workers
anchor chart

Vocabulary

Community worker

How to do it:

The day before this sharing or earlier in the week, have students brainstorm types of community workers (bank tellers, cashiers, doctors, environmental service workers, firefighters, judges, nurses, police officers, teachers). List students' ideas on chart paper to create an anchor chart.

1 On the day of the sharing, post the anchor chart where everyone can see it. Assign partners or have students pair up.

2 Introduce the sharing: "Today, you're going to work with a partner to create a riddle about one type of community worker. Pick a community worker from the anchor chart, and come up with two clues about them. Here's an example: 'I might work inside or outside a building. Part of my job is spraying water from a hose. Who am I?' Give a thumbs-up when you and your partner are ready to share your riddle."

3 When everyone gives their thumbs-up, go around the circle and have each pair say their riddle. Give the other students a few chances to guess. If no one figures out the correct community worker after a couple tries, have the pair share the answer.

VARIATION

■ Have individual students write their own community worker riddles.

**EXTENDING THE SOCIAL STUDIES LEARNING
BEYOND MORNING MEETING**

■ As a class, choose a type of community worker that students want to learn more about. Have them write down interview questions. Then invite someone who works in that field to come in and speak about their job and answer students' questions.

Eyes-Closed True or False

Social Studies Content

State geography

NCSS Standards Theme

People, Places, and
Environments

C3 Framework

D2.Geo.6.K–2 Identify some
cultural and environmental
characteristics of specific
places.

Common Core Standards

SL.2.2 Recount or describe
key ideas or details from a text
read aloud or information
presented orally or through
other media.

Materials Needed

Map of the United States

Map of the state you live in

Vocabulary

False
True

How to do it:

1 Introduce the activity: "I'm going to read a sentence about California, the state we live in. Listen carefully to decide if this statement is true or false." Clarify as needed so the class has a common understanding of "true" and "false."

2 Start with a simple true statement: "We attend elementary school in California." Have students close their eyes and show their response using a thumbs-up for "true" or thumbs-down for "false." Say: "I see all of you knew that was a true statement because you showed me a thumbs-up."

3 Give a simple false statement: "Our state borders the Atlantic Ocean." After all students respond, say: "I see many people knew that statement was false. Will someone turn it into a true statement?" Continue with other statements about your state's geography. For example:

➤ There are deserts in California. (true)

➤ Yellowstone National Park is in California. (false)

➤ The Sierra Nevada Mountain Range is in Eastern California. (true)

4 End the activity by reinforcing students' learning: "Wow! I can tell that we have learned a lot of facts about the geography of our state!"

VARIATION

■ Have students prepare two true statements and one false statement about a given topic. Have students read their three statements aloud to the class and then call on volunteers to guess the false statement and change it into a "truth."

EXTENDING THE SOCIAL STUDIES LEARNING BEYOND MORNING MEETING

■ Record the true statements and corrected false statements on a class chart. Use this chart to review facts in preparation for a test or assessment.

Fidget Family Back Then

Social Studies Content

Everyday life in earlier times

NCSS Standards Theme

Time, Continuity, and Change

C3 Framework

D2.His.2.K–2 Compare life
in the past to life today.

Common Core Standards

SL.2.3 Ask and answer
questions about what a
speaker says in order to clarify
comprehension, gather
additional information, or
deepen understanding
of a topic or issue.

Materials Needed

None

Vocabulary

Apartment
Factory
High-button shoes
Lamplighter
Slate
Trolley

How to do it:

1 Introduce the activity: "For today's activity, we're going back to the 19th century with the Fidget Family. In the story I'll read you, the Fidget Family lives in a very big city in the 1880s. The story will remind you what we've learned about city life back then."

2 Assign students to the following roles: Mama Fidget, Papa Fidget, Grandpa Fidget, Grandma Fidget, Tommy Fidget, Bridget Fidget, Baby Fidget, lamplighters, gas lamps, horse-drawn trolley, apartment, factory, blocks. As needed, assign multiple students to the same role.

3 Explain how to do the activity: "Everyone is going to have a part in this story. When you hear your part, you will stand up, spin around, and sit back down. When you hear 'the whole Fidget Family,' everyone will stand up, spin around, and sit back down."

4 Model the actions as needed and remind students about safe movement: "Remember to stay in your own body space so we can keep everyone safe." Read the following story aloud slowly; pause when you get to a student's part.

The Fidget Family

Once upon a time, there was a family called the Fidget Family. The whole Fidget Family lived in an apartment in a building in a very big city. Every day, Papa Fidget woke up when the lamplighters turned the gas lamps off. After breakfast, he left the apartment and took a horse-drawn trolley all the way across the city to his job at a factory where people made brooms. After Papa Fidget left on the horse-drawn trolley to go to the factory, Bridget Fidget and Tommy Fidget pulled on their high-buttoned shoes and walked three blocks down and four blocks over to school, where they sat in desks in long rows. Bridget Fidget and Tommy Fidget and their classmates got out their slates and practiced their times tables. Back at the apartment where the whole Fidget Family lived, Mama Fidget put Baby Fidget in a basket and took a horse-drawn trolley with Grandpa Fidget and Grandma Fidget to the outdoor market, which was just two blocks away from the factory where people made brooms. Dark rain clouds blew in, and the lamplighters turned the gas lamps on again. Baby Fidget wanted an apple, but Mama Fidget said, "Not today." Then Mama Fidget, Baby Fidget, Grandpa Fidget, and Grandma Fidget took the horse-drawn trolley back to the apartment where the whole Fidget Family lived. The sun came out and the lamplighters turned the gas lamps off. Grandpa Fidget heated water on the wood-burning stove so Grandma Fidget could wash clothes in a big metal tub. Mama Fidget gave Baby Fidget a rag doll to play with while she cooked dinner. At four o'clock, Bridget Fidget and Tommy Fidget walked four blocks over and three blocks up to the apartment where the whole Fidget Family lived. Bridget Fidget and Tommy Fidget rolled hoops outside on the sidewalk in front of their apartment until the lamplighters turned the gas lamps on again. Papa Fidget took the horse-drawn trolley home from the factory. Then the whole Fidget Family sat down to eat dinner together.

(This activity is adapted from *Energizers! 88 Quick Movement Activities That Refresh and Refocus, K–6*, published by Center for Responsive Schools. You can lengthen or shorten the story as needed.)

5 Ask: "What things in this story let you know that the Fidget Family lived in the 19th century?"

VARIATION

■ Have students think of a different motion to represent their character.

**EXTENDING THE SOCIAL STUDIES LEARNING
BEYOND MORNING MEETING**

■ Work as a class to create other versions of the "Fidget Family" to reflect another time period, and then compare similarities and differences.

National Symbols Loop Cards

Social Studies Content

American symbols

NCSS Standards Theme

Civic Ideals and Practices

C3 Framework

D2.Civ.8.K–2 Describe democratic principles such as equality, fairness, and respect for legitimate authority and rules.

Common Core Standards

SL.2.1 Participate in collaborative conversations with diverse partners about grade 2 topics and texts with peers and aduts in small and larger groups.

SL.2.3 Ask and answer questions about what a speaker says in order to clarify comprehension, gather additional information, or deepen understanding of a topic or issue.

Materials Needed

Pre-written paper strips or cards with factual statements and questions about American symbols

Vocabulary

National
Symbol

How to do it:

In advance, prepare a set of "loop cards." (A sample set is available to download; see page 12.) There should be one card for each student, plus the starting card for the teacher. Mix up the cards (or paper strips) before handing them out.

1 Introduce the activity: "We've been having fun learning about national symbols—those things that stand for or remind us about our country. For our activity today, we'll play a game using some of those symbols."

2 Explain how to do the activity: "Everyone will have a card that has one statement and one question. I'll begin by standing up, reading the question on my card, and sitting down. If the statement on your card is the answer to the question I ask, you will stand up and read the statement. Then you'll read the question on your card and sit down. We'll continue this way until we reach the card that says 'I have the last card.'"

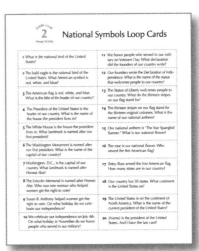

3 Give each student a card. Stand and read the first card in a loud, clear voice: "What is the national bird of the United States?" After reading, sit down. The student whose card answers the question then stands and reads their card: "The bald eagle is the national bird of the United States. What American symbol is red, white, and blue?"

4 If no one responds, have students check again to see if their card matches the clue. When the final question is answered and the last student says "I have the last card," reinforce students' efforts: "We finished our loop. Our activity went smoothly because everyone listened carefully to the questions!"

VARIATIONS

■ Create (or have students create) more sets of "loop cards" to review other units of study or to go even deeper into a specific topic, such as a historic event or geographic feature.

■ Add images to the cards to help struggling or emerging readers.

EXTENDING THE SOCIAL STUDIES LEARNING BEYOND MORNING MEETING

■ Read the book *O, Say Can You See: America's Symbols, Landmarks, and Inspiring Words* by Sheila Keenan, illustrated by Ann Boyajian, or ask your school librarian to recommend a similar title. Have students work in small groups to create a poster that showcases important facts about one American symbol from the book. Display the posters in the classroom.

We Wonder . . .

Social Studies Content

Countries

NCSS Standards Theme

People, Places, and
Environments

C3 Framework

D2.Geo.6.K–2 Identify some
cultural and environmental
characteristics of specific
places.

Common Core Standards

W.2.8 Recall information
from experiences or gather
information from provided
sources to answer a question.
(Extending the learning)

SL.2.1 Participate in
collaborative conversations
with diverse partners about
grade 2 topics and texts with
peers and adults in small and
larger groups.

Materials Needed

Chart paper

Markers

Vocabulary

Will vary depending on the
country used in the activity

How to do it:

In advance, post sheets of chart paper around the room (one chart per group of three to four students).

1 Introduce the activity: "In our new social studies unit, we'll be studying other communities around the world. Today, we're going to get our brains ready for this unit by doing some wondering about communities in Brazil. For example, I wonder: what kinds of food do people in Brazil eat?"

2 Assign groups of three or four students to each chart and explain how to do the activity: "Each of you will think of at least one thing you wonder about communities in Brazil, and then write or draw your idea on the chart."

3 After students complete their charts, give them a few minutes to walk around and examine the other groups' charts. Have them think about this question: "What are some ways we might investigate these wonderings?"

VARIATION

■ Use this activity at the end of a unit of study by asking: "What is the most interesting thing you learned about Brazil, and why?"

**EXTENDING THE SOCIAL STUDIES LEARNING
BEYOND MORNING MEETING**

■ Save these charts and review them throughout your unit of study. Check off any wonderings that have been addressed and add any new wonderings as they come up.

Classroom Grid

Social Studies Content

Map grids

NCSS Standards Theme

People, Places, and Environments

C3 Framework

D2.Geo.2.K–2 Use maps, graphs, photographs, and other representations to describe places and the relationships and interactions that shape them.

Common Core Standards

SL.2.1 Participate in collaborative conversations with diverse partners about grade 2 topics and texts with peers and adults in small and larger groups.

Materials Needed

None

Vocabulary

Coordinates
Grid
Map
Mapmaker

How to do it:

1 Display a message like the one below:

Dear Mapmakers,

We've learned that mapmakers use grids to help us find things on maps. Look at the grid below. Think about what the coordinates are for each of these four areas of our classroom. (Hint: The whiteboard is at B1.)

	1	2
A	Science area	Reading area
B	Whiteboard	Classroom bulletin board

2 Read the message chorally. Ask for volunteers to name the coordinates for the other three classroom areas.

3 Say: "Take a look at the grid again. I'm going to call out a set of coordinates. Raise your hand when you can tell me something you can find in that location. For example, if I call out B1, one answer might be the projector." Ask other questions using the coordinates, such as:

➤ What is one thing we might need when we go to A2?

➤ What is something we recently added to B2?

➤ What time of the day might we go to A1?

EXTENDING THE SOCIAL STUDIES LEARNING BEYOND MORNING MEETING

■ Give students blank map grids and have them fill in the names of objects or areas in other parts of the school, such as the library or auditorium.

■ Have students create their own classroom maps with grids. Students can pair up and take turns identifying classroom features on the map grid.

Climate Conversation

Social Studies Content

Climate

NCSS Standards Theme

People, Places, and Environments

C3 Framework

D2.Geo.3.K–2 Use maps, globes, and other simple geographic models to identify cultural and environmental characteristics of places.

D2.Geo.4.K–2 Explain how weather, climate, and other environmental characteristics affect people's lives in a place or region.

Common Core Standards

SL.2.2 Recount or describe key ideas or details from a text read aloud or information presented orally or through other media.

Materials Needed

Picture of a place in a climate zone (desert, tropical forest, etc.) that students are studying

Vocabulary

Climate
Environment

How to do it:

1 Display a message like the one below:

Greetings, Students!

Climate is the normal weather in a place over a long time. We have learned that places on Earth have different climates. Look at the picture below. What would you need to live in this climate? Add your idea to the bottom of this message.

2 Read the message chorally; then read students' ideas aloud. Reinforce students' thoughtful responses: "You came up with a lot of ideas about how to live in this climate!"

3 Ask students to reflect: "How would you describe the climate in this picture? Who remembers where we might find a climate like this?" Use a globe to discuss where the climate might be found.

VARIATION

■ On your message, post a picture of a type of extreme weather (such as a tornado or hurricane). Have students write a fact or question about this type of weather. Use a map or globe to show some places where this type of weather is typically found.

EXTENDING THE SOCIAL STUDIES LEARNING BEYOND MORNING MEETING

■ Have students create a classroom display showing pictures of items people need in a specific climate. For example: A display about a desert climate might have sunscreen, water, sunglasses, head coverings, etc.

Country Commonalities

Social Studies Content

Geography

NCSS Standards Theme

People, Places, and
Environments

C3 Framework

D2.Geo.6.K–2 Identify some
cultural and environmental
characteristics of specific
places.

D2.Geo.8.K–2 Compare how
people in different types of
communities use local and
distant environments to meet
their daily needs.

Common Core Standards

W.2.6 With guidance and
support from adults, use a
variety of digital tools to
produce and publish writing,
including in collaboration
with peers. (Extending
the learning)

SL.2.2 Recount or describe
key ideas or details from a text
read aloud or information
presented orally or through
other media.

Materials Needed

None

Vocabulary

Culture
Differences
Geography
Similarities

How to do it:

1 Display a message like the one below:

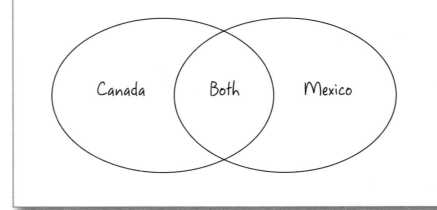

Good Morning, Geographers,

We've learned so much about our neighbors, Canada and Mexico!
On the Venn diagram below, write a fact that is true about Canada
or Mexico or both. To get ideas, think about culture and geography.

2 Going around the circle, have each student read one word of the message
until the whole message is read. Point to each word as it's read. Then read
students' ideas aloud. Reinforce their efforts: "You've included a lot of
specific details in these facts!"

3 Prompt deeper reflection with an open-ended question: "Look at our diagram. What do you notice?" Invite a few volunteers to share observations.

VARIATIONS

■ As a class, categorize the ideas on the chart. For example, put a yellow
circle around ideas that have to do with culture, and put a green circle
around ideas that relate to geography.

■ Use the Venn diagram to compare and contrast two important figures in
history, two events, or two other topics of study.

EXTENDING THE SOCIAL STUDIES LEARNING BEYOND MORNING MEETING

■ Have students work in groups to make a slide show presentation that
highlights key similarities and differences between Canada and Mexico.

History by the Numbers

Social Studies Content
U.S. landmarks

NCSS Standards Theme
Time, Continuity, and Change

C3 Framework
D2.His.14.K–2 Generate possible reasons for an event or development in the past.

Common Core Standards
SL.2.1 Participate in collaborative conversations with diverse partners about grade 2 topics and texts with peers and adults in small and larger groups.

Materials Needed
None

Vocabulary
Historian
Landmark

How to do it:

1 Display a message like the one below:

> Hello, New York City Historians:
>
> We've been studying historic landmarks like the Empire State Building and the USS Intrepid. Yesterday, you collected information about the Brooklyn Bridge. Later today, you will share your findings with Mr. Brown's class!
>
> Thinking Challenge: Here are three numbers that relate to the Brooklyn Bridge. Think about what they might mean! We'll talk about them at Morning Meeting.
>
> 5,989   1883   14

2 Invite a student volunteer to read the message aloud, with help from you and classmates as needed.

3 Give students a minute or so to share their ideas with a partner. Invite students to share out. Reinforce students' thoughtful responses: "Wow! You really thought of lots of different ways those numbers might relate to the Brooklyn Bridge!"

4 Reveal how each number relates to the Brooklyn Bridge: "The length of the bridge is 5,989 feet. 1883 is the year the bridge officially opened. It took 14 years to construct the bridge."

VARIATION

■ Do not reveal how each number relates to the bridge. Instead, have students work in pairs and look up the answers using their social studies resources.

EXTENDING THE SOCIAL STUDIES LEARNING BEYOND MORNING MEETING

■ Have students research three other numerical facts about the Brooklyn Bridge or another unit of study. Use their numbers in future messages.

School Tools Long Ago

Social Studies Content

How institutions such as schools change over time

NCSS Standards Theme

Time, Continuity, and Change

C3 Framework

D2.His.2.K–2 Compare life in the past to life today.

Common Core Standards

W.2.2 Write informative/ explanatory texts in which they introduce a topic, use facts and definitions to develop points, and provide a concluding statement or section.

SL.2.1 Participate in collaborative conversations with diverse partners about grade 2 topics and texts with peers and adults in small and larger groups.

Materials Needed

Picture of something found in a 19th-century classroom

Sticky notes

Vocabulary

Society

How to do it:

1 Display a message like the one below:

Hello, Historians of the 19th Century,

We have learned how society changes over time. Many years ago, people had different tools, ideas, and ways of doing things. Look at the picture below. On a sticky note, write one way this 19th-century writing tool is the same as our writing tools today and one way it is different. Bring your sticky note to our meeting.

2 Invite student volunteers to each read one sentence of the message aloud. Then have students turn to the person next to them and refer to their sticky notes as they discuss their ideas. After a minute or two, have each pair share with the class one similarity or difference they discussed.

3 Invite deeper thought: "Which do you think would be easier: to be a student now or in the 19th century? Why?" Give partners a minute or so to share their ideas.

VARIATION

■ Post a photograph of your school, town, or city from long ago. Have students discuss ways your community has changed and reasons why those changes might have happened.

EXTENDING THE SOCIAL STUDIES LEARNING BEYOND MORNING MEETING

■ Have students work in groups to investigate other classroom tools from now and long ago and create T-charts with similarities on one side and differences on the other. Do a museum walk so students can see class-mates' findings.

Are You My Capital?

Social Studies Content

U.S. states and capitals

NCSS Standards Theme

People, Places, and
Environments

C3 Framework

D2.Geo.2.3–5 Use maps,
satellite images, photographs,
and other representations to
explain relationships between
the locations of places and
regions and their
environmental characteristics.

Common Core Standards

SL.3.1 Engage effectively in a
range of collaborative
discussions (one-on-one, in
groups, and teacher-led) with
diverse partners on grade 3
topics and texts, building on
others' ideas and expressing
their own clearly.

Materials Needed

State names on index
cards/slips of paper

State capitals on index
cards/slips of paper

Vocabulary

Capital

State

How to do it:

In advance, display a map of the United States and its capitals. Prepare enough cards that there's one for each student. Write the name of a state on half the cards, and the names of those states' capitals on the other cards. (A sample set of cards is available to download; see page 12.)

1 Introduce the greeting: "During our mix-and-mingle greeting today, we'll polish up our knowledge of states and capitals."

2 Hand out a card to each student and explain how to do the greeting: "Mingle and greet classmates until you find your state or capital match. If you greet someone who's not your match, say 'Sorry, no match!' and keep mingling. When you find your match, give them a gentle high-five and return to your seat."

Alabama	Montgomery
Alaska	Juneau
Arizona	Phoenix
Arkansas	Little Rock
California	Sacramento
Colorado	Denver
Connecticut	Hartford
Delaware	Dover
Florida	Tallahassee
Georgia	Atlanta

3 Model a "match" greeting with a volunteer: "Good morning, Josey! I'm Nevada. Are you my capital?" The student will respond: "Good morning, Ms. O'Donnell! Yes, I'm Carson City!"

4 Signal students to begin mixing and mingling. Reinforce positive behaviors you notice: "I hear people greeting each other in a friendly way by using each other's names." End the greeting after all students have found their matches and returned to their seats.

VARIATIONS

- Use countries and their capitals or continents.

- Use states and their national parks, prominent landforms, or major industries.

EXTENDING THE SOCIAL STUDIES LEARNING BEYOND MORNING MEETING

- Have students research and report on how the states used during Morning Meeting acquired their nicknames. For example: Ohio is nicknamed the "Buckeye State" because buckeye trees once covered the state's plains and hills.

Around the World

How to do it:

In advance, display a world map or globe where everyone can see it. If needed, check online for correct pronunciations of greetings in various languages.

1 Introduce the greeting: "We've learned that all languages have words people use to greet each other. This week, we'll practice greetings from different parts of the world. Each day, we'll write the day's greeting on a sticky note and put it on a country where that language is spoken."

2 Explain how to do the greeting: "Today, we're going to greet each other in Japanese. Here's one way that people in Japan greet each other: 'Ohayo.' Everyone say 'Ohayo' back to me." Wait for students to say it back.

3 Send "Ohayo" around the circle. Remind students how to greet each other respectfully: "Remember to look your neighbor in the eye, smile, and say their name as you greet them."

4 When the greeting has traveled around the circle, invite a volunteer to find Japan on the map or globe and mark it with a sticky note that says "Ohayo."

VARIATION

■ Use greetings from students' home countries or cultures (where they, their parents, or ancestors came from). After the greeting travels around the circle, have that student or group of students mark the map.

EXTENDING THE SOCIAL STUDIES LEARNING BEYOND MORNING MEETING

■ Have students work in small groups to research facts about one of the marked countries. Students can create brochures showing what they've learned and share them at future Morning Meetings.

Social Studies Content

World languages

NCSS Standards Themes

Global Connections

People, Places, and Environments

C3 Framework

D2.Geo.3.3–5 Use maps of different scales to describe the locations of cultural and environmental characteristics.

D2.Geo.4.3–5 Explain how culture influences the way people modify and adapt to their environments.

Common Core Standards

W.3.2 Write informative/ explanatory texts to examine a topic and convey ideas and information clearly. (Extending the learning)

SL.3.4 Report on a topic or text, tell a story, or recount an experience with appropriate facts and relevant, descriptive details, speaking clearly at an understandable pace.

Materials Needed

World map or globe

Vocabulary

Culture

Greeting

Beach Ball Review

Social Studies Content

Various, depending on unit being studied

NCSS Standards Theme

Varies

C3 Framework

D2.Civ.7.3–5 Apply civic virtues and democratic principles in school settings.

Common Core Standards

W.3.2 Write informative/ explanatory texts to examine a topic and convey ideas and information clearly. (Extending the learning)

SL.3.1 Engage effectively in a range of collaborative discussions (one-on-one, in groups, and teacher-led) with diverse partners on grade 3 topics and texts, building on others' ideas and expressing their own clearly.

L.3.6 Acquire and use accurately grade-appropriate conversational, general academic, and domain-specific words and phrases, including those that signal spatial and temporal relationships (e.g., After dinner that night we went looking for them).

Materials Needed

Beach ball

Vocabulary

Varies

How to do it:

In advance, write a vocabulary word from your unit of study on each panel of a beach ball and on the small circles at the top and bottom (or write on strips of paper and tape them to the ball).

1 Introduce the greeting: "Today, you'll each toss the beach ball to a class-mate to greet each other and review our unit's vocabulary words."

2 Explain and model how to do the greeting: "When you get the ball, greet someone in the circle with the word closest to one hand. Use the word in a sentence, and then toss the ball to the person you greeted, and sit down. I'll start. Good morning, Avery. My word is 'colony.' Virginia was a colony before it became a state." Toss the ball to the student you greeted, and sit down. "Now, it's Avery's turn."

3 After everyone has been greeted, reinforce students' efforts: "I saw people making eye contact before tossing the ball, and I heard meaningful sentences. You all really know our vocabulary words."

VARIATIONS

■ Use historical events, figures, and dates instead of vocabulary words.

■ Have students come up with the words to write on the beach ball.

EXTENDING THE SOCIAL STUDIES LEARNING BEYOND MORNING MEETING

■ Have students write a paragraph using their vocabulary word and make an illustration to accompany it. The paragraph should include facts they learned during their unit of study. Compile students' illustrated paragraphs to create a class book they can use as a reference.

Latitude and Longitude

How to do it:

In advance, prepare "latitude" and "longitude" cards. Optional: Display a map with latitude and longitude lines in the meeting area during Morning Meeting. (A sample set of cards is available to download; see page 12.)

1 Introduce the greeting: "Today, you'll greet each other by lines of latitude and longitude."

2 Give each student a "latitude" or "longitude" card, and then explain and model how to do the greeting: "When I say 'Prime meridian,' everyone who has a 'longitude' card will come into the circle to greet classmates by stretching one arm overhead like a line of longitude, saying 'Hello' and the person's name, and giving a high-five. When I say 'Equator,' everyone who has a 'latitude' card will come into the circle to greet classmates by stretching one arm out in front of you like a line of latitude, saying 'Hello' and the person's name, and giving a handshake."

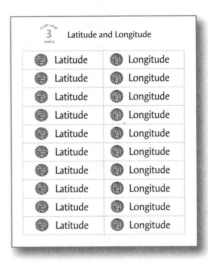

3 After everyone has had a chance to greet each other, reinforce their efforts: "I saw people making eye contact and smiling, and I heard people greeting each other with friendly voices."

VARIATION

■ As students greet each other, invite them to each name one place east or west of the prime meridian, or north or south of the equator. Students may use the displayed world map for reference.

EXTENDING THE SOCIAL STUDIES LEARNING BEYOND MORNING MEETING

■ Have students choose a country or state on a map and write down the lines of latitude and longitude to provide the coordinates. Include students' coordinates in morning messages throughout the week for the class to solve.

Social Studies Content

Location

NCSS Standards Theme

People, Places, and Environments

C3 Framework

D2.Geo.1.3–5 Construct maps and other graphic representations of both familiar and unfamiliar places.

Common Core Standards

L.3.6 Acquire and use accurately grade-appropriate conversational, general academic, and domain-specific words and phrases, including those that signal spatial and temporal relationships (e.g., After dinner that night we went looking for them).

Materials Needed

One prewritten index card for each student: half with the word "latitude;" half with "longitude"

Optional: A world map with latitude and longitude lines

Vocabulary

Equator
Latitude
Longitude
Prime meridian

Needs and Wants

Social Studies Content

Distinguish between needs and wants

NCSS Standards Theme

Production, Distribution, and Consumption

C3 Framework

D2.Eco.1.3–5 Compare the benefits and costs of individual choices.

D2.Eco.2.3–5 Identify positive and negative incentives that influence the decisions people make.

Common Core Standards

SL.3.1 Engage effectively in a range of collaborative discussions (one-on-one, in groups, and teacher-led) with diverse partners on grade 3 topics and texts, building on others' ideas and expressing their own clearly.

Materials Needed

One index card for each student: half with the word "need" on it; half with the word "want" on it

Vocabulary

Needs
Wants

How to do it:

In advance, prepare "need" and "want" cards. (A sample set of cards is available to download; see page 12.)

1 Introduce the greeting: "In today's mix-and-mingle greeting, you'll think about needs and wants while saying 'Good morning' to classmates." As a class, review the difference between a "need" and a "want." Post an anchor chart with a brief definition of each.

2 Give each student a "need" or "want" card, and explain how to do the greeting: "As you mix and mingle, say 'Good morning' to as many classmates as you can and share one example of a need or a want. For example, if I have a 'need' card, I might say 'Good morning, Maya. I need vegetables to eat because they keep me healthy.'" Let students know they can refer to the anchor chart if they get stuck.

3 Encourage students to choose a different need or want with each greeting, and remind them to greet each other respectfully: "Remember to make eye contact and use a friendly tone of voice when you greet your partner."

Grade Level **3** Greeting	Needs and Wants
Need	Want
Need	Want
Need	Want
Need	Want
Need	Want
Need	Want
Need	Want
Need	Want
Need	Want
Need	Want

4 After several minutes, signal for students to return to the circle. Invite a few students to share out a need or a want they heard.

VARIATION

- Use cards with examples of needs (such as a glass of water or a winter jacket) and wants (such as a baseball glove or a vacation trip). Have students mix and mingle, greeting partners and sharing whether they think their card is a need or a want, and why.

EXTENDING THE SOCIAL STUDIES LEARNING BEYOND MORNING MEETING

- Have students brainstorm lists of needs and wants they'd pack for a historical expedition or a visit to a country they've been studying.

Community News Desk

Social Studies Content

Current events

NCSS Standards Theme

Civic Ideals and Practices

C3 Framework

D2.Civ.6.3–5 Describe ways in which people benefit from and are challenged by working together, including through government, workplaces, voluntary organizations, and families.

Common Core Standards

RI.3.2 Determine the main idea of a text; recount the key details and explain how they support the main idea.

W.3.2 Write informative/ explanatory texts to examine a topic and convey ideas and information clearly. (Extending the learning)

SL.3.4 Report on a topic or text, tell a story, or recount an experience with appropriate facts and relevant, descriptive details, speaking clearly at an understandable pace.

Materials Needed

Newspapers

News websites

Vocabulary

Citizen
Community
News
News anchor

How to do it:

In advance, place a desk or table and chair—the "Community News Desk"—near the meeting area and plan to have one or two students share each day. A day or two before students share, have them find an article from a local newspaper (be sure to give clear guidelines about appropriate news items to share). Have students write a brief summary of their news in a format like this:

> I'm news anchor Leah Carson. Here's some news from Springfield. Firefighters held a holiday toy drive for children who are ill. They collected almost 400 toys. They gave the toys to patients at two local children's hospitals.

Review students' items before Morning Meeting and be ready to read a news item of your own to the class.

1 Introduce the sharing: "Today, we start our 'Community News Desk' sharing! As responsible citizens, it's important to know what's going on in our community and our world. Each of you will have a chance to share some news you've read about. We'll have two sharers today."

2 Explain and model how to do the sharing: "You will share the news like a real news anchor. News anchors are the people who tell us the news on the radio or television. They read the news in clear, firm voices." Read your own news in an emphatic news-anchor style.

3 Begin the student sharing. Reinforce students' efforts: "Today's sharers used strong, clear voices so we could hear their community news."

4 Invite reflection with an open-ended question: "What more would you like to know about the news that classmates shared today?"

VARIATION

- Have students act as weather reporters and share about the climate and weather of a particular geographic region.

EXTENDING THE SOCIAL STUDIES LEARNING BEYOND MORNING MEETING

- Have students work in pairs to write and present their own school news articles. These can also be shared at the Community News Desk during Morning Meetings.

Get Out the Vote

Social Studies Content

Voting

NCSS Standards Theme

Civic Ideals and Practices

C3 Framework

D2.Civ.2.3–5 Explain how a democracy relies on peoples' responsible participation, and draw implications for how individuals should participate.

Common Core Standards

SL.3.1 Engage effectively in a range of collaborative discussions (one-one-one, in groups, and teacher-led) with diverse partners on grade 3 topics and texts, building on others' ideas and expressing their own clearly.

SL.3.6 Speak in complete sentences when appropriate to task and situation in order to provide requested detail or clarification.

Materials Needed

Students' premade paper buttons

Tape

Optional: Sample buttons (or images of buttons)

Vocabulary

Citizen

Vote

How to do it:

The day before this sharing or earlier in the week, have students create buttons with words and pictures that encourage citizens to vote. If possible, show them some sample buttons (or images of buttons) and discuss different ways the designers got their message across (for example, by using humor, catchy phrases, bright colors, etc.). Have students tape on their buttons to wear to Morning Meeting.

1 Introduce the sharing: "For today's sharing, you'll take turns telling a partner about the button you created to encourage people to vote. One person will explain the words and pictures on their button. Then their partner will give them a compliment about their work. Then you'll switch roles."

2 Have partners sit facing each other and begin sharing. Reinforce positive behaviors: "I hear students politely asking each other who would like to go first."

3 After all students have shared, have them return to the circle. Invite students to dig deeper: "Why is it important for all citizens to vote? What might happen if people did not vote?"

VARIATION

■ Have students create and share about buttons that support causes they care about.

EXTENDING THE SOCIAL STUDIES LEARNING BEYOND MORNING MEETING

■ Explain to students that when our Constitution was first written, not all citizens had the right to vote. Have small groups investigate how different groups of people received this important right.

Grade Level

3

Sharing

What's Your Perspective?

How to do it:

In advance, prepare index cards that have one of the following roles: third grader, teacher, cafeteria monitor, and custodian. Make enough for each student to have one.

1 Introduce the sharing: "Today, we're going to play the role of different people in our school and imagine what we might do in different situations."

2 Explain how to do the sharing: "We'll all stand up, and I'll give each of you a role card. Then I'll name different situations that might happen here at school. If I call your role, give a thumbs-up. For each situation, I'll call on one or two people in different roles to share their ideas about what they would do. After you share, sit down."

3 Pass out the role cards and ask: "What are some ways we can be respectful to one another as we share?"

4 Pose a situation: "You notice that it is getting very loud in the cafeteria during lunch time. What might you do to help students enjoy their lunch in a quieter way?" Give students time to think.

5 Say: "Teacher, what's your perspective?" Call on one or two students with a teacher role card to share. Continue to pose different situations and call out different roles until all students have shared.

VARIATION

■ Substitute other school roles such as principal, guidance counselor, art teacher, or athletic coach.

EXTENDING THE SOCIAL STUDIES LEARNING BEYOND MORNING MEETING

■ Invite students to brainstorm other school situations with different roles and perspectives, and use those for a future sharing.

Social Studies Content

Understanding group roles

NCSS Standards Theme

Individuals, Groups, and Institutions

C3 Framework

D2.Civ.10.3–5 Identify the beliefs, experiences, perspectives, and values that underlie their own and others' points of view about civic issues.

Common Core Standards

SL.3.1 Engage effectively in a range of collaborative discussions (one-one-one, in groups, and teacher-led) with diverse partners on grade 3 topics and texts, building on others' ideas and expressing their own clearly.

SL.3.6 Speak in complete sentences when appropriate to task and situation in order to provide requested detail or clarification.

Materials Needed

Premade index cards or slips of paper with the following roles: teacher, third grader, cafeteria monitor, custodian

Vocabulary

Perspective
Role

Citizen Chant

Social Studies Content

Rights and responsibilities of citizens

NCSS Standards Theme

Civic Ideals and Practices

C3 Framework

D2.Civ.8.3–5 Identify core civic virtues and democratic principles that guide government, society, and communities.

Common Core Standards

SL.3.1 Engage effectively in a range of collaborative discussions (one-on-one, in groups, and teacher-led) with diverse partners on grade 3 topics and texts, building on others' ideas and expressing their own clearly.

Materials Needed

Words to the chant on chart paper or whiteboard

Vocabulary

Citizen
Responsibilities
Rights

How to do it:

In advance, post the chant below where everyone can see it, with the stanzas numbered 1 through 4.

1 Divide the class into four groups and assign each one a number. Then introduce the activity: "Today, we're going do a chant that will help us remember the rights and responsibilities that go along with being a citizen."

2 Explain how to do the activity: "Each group will come up with one or more motions to match your part of the chant. Then we'll say the chant together with each group doing their motions."

3 Give groups a couple of minutes to come up with motions for their stanza. Then as a class, read the chant chorally—each group doing their motion when their stanza is chanted.

> *Citizens, citizens*
> *It's our responsibility*
> *To follow all the rules and laws*
> *Within the whole community.*
>
> *Community, community*
> *We help in our community*
> *By being kind and neighborly*
> *And learning to cooperate.*
>
> *Cooperate, cooperate*
> *We work hard to cooperate*
> *Inside our homes and in our school*
> *Respecting people's lawful rights.*
>
> *Lawful rights, lawful rights*
> *Citizens have lawful rights*
> *To justice and equality*
> *To safety and to liberty.*

4 Reinforce students' efforts: "You came up with meaningful motions and chanted with such enthusiasm!"

EXTENDING THE SOCIAL STUDIES LEARNING BEYOND MORNING MEETING

■ Have students consider specific examples of rights and responsibilities they have at school. Post their ideas and refer to them as the class goes about its daily life, such as during other lessons and activities.

Continent Chant

Social Studies Content

Names of the continents

NCSS Standards Theme

People, Places, and Environments

C3 Framework

D2.Geo.2.3–5 Use maps, satellite images, photographs, and other representations to explain relationships between the locations of places and regions and their environmental characteristics.

Common Core Standards

SL.3.1 Engage effectively in a range of collaborative discussions (one-on-one, in groups, and teacher-led) with diverse partners on grade 3 topics and texts, building on others' ideas and expressing their own clearly.

Materials Needed

World map

Words to the chant on chart paper or whiteboard

Vocabulary

Continent

Prominent

How to do it:

1 Introduce the activity: "Today, we are going to learn a chant that will help us remember the seven continents."

2 First, have the whole class chant together while you point to the continents on the map. Then invite student volunteers to point to the continents as the class chants.

> *Earth has seven continents*
> *On a globe they're prominent*
> *North and South America*
> *Europe, Asia, Africa*
> *To the south Antarctica*
> *The smallest one is Australia*

3 After the class has done the chant several times, remove the chart and have them try the chant from memory.

VARIATION

■ With the chart removed, divide the class into four groups. Have everyone say the first two lines together, then point to the groups one by one to say the remaining four lines. Repeat as time allows, varying which group says which line.

EXTENDING THE SOCIAL STUDIES LEARNING BEYOND MORNING MEETING

■ Have students work in small groups to look up facts about one of the continents. Groups can share what they learn at a future Morning Meeting.

Ellis Island Timeline

Social Studies Content

Immigration

NCSS Standards Theme

Time, Continuity, and Change

C3 Framework

D2.His.1.3–5 Create and use a chronological sequence of related events to compare developments that happened at the same time.

Common Core Standards

RI.3.3 Describe the relationship between a series of historical events, scientific ideas or concepts, or steps in technical procedures in a text, using language that pertains to time, sequence, and cause/effect.

W.3.3 Write narratives to develop real or imagined experiences or events using effective technique, descriptive details, and clear event sequences. (Extending the learning)

Materials Needed

Timeline cards (one set per group of three to five students)

Vocabulary

Ellis Island
Immigrant
Immigration
Timeline

How to do it:

In advance, create a set of timeline cards for each group of three to five students. For example:

➤ Board a ship and spend days at sea

➤ See the Statue of Liberty for the first time

➤ Take a ferry or barge

➤ Arrive at Ellis Island

➤ Go through a health check

➤ Answer many questions from immigration officers

➤ Get your landing card

1 Introduce the activity: "Today, we're going to work in small groups to create timelines that show what happened when an immigrant arrived at Ellis Island in the early 1900s. First, let's refresh our memory. What is a timeline? What can a timeline tell us?" Clarify any misunderstandings.

2 Put students into groups, and give each group a set of cards. Explain how to do the activity: "Read your cards and work together to put the events in the order in which they would have happened." Remind students about working cooperatively: "What are ways you can make sure that everyone in your group has a turn to contribute ideas?"

3 When timelines are complete, have students return to the circle. Invite deeper thinking with an open-ended question: "How might people have felt about leaving their homelands and creating a home in a new place?"

EXTENDING THE SOCIAL STUDIES LEARNING BEYOND MORNING MEETING

■ Have students create graphic stories depicting the events on the cards.

■ Have students investigate individual experiences at Ellis Island by reading a book like *At Ellis Island: A History in Many Voices* by Louise Peacock, illustrated by Walter Lyon Krudop.

Guess My State!

Social Studies Content

The 50 states of the U.S.

NCSS Standards Theme

People, Places, and Environments

C3 Framework

D1.4.3–5 Explain how supporting questions help answer compelling questions in an inquiry.

D2.Geo.2.3–5 Use maps, satellite images, photographs, and other representations to explain relationships between the locations of places and regions and their environmental characteristics.

Common Core Standards

SL.3.3 Ask and answer questions about information from a speaker, offering appropriate elaboration and detail.

SL.3.4 Report on a topic or text, tell a story, or recount an experience with appropriate facts and relevant, descriptive details, speaking clearly at an understandable pace. (Extending the learning)

Materials Needed

Map of the United States

Vocabulary

Border
Landmark

How to do it:

In advance, display a map of a region of the United States that the class is studying (for example, New England), or outline the area on a map of the United States.

1 Introduce the activity: "Today, we're going to play Guess My State!"

2 Explain how to do the activity: "I'm going to think of one New England state. I'll call on five students to ask a question about the state. They should be questions I can answer with 'Yes' or 'No.' Then I'll call on up to three students to guess my state."

3 Give students a few examples of questions to ask: "You might ask whether I border a certain state or a body of water, if a certain city is in the state, or if the state is home to a specific famous landmark."

4 Call on five students to ask questions and then up to three students to guess. If no one guesses the state, give additional clues or name the state and point it out on the map. Play additional rounds as time allows.

VARIATION

■ Have student volunteers think of a state, answer questions, and take guesses. This activity can be extended over several Morning Meetings to give all students a chance to be the leader.

EXTENDING THE SOCIAL STUDIES LEARNING BEYOND MORNING MEETING

■ Have students work in small groups to research facts about a state (history, famous people, and so on). Have them prepare an oral presentation using a question-and-answer format to share their findings.

History Wordsmiths

Social Studies Content

Settlement

NCSS Standards Themes

Culture and Cultural Diversity

People, Places, and
Environments

C3 Framework

D2.His.2.3–5 Compare life
in specific historical time
periods to life today.

Common Core Standards

W.3.6 With guidance and
support from adults, use
technology to produce and
publish writing (using
keyboarding skills) as well as
to interact and collaborate
with others. (Extending
the learning)

L.3.6 Acquire and use
accurately grade-appropriate
conversational, general
academic, and domain-specific
words and phrases, including
those that signal spatial and
temporal relationships
(e.g., After dinner that night
we went looking for them).

Materials Needed

Chart paper or whiteboard

Paper

Pens or pencils

Vocabulary

Wordsmith

How to do it:

1 Introduce the activity: "You'll be working in small groups to share some things you know about the Plymouth colony. Each group will get a vocabulary word related to the Plymouth colony and will work together on three tasks." Display the tasks on chart paper or a whiteboard:

➤ Write a definition of your word.

➤ Write a sentence using your word.

➤ Write one thing about this word you would like to know more about.

2 Divide students into groups of three. Assign a vocabulary word to each group and give them paper for recording their ideas. Reinforce students' cooperation: "I see lots of students listening to one another and sharing ideas."

3 When time is up, have each group count off by threes. Ones will share their group's word and definition, twos will share their group's sentence, and threes will share what their group would like to know more about. Choose one group to share first and continue until all groups have shared. (You may want to spread this activity out over several days.)

4 Prompt students to reflect on how life in the Plymouth Colony was different than life today.

EXTENDING THE SOCIAL STUDIES LEARNING BEYOND MORNING MEETING

■ Have each group create three digital slides showing their word with its definition, their sentence, and what they wanted to learn more about. Use these slides as part of a unit review.

Personal Hero Postage Stamps

Social Studies Content

Personal heroes

NCSS Standards Themes

Civic Ideals and Practices

Individual Development and Identity

C3 Framework

D2.His.3.3–5 Generate questions about individuals and groups who have shaped significant historical changes and continuities.

Common Core Standards

SL.3.1 Engage effectively in a range of collaborative discussions (one-on-one, in groups, and teacher-led) with diverse partners on grade 3 topics and texts, building on others' ideas and expressing their own clearly.

Materials Needed

Examples of postage stamps commemorating significant American figures (actual stamps, printouts, or digital images)

Paper

Markers and/or colored pencils

Vocabulary

Commemorate

Honor

Personal hero

Postage stamp

How to do it:

In advance, show students examples or images of commemorative stamps.

1 Introduce the group activity: "The United States Postal Service commemorates or honors people who have made important contributions to our country by putting their image on postage stamps. Today, you'll each get to create a stamp for someone who is a hero of yours. It could be someone you know, like a family member, or someone you don't know personally but whose work or actions you admire. The stamp doesn't have to include the person's face—you can also use symbols and words to represent the person."

2 Model the activity by showing a stamp you created: "Here is the postage stamp I created for my mom. She is my hero because she became an electrician at a time when men usually did that job. She didn't let anything stop her from doing what she wanted to do." Ask for a few questions and comments.

3 Provide each table group with paper and markers or colored pencils. Give students a minute to think of someone they admire. Then give them five minutes or so to create their stamps.

4 Have several students share each day until everyone has shared.

VARIATION

■ Have students work in small groups to create a postage stamp to commemorate a historical figure they are learning about. Have a few groups share each day until everyone has shared.

EXTENDING THE SOCIAL STUDIES LEARNING BEYOND MORNING MEETING

■ Have students choose a person or place that has been commemorated on a United States postage stamp and research why the person or place is significant. They can share their information at a future Morning Meeting.

Pin the Capital

Social Studies Content

Location, cardinal directions, state capitals

NCSS Standards Theme

People, Places, and Environments

C3 Framework

D2.Geo.2.3–5 Use maps, satellite images, photographs, and other representations to explain relationships between the locations of places and regions and their environmental characteristics.

Common Core Standards

SL.3.6 Speak in complete sentences when appropriate to task and situation in order to provide requested detail or clarification.

L.3.6 Acquire and use accurately grade-appropriate conversational, general academic, and domain-specific words and phrases, including those that signal spatial and temporal relationships (e.g., After dinner that night we went looking for them).

Materials Needed

Map of your state

Stickers or colored tape

Optional: Cloth or bandana to cover eyes

Vocabulary

Capital
Cardinal directions
East
Location
North
South
West

How to do it:

In advance, display a large map of your state on the wall.

1 Introduce the activity: "Today, you'll help different classmates follow cardinal directions to pin our state's capital on the map without looking."

2 Explain how to do the activity: "When the person at the map says 'Help me navigate,' I'll call on students to give a cardinal direction, such as 'Move your hand a little north.' We will continue giving directions until the volunteer's hand is over the capital. Then as a class, we'll say 'Pin the capital.'"

3 Select a volunteer and give them a sticker or piece of colored tape for marking the capital. Tie a soft cloth loosely over their eyes or have them close their eyes. Then turn the student around three times and position them in front of the map.

4 As students offer clues, reinforce positive behaviors: "You are giving specific directions to help our volunteer get the exact location."

5 After the volunteer places the sticker on the map, they remove their blindfold or open their eyes. Repeat with one or two more volunteers.

6 If time allows, ask students to reflect: "What is one thing that made this activity challenging or easy for you? What are some things we did to support one another?"

VARIATION

- Use a map of the United States and have a volunteer choose a state (or state capital) for the student to pin. Repeat throughout the week until all students have a chance to "pin the capital."

EXTENDING THE SOCIAL STUDIES LEARNING BEYOND MORNING MEETING

- Have students work in small groups to create a set of directions for how to locate the state capital on a map, starting from their town or city. They can use the state map and other social studies and classroom resources for reference.

Spend It or Save It?

Social Studies Content

Spending and saving

NCSS Standards Theme

Production, Distribution, and Consumption

C3 Framework

D2.Eco.1.3–5 Compare the benefits and costs of individual choices.

D2.Eco.2.3–5 Identify positive and negative incentives that influence the decisions people make.

Common Core Standards

SL.3.1 Engage effectively in a range of collaborative discussions (one-on-one, in groups, and teacher-led) with diverse partners on grade 3 topics and texts, building on others' ideas and expressing their own clearly.

SL.3.3 Ask and answer questions about information from a speaker, offering appropriate elaboration and detail.

Materials Needed

None

Vocabulary

Save
Spend

How to do it:

1 Introduce the activity: "When we earn money or receive it as a gift, we have to choose whether to spend the money or to save it. Each of us has things we need and want, so we make different choices about our money."

2 Explain how to do the activity: "I'll describe a scenario about how you might receive money, and then I'll ask 'Would you spend it or save it?' If you'd spend the money, move to the left side of the room. If you'd save it, move to the right side. Then partner up and share ideas about why you made your choice."

3 Describe a scenario such as one of the following, and ask: "Would you spend it or save it?"

➤ You earn $5 for doing extra chores at home.

➤ It's your birthday. Your uncle gives you $10 as a gift.

➤ You're walking in the park and find a $1 bill on the ground.

4 Give students a minute or two to move to their chosen side and partner up for discussion. After signaling for everyone to return to the circle, invite a few students to share out why they made their choice. Repeat with other scenarios as time allows.

·VARIATION

■ Add the option "give it away" to some scenarios. Discuss why people donate money to various causes and organizations.

EXTENDING THE SOCIAL STUDIES LEARNING BEYOND MORNING MEETING

■ Use library and online resources to help students create spending and savings plans, such as weekly budgets and long-term savings goals.

ABCs of History

Social Studies Content

Indigenous cultures

NCSS Standards Theme

Culture and Cultural Diversity

C3 Framework

D2.His.2.3–5 Compare life
in specific historical time
periods to life today.

Common Core Standards

W.3.8 Recall information
from experiences or gather
information from print and
digital sources; take brief notes
on sources and sort evidence
into provided categories.

Materials Needed

None

Vocabulary

Culture
Lenape

How to do it:

1 Display a message like the one below:

Dear Historians,

This month we have learned a lot about the Lenape culture.
Add one word or short phrase to the alphabet below to help us
summarize our learning about the Lenape culture. Be creative!

A	M
B	N Natural Resources
C	O
D	P
E	Q
F Farming	R
G	S
H Hunting	T Tools
I	U
J	V
K	W
L Longhouses	X, Y, Z

2 Read the message chorally. Reinforce students' thinking: "You really
stretched your brains to think of details that show our learning!"

3 Review the words and phrases students listed. Brainstorm words and
phrases for any missing letters.

4 Call on volunteers to use a word on the chart in a sentence. Then invite
students to reflect on how life in the Lenape culture compares to their
own lives today.

**EXTENDING THE SOCIAL STUDIES LEARNING
BEYOND MORNING MEETING**

■ Choose key words from the chart and have groups of students work
cooperatively to create acrostic poems.

Express Your Thoughts

How to do it:

1 Display a message like the one below:

Dear Responsible Citizens,

We are <u>interdependent</u> at school! That means we rely on one another to help care for our school and the people in it. Draw an emoji below to show how you feel our class is doing with helping make our school a safe learning place for everyone.

2 Read the message chorally. Call on student volunteers to explain the reasons for the emoji they drew.

3 As a whole group, generate a list of ways the class can help out more in the school. Ask: "What do you notice about the list we created?"

VARIATION

- Have students submit their emoji anonymously by drawing it on a slip of paper, crumpling it up, and tossing it into the middle of the room. Students pick up a paper near them and share the emoji with the class.

EXTENDING THE SOCIAL STUDIES LEARNING BEYOND MORNING MEETING

- Have students create a plan for a service they want to provide to the school, such as setting up a recycling or composting program. Have students share their plan with the class at future Morning Meetings.

Social Studies Content

Responsibilities of a citizen

NCSS Standards Theme

Individuals, Groups, and Institutions

C3 Framework

D2.Civ.2.3–5 Explain how a democracy relies on people's responsible participation, and draw implications for how individuals should participate.

Common Core Standards

SL.3.1 Engage effectively in a range of collaborative discussions (one-on-one, in groups, and teacher-led) with diverse partners on grade 3 topics and texts, building on others' ideas and expressing their own clearly.

Materials Needed

None

Vocabulary

Citizen
Interdependent
Rely
Responsible
Responsibility
Role

Tell Me More

Social Studies Content

War of 1812

NCSS Standards Theme

Time, Continuity, and Change

C3 Framework

D2.His.3.3–5 Generate questions about individuals and groups who have shaped significant historical changes and continuities.

Common Core Standards

SL.3.6 Speak in complete sentences when appropriate to task and situation in order to provide requested detail or clarification.

Materials Needed

None

Vocabulary

War of 1812

How to do it:

1 Display a message like the one below:

Hello, Historians,

We are deep in our study of the War of 1812! Below are names of people we are learning about. Which person would you like to learn more about, and why? Be prepared to share.

Andrew Jackson

Dolley Madison

Robert Ross

Tecumseh

James Madison

2 Invite student volunteers to each read one sentence of the message. Have the whole class call out each of the names as you point to them. Then, going around the circle, have students share which person they'd like to learn more about and one or two reasons why.

VARIATION

■ Include names of objects and places important to the War of 1812, such as "Old Ironsides" and Chesapeake Bay.

EXTENDING THE SOCIAL STUDIES LEARNING BEYOND MORNING MEETING

■ Invite students to research three additional facts about the person they chose and present them during a future Morning Meeting.

Use the Map

How to do it:

In advance, draw or find a map of your school building to post below the morning message.

1 Display a message like the one below:

Dear Map Readers,

Below is a map of our school building. Think about the following questions:

• What symbols or labels on this map help you find things easily?

• What would you add to make the map easier to use?

Write an idea about one of these questions on a sticky note and bring it to Morning Meeting.

---

2 Read one sentence at a time and have students echo-read it back. Ask: "What are some things you noticed about this map?" Take a few answers.

3 Have students pair up and share the responses on their sticky notes. As you listen to partners sharing, encourage them to go deeper with their thinking: "What's one reason why it might be important to be able to read a map easily?"

EXTENDING THE SOCIAL STUDIES LEARNING BEYOND MORNING MEETING

■ Invite students to construct a map of the classroom and add symbols, labels, and other features that will make their maps easier to read, such as a map key or a compass rose.

Social Studies Content

Working with maps

NCSS Standards Theme

People, Places, and Environments

C3 Framework

D2.Geo.2.3–5 Use maps, satellite images, photographs, and other representations to explain relationships between the locations of places and regions and their environmental characteristics.

Common Core Standards

RI.3.7 Use information gained from illustrations (e.g., maps, photographs) and the words in a text to demonstrate understanding of the text (e.g., where, when, why, and how key events occur).

SL.3.1 Engage effectively in a range of collaborative discussions (one-on-one, in groups, and teacher-led) with diverse partners on grade 3 topics and texts, building on others' ideas and expressing their own clearly.

Materials Needed

Map of your school building or another place to attach to the message

Sticky notes

Vocabulary

Map
Symbol

Cardinal Directions

Social Studies Content

Cardinal directions

NCSS Standards Theme

People, Places, and
Environments

C3 Framework

D2.Geo.1.3–5 Construct
maps and other graphic
representations of both
familiar and unfamiliar places.

Common Core Standards

SL.4.1 Engage effectively in a
range of collaborative
discussions (one-on-one, in
groups, and teacher-led) with
diverse partners on grade 4
topics and texts, building on
others' ideas and expressing
their own clearly.

Materials Needed

Optional: Twine, yarn, or tape;
index cards or slips of paper

Vocabulary

Equator
Latitude
Longitude
Northeast
Northwest
Prime meridian
Southeast
Southwest
Quarter

How to do it:

If desired, in advance, use twine, yarn, or tape to mark the prime meridian
and the equator. You may also want to use index cards or slips of paper to
label the cardinal directions.

1 Introduce the activity: "Today, we'll be greeting people according to their
relative location in our meeting circle. I'll walk a line of longitude for the
prime meridian to divide the circle in half. Then I'll walk a line of latitude
for the equator to divide the circle into quarters."

2 Walk the imaginary longitude and latitude lines through the circle. Ask
the students on either side of each line to scoot away from each other a
bit so the class can clearly see where the lines are located.

3 Explain how to do the greeting: "If I say 'Everyone in the northeast, greet
each other,' everyone who is in the quarter that is east of the prime meridian and north of the equator will greet each other with a gentle high-five."
Model how to do this if necessary.

4 Call out varying locations until all students are greeted.

VARIATIONS

For either of these variations, have a globe or map available for students to
reference.

- As students greet each other, invite them to share the name of one country
  or continent located in their quarter of the world.

- Call out a country. Students in the hemisphere where that country is
  located will turn and greet a partner. Continue for several rounds, with
  students greeting different partners each time.

**EXTENDING THE SOCIAL STUDIES LEARNING
BEYOND MORNING MEETING**

- Have students research a country or continent in their greeting quarter or
  hemisphere and share their findings at a future Morning Meeting.

Institutional Greeting

Social Studies Content

Institutional roles

NCSS Standards Theme

Individuals, Groups, and
Institutions

C3 Framework

D2.Civ.6.3–5 Describe ways
in which people benefit from
and are challenged by
working together, including
through government,
workplaces, voluntary
organizations, and families.

Common Core Standards:

SL.4.1 Engage effectively in a
range of collaborative
discussions (one-on-one, in
groups, and teacher-led) with
diverse partners on grade 4
topics and texts, building on
others' ideas and expressing
their own clearly.

Materials Needed

Chart paper or whiteboard

Vocabulary

Institution
Types of institutions studied

How to do it:

In advance, display the following sentence stem on chart paper or a white-board in the meeting area: "_____ are institutions that _____."

1 Introduce the greeting: "We've learned that institutions are groups that work toward taking care of an important need shared by many people in a society. Today, our greeting will give everyone a chance to say 'Good morning' to a partner and review what we've studied about institutions."

2 Explain how to do the greeting: "I'll assign each of you an institution we've studied. You'll greet the person next to you and use this sentence stem to name one of the things your institution does. For example, when it's my turn, I would say 'Good morning, Isaiah. Banks are institutions that lend people money to buy homes.' Then Isaiah would greet me the same way using his institution."

3 As you listen to students' greetings, reinforce their efforts: "I saw people making eye contact and using friendly voices. And I heard lots of interesting facts about institutions!"

EXTENDING THE SOCIAL STUDIES LEARNING
BEYOND MORNING MEETING

■ Invite students to gather facts about an institution in their community. These facts could include when the institution was founded, who leads it, what services it provides, and who benefits from it.

Landform Greeting

Social Studies Content

Landforms

NCSS Standards Theme

People, Places, and Environments

C3 Framework

D2.Geo.2.3–5 Use maps, satellite images, photographs, and other representations to explain relationships between the locations of places and regions and their environmental characteristics.

Common Core Standards

SL.4.1 Engage effectively in a range of collaborative discussions (one-on-one, in groups, and teacher-led) with diverse partners on grade 4 topics and texts, building on others' ideas and expressing their own clearly.

Materials Needed

Optional: Chart showing landform symbols

Vocabulary

Gesture
Island
Landform
Mountain
Plain
Plateau
Valley

How to do it:

1 Introduce the greeting: "Today, you'll greet classmates with gestures that make the shapes of landforms we've been studying."

Model landform gestures for mountain, plateau, valley, island, and plain, using hands and arms (some possible shapes are shown below). Have the whole class make each shape as you model it. You may also want to display a chart showing the shapes.

Plateau   Island   Valley

2 Have students count off by fives around the circle. Assign each number a landform: "Ones are mountains, two are plateaus," and so forth.

3 Explain how the greeting will work: "When I call out the names of two landforms, those students will come to the middle of the circle, make the shape of their landform, and greet each other with "Hello" and their landform names—for example, 'Hello, mountain!' and 'Hello, plain!" Then I'll say 'Landforms return,' and I'll call out two more landforms."

4 Call out different pairs of landforms until everyone has been greeted.

VARIATION

■ Have students choose the landforms and create the hand motions.

EXTENDING THE SOCIAL STUDIES LEARNING BEYOND MORNING MEETING

■ Assign small groups of students one landform to research. They might create a narrated slideshow or booklet of images and text about the landform and places in the world where it can be found.

Musical Questions

Social Studies Content

Major historical events

NCSS Standards Theme

Time, Continuity, and Change

C3 Framework

D2.His.3.3–5 Generate questions about individuals and groups who have shaped significant historical changes and continuities.

Common Core Standards

SL.4.1 Engage effectively in a range of collaborative discussions (one-on-one, in groups, and teacher-led) with diverse partners on grade 4 topics and texts, building on others' ideas and expressing their own clearly.

Materials Needed

Music (Civil War–era music or songs, if desired)

Vocabulary

Civil War

How to do it:

1 Introduce the greeting: "Today, you'll mix and mingle to music to greet classmates and share about the Civil War."

2 Explain how the greeting will work: "I will pose a question about our study of the Civil War. You'll walk around the room until the music stops, then find a partner close to you, greet each other by name, and take turns sharing your reflections about the question. Then I'll pose another question. The first question is, 'If you could be any Civil War figure, who would it be, and why?'"

3 Start and stop the music for several rounds, using questions such as these:

➤ What's one thing about the Civil War you are looking forward to learning more about?

➤ What's one thing you've learned so far about the Civil War that surprised you?

4 Have students return to their circle spots. Invite a few volunteers to share with the class one reflection they heard.

VARIATION

■ Do this greeting/sharing using inside-outside circles.

EXTENDING THE SOCIAL STUDIES LEARNING BEYOND MORNING MEETING

■ Have students write an essay about the Civil War, including at least one fact they heard during the greeting/sharing.

Compare and Contrast

Social Studies Content

Meeting similar needs and concerns

NCSS Standards Theme

Culture and Cultural Diversity

C3 Framework

D2.His.4.3–5 Explain why individuals and groups during the same historical period differed in their perspectives.

Common Core Standards

W.4.7 Conduct short research projects that build knowledge through investigation of different aspects of a topic. (Extending the learning)

SL.4.1 Engage effectively in a range of collaborative discussions (one-on-one, in groups, and teacher-led) with diverse partners on grade 4 topics and texts, building on others' ideas and expressing their own clearly.

Materials Needed

None

Vocabulary

Indigenous people
Jamestown
Powhatans
Settlers
Similar

How to do it:

1 Introduce the sharing: "Today, we will compare and contrast the different groups of people who lived in the Jamestown area in 1607."

2 Explain how the sharing will work: "I'll give you a question to think about. Then you'll mix and mingle and partner up with someone to share your thoughts."

3 Remind students to take care of each other: "Everyone needs to have a partner for sharing. What are some ways we can meet this goal?" (Possible answers: Say yes if someone asks to share with you. Try to share with people besides your close friends.)

4 Say: "Compare the needs of the Jamestown settlers to those of the Powhatans, the indigenous people who lived in that area of Virginia. How were they similar?" Allow a minute or two for partnering and discussion.

5 Repeat with additional questions. For example: "Contrast the needs of the Powhatans and the needs of the Jamestown settlers. How were they different?"

EXTENDING THE SOCIAL STUDIES LEARNING BEYOND MORNING MEETING

- Invite students to research some of the questions generated during sharing and report their findings to the class.

Culture Brainstorm

Social Studies Content

Defining culture

NCSS Standards Theme

Culture and Cultural Diversity

C3 Framework

D2.Geo.7.3–5 Explain how cultural and environmental characteristics affect the distribution and movement of people, goods, and ideas.

Common Core Standards

SL.4.1 Engage effectively in a range of collaborative discussions (one-on-one, in groups, and teacher-led) with diverse partners on grade 4 topics and texts, building on others' ideas and expressing their own clearly.

Materials Needed

List of different elements of culture

Vocabulary

Culture

How to do it:

In advance, list some of the different areas that define a culture.

1 Introduce the sharing: "Culture is the shared way of life of a specific group of people. Culture is defined by many things, such as language, religion, food, celebrations, beliefs, and traditions. We've been studying Japan, so we're going to share about Japanese culture."

2 Explain how to do the sharing: "You and a partner will brainstorm three examples of Japanese culture. Check the chart if you need to. You'll have a minute or so for discussion."

3 Have students pair up. Move from pair to pair, listening as students share. Reinforce their efforts: "I see that you and your partner are taking turns to make sure each person's ideas are heard." Or coach as needed: "What do you know about Japanese culture that can help you with some ideas for your brainstorming?"

4 After about a minute, signal for students to wrap up. Have a few pairs share one example with the whole class. Then ask: "What are some elements of Japanese culture that have traveled to our country?"

EXTENDING THE SOCIAL STUDIES LEARNING BEYOND MORNING MEETING

■ Assign small groups different aspects of a culture you're studying—for example, food or language. Have each group brainstorm that aspect on chart paper. Have students walk around the room and review each other's lists.

Scientifically Speaking

Social Studies Content

Impact of science and technology

NCSS Standards Theme

Science, Technology, and Society

C3 Framework

D4.2.3–5 Construct explanations using reasoning, correct sequence, examples, and details with relevant information and data.

Common Core Standards

W.4.2 Write informative/ explanatory texts to examine a topic and convey ideas and information clearly. (Extending the learning)

SL.4.1 Engage effectively in a range of collaborative discussions (one-on-one, in groups, and teacher-led) with diverse partners on grade 4 topics and texts, building on others' ideas and expressing their own clearly.

Materials Needed

None

Vocabulary

Science
Technology

How to do it:

1 Introduce the sharing: "Imagine a future where people live on Mars. Today, you're going to think of an invention that can help make life better for them."

2 Explain how to do the sharing: "I'll give you a minute to think about what people on Mars might need in order to thrive. For example, you might invent a technology for growing crops that could live in Martian soil. You'll share your idea in small groups. Make sure everyone has a chance to share."

3 Give students some think time and then have them count off by fives and form their groups. As you listen, reinforce their efforts: "Your ideas show that you're remembering how social studies connects to science and technology."

4 End the sharing when everyone has had a turn to speak. Invite a few volunteers to share their group's ideas with the class.

EXTENDING THE SOCIAL STUDIES LEARNING BEYOND MORNING MEETING

■ Have students write a journal entry about their idea, using detailed sentences about how they think it could help people living on Mars.

Landform Chatter

Social Studies Content

Landforms

NCSS Standards Theme

People, Places, and Environments

C3 Framework

D2.Geo.10.3–5 Explain why environmental characteristics vary among different world regions.

Common Core Standards

SL.4.1 Engage effectively in a range of collaborative discussions (one-on-one, in groups, and teacher-led) with diverse partners on grade 4 topics and texts, building on others' ideas and expressing their own clearly.

SL.4.4 Report on a topic or text, tell a story, or recount an experience in an organized manner, using appropriate facts and relevant, descriptive details to support main ideas or themes; speak clearly at an understandable pace. (Extending the learning)

Materials Needed

One six-sided die

Vocabulary

Landform

How to do it:

In advance, create and display a Sharing Chart with the following options (A sample sharing chart is available to download; see page 12):

If you roll a 1, describe it: "What does it look like?"

If you roll a 2, provide examples: "What are some examples of it?"

If you roll a 3, compare/contrast: "What is it the same as or different from?"

If you roll a 4, make connections: "What does it make you think of?"

If you roll a 5, use prior knowledge: "What did you already know about it?"

If you roll a 6, state your preferences: "What aspect of it would you like to know more about?

1 Introduce the sharing/group activity: "Today, you'll share your thoughts and knowledge about mountains." Divide the class in two and have students form an inner circle facing out and an outer circle facing in, so each student faces a partner.

2 Explain how to do the sharing/group activity: "What you'll share depends on the number I roll. For example, if I roll a 1, you and your partner will share descriptions of what a mountain looks like. If I roll a 5, you'll share what you already know about mountains."

3 Roll the die and call out the number. Allow a minute or so for each student to share.

4 Have the outside circle step one person to the left to a new partner. Repeat as time allows.

VARIATION

■ Change the landform with each roll of the die.

EXTENDING THE SOCIAL STUDIES LEARNING BEYOND MORNING MEETING

■ Have students choose and research one example of a landform from any area of the world (or a specific area you assign). Students can share their findings at a future Morning Meeting.

Economic Minds

Social Studies Content

Key economic terms

NCSS Standards Theme

Production, Distribution, and
Consumption

C3 Framework

D2.Eco.3.3–5 Identify
examples of the variety of
resources (human capital,
physical capital, and natural
resources) that are used to
produce goods and services.

D2.Eco.11.3–5 Explain the
meaning of inflation, deflation,
and unemployment.

Common Core Standards

SL.4.1 Engage effectively in a
range of collaborative
discussions (one-on-one, in
groups, and teacher-led) with
diverse partners on grade 4
topics and texts, building on
others' ideas and expressing
their own clearly.

Materials Needed

Index cards

Vocabulary

Consumers
Deflation
Goods
Inflation
Opportunity cost
Producers
Scarcity
Services

How to do it:

In advance, prepare a set of cards labeled with vocabulary words and
phrases that relate to economics, such as those listed in the panel at left.
Stack the cards in the center of the circle with the words face down.

1 Introduce the activity: "In today's activity, you'll give clues to help someone guess which economic concept is on the card they're holding."

2 Explain and model the activity: "One person will take a card and hold it
like this." Take a card from the stack without looking at it and hold it
against your forehead with the word or phrase visible to the class (you
may need to ask if it is right-side up). Turn slowly so all students can see
the word.

3 Say: "You'll then call on a classmate who has a hand raised, and they will
give you a clue to help you guess the word or phrase. If you can't guess
your word, call on another classmate. If you haven't guessed the word
after three clues, you can look at the card."

4 Remind students to give helpful clues: "What are some ways to give clues
that mention key ideas but don't give away the answer?"

5 Choose a student to pick a card. Play as many rounds as time allows.

VARIATION

■ Focus on a single economic concept, such as services, by making all the
cards examples of that concept.

EXTENDING THE SOCIAL STUDIES LEARNING
BEYOND MORNING MEETING

■ Have students research the connection between one of the economic
concepts and a specific event in history.

History Mystery

Social Studies Content

Significant historical figures and groups

NCSS Standards Theme

Time, Continuity, and Change

C3 Framework

D2.His.3.3–5 Generate questions about individuals and groups who have shaped significant historical changes and continuities.

Common Core Standards

SL.4.1 Engage effectively in a range of collaborative discussions (one-on-one, in groups, and teacher-led) with diverse partners on grade 4 topics and texts, building on others' ideas and expressing their own clearly.

Materials Needed

None

Vocabulary

None

How to do it:

1 Introduce the activity: "Today's activity is a history guessing game. One student will leave the room, and I'll name a person from the historical period we've been studying. When the student comes back, we'll take turns giving clues to help them guess who the mystery person is."

2 Choose a volunteer guesser and send them outside the room. While the student is gone, name a historical figure—for example, Harriet Tubman. Give students a minute to brainstorm clues. Explain that when they share their clue, they'll replace Harriet Tubman's name with "the mystery person." For example: "The mystery person was a conductor on the Underground Railroad."

3 Invite the guesser back and have them call on student volunteers to give clues. Reinforce students' positive efforts: "You're choosing details that will help the guesser figure out our historical figure."

4 After four clues, the guesser may guess the mystery person's name or ask for the answer. Repeat with other guessers and historical figures as time allows.

VARIATION

■ Choose a student to pretend to be the mystery person, and have them call on volunteers to ask yes or no questions about that person. After four or five questions, have a few students guess who the person is. If they don't guess correctly, the student can reveal the mystery person.

EXTENDING THE SOCIAL STUDIES LEARNING BEYOND MORNING MEETING

■ Have students write "Who am I?" riddles about significant people from a historical period. Use the riddles in a future Morning Meeting.

Human Compass

Social Studies Content

Maps

NCSS Standards Theme

People, Places, and
Environments

C3 Framework

D2.Geo.1.3–5 Construct
maps and other graphic
representations of both
familiar and unfamiliar places.

D2.Geo.2.3–5 Use maps,
satellite images, photographs,
and other representations to
explain relationships between
the locations of places and
regions and their
environmental characteristics.

Common Core Standards

SL.4.1 Engage effectively in a
range of collaborative
discussions (one-on-one, in
groups, and teacher-led) with
diverse partners on grade 4
topics and texts, building on
others' ideas and expressing
their own clearly.

Materials Needed

N, E, S, W signs to post

Vocabulary

Compass
Northeast
Northwest
Southeast
Southwest

How to do it:

In advance, make a sign for each cardinal direction and post it on the appropriate wall. (Note: You can download a free compass app for your smartphone or tablet to help you identify the directions of your classroom.)

1 Introduce the activity: "Today, we will be human compasses and move
our bodies to identify the direction we would travel to get from one location to another."

2 Have students spread out in the circle area, starting out all facing north.
Explain how to do the activity: "I'll ask a question, and you'll respond by
turning to face the correct direction. For example, if I ask, 'In what direction would you travel to get from California to Virginia?' you would turn
and face east."

3 Pose six to ten questions, using the examples below or other questions
that you compose based on what students are studying.

➤ In what direction would you travel to get from Japan to Australia?

➤ If you were one of the first Jamestown settlers, in what direction would
you sail to reach the New World?

➤ In what direction did Columbus travel when he left Spain?

4 Ask students an open-ended question for reflection: "What are some ways
we use directions in our daily lives?" Invite a few volunteers to share their
ideas.

VARIATION

■ Increase the challenge by including intermediate directions—northeast,
southwest, etc.

**EXTENDING THE SOCIAL STUDIES LEARNING
BEYOND MORNING MEETING**

■ Have students write a series of their own direction questions and use
them in a future Morning Meeting or as part of a review.

Loyalist and Patriot Song

How to do it:

In advance, post the song lyrics where all students can easily read them.

1 Introduce the activity: "Today, we're going to sing a song about the Revolutionary War. The song reminds us that both patriots and loyalists were fighting for ideas in which they believed very strongly."

2 Have students count off by twos. Ones move to one side of the circle, and twos move to the other side.

3 Explain how to do the activity: "We'll sing this song to the tune of 'Row, Row, Row Your Boat.' The ones will play the part of patriots—you'll sing verses 1 and 3. The twos will play the part of loyalists—you'll sing verses 2 and 4."

4 Sing the song through once, with the groups alternating verses. Then have students march while they sing.

> *I am a patriot:*
> *Let our freedom ring.*
> *Liberty, liberty, liberty, liberty*
> *That's the song we sing!*
>
> *I am a loyalist:*
> *We support the king.*
> *Monarchy, monarchy, monarchy, monarchy*
> *That's the song we sing!*
>
> *I am a patriot:*
> *United we will stand.*
> *We will fight to have the right*
> *To make laws for our land!*
>
> *I am a loyalist:*
> *United we will stand.*
> *We should obey the laws we have*
> *The king should rule this land!*

VARIATION

■ Have students come up with motions to go with the words of the song.

EXTENDING THE SOCIAL STUDIES LEARNING BEYOND MORNING MEETING

■ Have students research songs, poems, or artwork from the American Revolution and share what they learned at a future Morning Meeting.

Made in Our State!

Social Studies Content

Products and industries

NCSS Standards Theme

Production, Distribution, and Consumption

C3 Framework

D2.Eco.3.3–5 Identify examples of the variety of resources (human capital, physical capital, and natural resources) that are used to produce goods and services.

Common Core Standards

SL.4.1 Engage effectively in a range of collaborative discussions (one-on-one, in groups, and teacher-led) with diverse partners on grade 4 topics and texts, building on others' ideas and expressing their own clearly.

Materials Needed

Timer

Chart paper or whiteboard

Index cards or slips of paper

Vocabulary

Industry
Product

How to do it:

In advance, prepare index cards or slips of paper, each with an industry in your state or a product that industry makes.

1 Introduce the activity: "Our activity today is a guessing game. I've written down the names of some industries located in our state and some products they make. I'm going to ask a volunteer to help us guess these industries and products by drawing a picture of each. As this person is drawing, you'll raise your hand if you want to guess the product or industry."

2 Explain how to do the activity: "The volunteer will look at the first card and draw a quick sketch with just the most important details. They'll have up to 30 seconds to finish their drawing. Then you'll guess what it is."

3 Ask for a volunteer who feels comfortable drawing. Check that all students can see the drawing. Show the volunteer the first card and have them begin to draw. Set the timer for 30 seconds.

4 When the volunteer finishes their sketch, call on students for their guesses. Repeat with additional rounds as time allows.

VARIATION

■ Use other economic vocabulary (for example, services).

EXTENDING THE SOCIAL STUDIES LEARNING BEYOND MORNING MEETING

■ Have students choose and research other industries in your state and the products they make.

Two Facts and a Falsehood

Social Studies Content

Explorers

NCSS Standards Theme

Time, Continuity, and Change

C3 Framework

D2.His.3.3–5 Generate questions about individuals and groups who have shaped significant historical changes and continuities.

Common Core Standards

SL.4.1 Engage effectively in a range of collaborative discussions (one-on-one, in groups, and teacher-led) with diverse partners on grade 4 topics and texts, building on others' ideas and expressing their own clearly.

Materials Needed

Chart paper or whiteboard

Vocabulary

Explorer
Fact
Falsehood

How to do it:

Have students come to Morning Meeting prepared to share two facts and one falsehood about an explorer.

1 Introduce the activity: "Today, we'll see what we know about the explorers we've been studying. When it's your turn, you'll share two true statements and one false statement about an explorer, and we'll try to guess which statement is false."

2 Explain and model how to do the activity: "Here's an example of two true statements and one false: 'Columbus wanted to travel from Europe to Asia by sailing west. Columbus was a French explorer. Columbus made four voyages across the Atlantic Ocean.' Which statement is false?" Call on a few students to guess. (Answer: "Columbus was a French explorer" is a falsehood.)

3 Have the first student give their true and false statements and call on volunteers to guess. Have other students take their turn (continue at future Morning Meetings, if necessary). Reinforce students' efforts: "You worked hard to come up with detailed statements about each explorer. That made the guessing part more challenging!"

EXTENDING THE SOCIAL STUDIES LEARNING BEYOND MORNING MEETING

■ Select one explorer and challenge students to see how many facts they can list about that explorer, using resources in the classroom or school library. Combine all the facts into a chart students can use for review.

We're All in This Together

Social Studies Content

Interdependence

NCSS Standards Theme

Production, Distribution, and Consumption

C3 Framework

D2.Eco.15.3–5 Explain the effects of increasing economic interdependence on different groups within participating nations.

Common Core Standards

SL.4.1 Engage effectively in a range of collaborative discussions (one-on-one, in groups, and teacher-led) with diverse partners on grade 4 topics and texts, building on others' ideas and expressing their own clearly.

Materials Needed

A ball of yarn or string

Chart with the following words and their definitions: good, service, producer, consumer

Vocabulary

Consumer
Good
Interdependence
Producer
Service

How to do it:

In advance, display a chart defining "good," "service," "producer," and "consumer" for students' reference.

1 Introduce the activity: "In today's activity, we will make economic connections to see how we all depend on others and on the things they make or do. This is called interdependence. We will show these connections by making a web with this ball of yarn."

2 Explain how to do the activity: "I'll start by saying the name of a good, service, producer, or consumer. Then I'll name someone else in the circle. They will state a good, service, producer, or consumer and how it's connected to my word, and I'll roll the ball of yarn to them while holding on to one end. For example, if I say 'Farmer,' the person might say 'Potato,' which is a good that farmers produce. That person will call on someone else, and so on."

3 Begin the activity using a different example: "My word is 'paint.' Paint is a good." Choose someone to make the next connection, and roll the yarn to to them. Continue until all students have made a connection.

4 Ask students to reflect with an open-ended question: "Look at how the yarn is connected to everyone. What made this activity successful, and how does that relate to interdependence?"

EXTENDING THE SOCIAL STUDIES LEARNING BEYOND MORNING MEETING

■ Have students explore the supply chain (for example, farmer grows the corn, laborer harvests the corn, truck driver delivers the corn, etc.) and have students create a flow chart for each part.

At Your Service

Social Studies Content

Goods and services

NCSS Standards Theme

Production, Distribution, and Consumption

C3 Framework

D2.Eco.3.3–5 Identify examples of the variety of resources (human capital, physical capital, and natural resources) that are used to produce goods and services.

Common Core Standards

SL.4.1 Engage effectively in a range of collaborative discussions (one-on-one, in groups, and teacher-led) with diverse partners on grade 4 topics and texts, building on others' ideas and expressing their own clearly.

Materials Needed

None

Vocabulary

Organization
Service

How to do it:

1 Display a message like the one below:

> Dear Consumers,
>
> We've learned that services are actions a person does for someone else. For example, the mechanic who repairs my car provides me with a service. Can you think of services that start with each letter of the alphabet? Write or draw one service in the alphabet below.
>
> A   M
> B   N
> C   Car repair   O
> D   Dog walking   P   Painting
> E   Q
> F   R
> G   S
> H   Hair cutting   T   Taking care of animals
> I   U
> J   V
> K   W
> L   X, Y, Z

2 Read the message aloud or have a volunteer read it. Ask: "What do we call the people or organizations in our community that provide some of the services we listed?" "What services do you think are scarce in our community?" Call on a few student volunteers for ideas.

3 If any letters were left blank, brainstorm services that begin with those letters.

EXTENDING THE SOCIAL STUDIES LEARNING BEYOND MORNING MEETING

- Invite students to create their own advertisement poster of a service that they would like to provide for the school community. Give examples, such as editing a school newsletter and creating a community bulletin board.

Exploring Our Natural Resources

Social Studies Content

Regions and districts

NCSS Standards Theme

People, Places, and Environments

C3 Framework

D2.Eco.3.3–5 Identify examples of the variety of resources (human capital, physical capital, and natural resources) that are used to produce goods and services.

Common Core Standards

SL.4.1 Engage effectively in a range of collaborative discussions (one-on-one, in groups, and teacher-led) with diverse partners on grade 4 topics and texts, building on others' ideas and expressing their own clearly.

Materials Needed

None

Vocabulary

Natural resource

How to do it:

1 Display a message like the one below:

> Dear State Explorers,
>
> We've been learning about the many natural resources that make our state unique. Look at the list below. Place an "X" under the natural resource you'd like to learn more about. Be ready to share why during Morning Meeting.
>
> Forests   Salt mines   Fish

2 Chorally read the message. Review vocabulary as needed.

3 Invite several students to share their responses to the message and why they'd like to explore the natural resource they chose. Reinforce students' efforts: "I noticed how respectfully you listened to one another's responses; voices were still and eyes were on the speaker."

EXTENDING THE SOCIAL STUDIES LEARNING BEYOND MORNING MEETING

- Have students create a graph showing which natural resources students would like to explore using the data from the marked-up list.

- Give students opportunities to research the natural resource they marked.

111

My Favorite Scientist

Social Studies Content

Scientific achievements

NCSS Standards Theme

Science, Technology, and Society

C3 Framework

D2.His.3.3–5 Generate questions about individuals and groups who have shaped significant historical changes and continuities.

Common Core Standards

SL.4.1 Engage effectively in a range of collaborative discussions (one-on-one, in groups, and teacher-led) with diverse partners on grade 4 topics and texts, building on others' ideas and expressing their own clearly.

Materials Needed

None

Vocabulary

Scientist
Universe

How to do it:

1 Display a message like the one below:

> Dear Science Lovers,
>
> Scientific discoveries can help us learn about the world, the universe, and ourselves. If you could meet one of the scientists we've studied, who would you choose? Shade a bar on the graph below to show your choice. Be ready to explain your reason why.
>
> | | | | | |
> |---|---|---|---|---|
> | | | | | |
> | | | | | |
> | | | | | |
> | | | | | |
> | Astrophysicist Sara Seager | Neuroscientist Sebastian Seung | Climatologist Gavin Schmidt | Biologist Maydianne Andrade | Geophysicist Estella Atekwana |

To help students make connections, you could provide pictures of the scientists or add a sentence about their major discoveries to the chart.

2 Read the message aloud. Invite a few students to share which scientist they chose, and why.

3 Have students reflect: "What are some ways that scientists in these fields have made our society better or safer?"

EXTENDING THE SOCIAL STUDIES LEARNING BEYOND MORNING MEETING

■ Have students draft a list of questions they would ask their scientist and then choose one or two questions to research.

One Big World

Social Studies Content

Shared ideas, inventions, and products

NCSS Standards Theme

Global Connections

C3 Framework

D2.Geo.7.3–5 Explain how cultural and environmental characteristics affect the distribution and movement of people, goods, and ideas.

Common Core Standards

SL.4.1 Engage effectively in a range of collaborative discussions (one-on-one, in groups, and teacher-led) with diverse partners on grade 4 topics and texts, building on others' ideas and expressing their own clearly.

Materials Needed

None

Vocabulary

Invention
Product

How to do it:

1 Post a message like the one below:

Dear Global Citizens,

We've learned about many inventions and products that came to America from other parts of the world. Choose one from the list below that you think has had a big effect on American culture. Be ready to share your choice and a reason why at Morning Meeting.

Pizza (Italy)   Automobiles (Germany)

Toothpaste (Egypt)   Paper (China)

Democracy   Coffee (Ethiopia)
(Greece)   Peanut butter
                                                    (South America)

Alphabet (Middle East)

2 Have students read the message by using word turns (each student reads just one word). Then choose volunteers to share their choice and reason why with the class.

3 Prompt student reflection: "What are some inventions or products developed in the United States that are now used in other countries?"

EXTENDING THE SOCIAL STUDIES LEARNING BEYOND MORNING MEETING

▪ Have students research how and when their chosen product or invention traveled to the United States. They can share their findings at a future Morning Meeting.

113

Time Travel

Social Studies Content

Historical events/past
and present

NCSS Standards Theme

Time, Continuity, and Change

C3 Framework

D2.His.1.3–5 Create and use
a chronological sequence of
related events to compare
developments that happened
at the same time.

Common Core Standards

SL.4.1 Engage effectively in a
range of collaborative
discussions (one-on-one, in
groups, and teacher-led) with
diverse partners on grade 4
topics and texts, building on
others' ideas and expressing
their own clearly.

Materials Needed

Timeline of events recently
studied

Vocabulary

History
Timeline

How to do it:

1 Post a message like the one below:

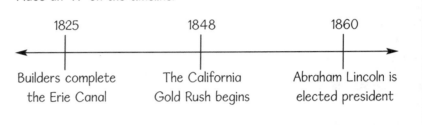

Dear Historians,

Studying the past helps us better understand the present. The timeline below shows events we have studied. If you could travel back in time, which event would you like to witness firsthand? Place an "X" on the timeline.

1825	1848	1860
Builders complete the Erie Canal	The California Gold Rush begins	Abraham Lincoln is elected president

2 Read the message aloud. Invite several students to share their responses.

3 Ask: "What other events could we add to this timeline?" Brainstorm for a minute or two with the class.

**EXTENDING THE SOCIAL STUDIES LEARNING
BEYOND MORNING MEETING**

■ Invite students to create their own timelines with three to five important events from a time period in history that interests them.

Branching Out

Social Studies Content

Branches of U.S. government

NCSS Standards Theme

Power, Authority, and Governance

C3 Framework

D2.Civ.1.3–5 Distinguish the responsibilities and powers of government officials at various levels and branches of government and in different times and places.

Common Core Standards

SL.5.1 Engage effectively in a range of collaborative discussions (one-on-one, in groups, and teacher-led) with diverse partners on grade 5 topics and texts, building on others' ideas and expressing their own clearly.

SL.5.5 Include multimedia components (e.g., graphics, sound) and visual displays in presentations when appropriate to enhance the development of main ideas of themes. (Extending the learning)

Materials Needed

Index cards

Optional: Chart showing branches of government and their responsibilities

Vocabulary

Executive
House of Representatives
Judicial
Legislative
President
Senate
Supreme Court

How to do it:

In advance, write each word or phrase below on a card. Prepare enough sets of cards so there's one card for each student. (A sample set of cards is available to download; see page 12.)

Executive Branch
Legislative Branch
Judicial Branch
President
Senate and House of Representatives
Supreme Court
Enforces the laws
Makes the laws
Interprets the laws

1 Introduce the greeting: "Today, we'll greet each other while sharpening our knowledge of the three branches of our government."

2 Explain how to do the greeting: "You'll each get a card that has the name of a branch of our government, or a word or phrase that is related to one of the branches. Then you'll find a partner, greet them with 'Good morning' and their name, and say which card you have. If your cards are related, give a high-five and say 'That's a match!' If not, say 'Sorry, no match.' Then mix and mingle to find new partners."

3 Pass out one card to each student, and begin the greeting. Reinforce friendly behaviors: "I hear people responding politely to each other if they're not sure they have a match."

4 End the greeting after all students have had a chance to greet four or five classmates, and everyone has made at least one match.

EXTENDING THE SOCIAL STUDIES LEARNING BEYOND MORNING MEETING

■ Have students create a chart, illustration, or concept map explaining one branch of government and its roles and responsibilities.

Geographical Connections

Social Studies Content

Landforms

NCSS Standards Theme

People, Places, and
Environments

C3 Framework

D2.Geo.2.3–5 Use maps,
satellite images, photographs,
and other representations
to explain relationships
between the locations of
places and regions and their
environmental characteristics.

Common Core Standards

SL.5.1 Engage effectively in a
range of collaborative
discussions (one-on-one, in
groups, and teacher-led) with
diverse partners on grade 5
topics and texts, building on
others' ideas and expressing
their own clearly.

Materials Needed

Index cards or slips of paper

Vocabulary

Varies, based on geographic
content

How to do it:

In advance, on index cards or slips of paper, write the names of specific geographical features, the types of landforms or bodies of water they are, and the continents on which they're found. For example, one set of cards might be "Amazon," "river," and "South America." (A sample set of cards is available to download; see page 12.)

1 Introduce the greeting: "Today, you'll greet people by making geographical connections."

2 Give each student a card, and explain how to do the greeting: "Each of you has a card that has two matches. You might have a card with the name of a specific geographical feature, a type of landform or body of water, or a continent. The goal is to find two classmates that match your card to form a group of three. For example, if someone has 'Everest,' they would need to find someone who has 'mountain' and then find someone who has 'Asia' because Mount Everest is a mountain in Asia. When I call out the type of card you have, go to the middle of the circle."

Grade Level 5 Greeting	Geographical Connections	
Amazon	desert	Africa
Andes	lake	Africa
Death	mountains	Asia
Ganges	mountains	Asia
Himalaya	rain forest	Europe
Mediterranean	river	North America
Nile	river	North America
Sahara	sea	South America
Superior	valley	South America

3 Say: "Specific geographical features to the middle." Then say: "Types of landforms and bodies of water to the middle to find your match." Finally: "Continents to the middle to find your matching pair. When your group of three is formed, greet each other by name." End the greeting when all students have found their connections and greeted each other.

**EXTENDING THE SOCIAL STUDIES LEARNING
BEYOND MORNING MEETING**

■ Invite students to create a geographical picture dictionary of the landforms used in the greeting for a younger grade level.

The Justices Speak

Social Studies Content

Judicial branch of
U.S. government

NCSS Standards Theme

Power, Authority, and
Governance

C3 Framework

D2.Civ.10.3–5 Identify
the beliefs, experiences,
perspectives, and values that
underlie their own and others'
points of view about civic
issues.

Common Core Standards

W.5.1 Write opinion pieces
on topics or texts, supporting
a point of view with reasons
and information. (Extending
the learning)

SL.5.1 Engage effectively in a
range of collaborative
discussions (one-on-one, in
groups, and teacher-led) with
diverse partners on grade 5
topics and texts, building on
others' ideas and expressing
their own clearly.

Materials Needed

Index cards or slips of paper

Vocabulary

Associate justice
Chief justice
Supreme Court

How to do it:

In advance, choose three quotes from various Supreme Court justices and write each quote on enough slips of paper or index cards that each student will have one. Use the following quotes or look online for others.

To listen well is as powerful a means of communication and influence as to talk well.

—Chief Justice John Marshall

Most of the things worth doing in the world had been declared impossible before they were done.

—Associate Justice Louis D. Brandeis

I firmly believe in the rule of law as the foundation for all of our basic rights.

—Associate Justice Sonia Sotomayor

1 Introduce the greeting: "Today, you'll greet several classmates and share your connections to quotes from some of our Supreme Court justices."

2 Hand out a quote to each student. Give students a minute to read their quote and think about ways it has meaning in their own life.

3 Invite students to mix and mingle, greeting each other and sharing their connections to the quotes. End the greeting when each student has greeted two or three classmates.

VARIATION

■ Give students quotes from influential scientists, inventors, explorers, artists, or others related to their social studies learning.

EXTENDING THE SOCIAL STUDIES LEARNING
BEYOND MORNING MEETING

■ Have students expand their connections into essays about specific ways in which the justices influenced American life and law.

They Should Pass a Law!

Social Studies Content

Legislative branch of
U.S. government

NCSS Standards Theme

Power, Authority, and
Governance

C3 Framework

D2.Civ.4.3–5 Explain how
groups of people make rules
to create responsibilities and
protect freedoms.

D2.Civ.12.3–5 Explain how
rules and laws change society
and how people change
rules and laws.

Common Core Standards

W.5.4 Produce clear and
coherent writing in which the
development and
organization are appropriate
to task, purpose, and
audience. (Extending the
learning)

SL.5.1 Engage effectively in a
range of collaborative
discussions (one-on-one, in
groups, and teacher-led) with
diverse partners on grade 5
topics and texts, building on
others' ideas and expressing
their own clearly.

Materials Needed

Chart paper and marker

Vocabulary

Law

How to do it:

1 Introduce the greeting/sharing: "This morning, we're going to greet several classmates and share an idea for a law that could make life in our country better."

2 Brainstorm with students about issues that concern them that the federal government could help fix. If needed, guide students to think of problems related to the environment, the economy, education, health care, the treatment of animals, working conditions, or civil rights. Chart their ideas for reference during sharing.

3 Explain how to do the greeting/sharing: "When I say 'Go,' you'll greet as many classmates as you can with 'Hello,' the student's name, and a handshake. When I say 'Stop,' you'll sit down with the last person you greeted and take turns sharing your idea for a new law."

4 Remind students to greet respectfully: "Remember that the quality of your greeting matters more than the number of people you greet. Give each person your full attention before moving on to the next person." Then signal to begin the greeting.

5 When everyone has greeted two or three classmates, say: "Stop! Now sit down with the person you're greeting and share your idea for a law." After a minute or so, invite a few pairs to share out their ideas.

VARIATION

■ Give students the name of a significant law they've studied, such as the Endangered Species Act, Civil Rights Act, or Americans with Disabilities Act, and invite them to share about how that law has affected their lives, their community or school, or the life of someone they know.

EXTENDING THE SOCIAL STUDIES LEARNING BEYOND MORNING MEETING

■ Have students draft letters to legislators about their proposed laws.

Build a Better Institution

Social Studies Content

Civic institutions

NCSS Standards Theme

Individuals, Groups, and Institutions

C3 Framework

D2.Civ.6.3–5 Describe ways in which people benefit from and are challenged by working together, including through government, workplaces, voluntary organizations, and families.

D4.6.3–5 Draw on disciplinary concepts to explain the challenges people have faced and opportunities they have created, in addressing local, regional, and global problems at various times and places.

Common Core Standards

SL.5.1 Engage effectively in a range of collaborative discussions (one-on-one, in groups, and teacher-led) with diverse partners on grade 5 topics and texts, building on others' ideas and expressing their own clearly.

Materials Needed

None

Vocabulary

Improve
Institution
United Nations

How to do it:

1 Introduce the sharing: "We've been learning about how institutions like schools, museums, banks, and hospitals can make our lives better or help us when we're in trouble. Today, you'll work in small groups to share your ideas about how to improve an institution."

2 Explain how to do the sharing: "I'm going to give each group an institution to talk about improving. For example, if your institution is 'bank,' you'll discuss ways that banks could serve people better."

3 Ask: "What will it sound like if group members are being respectful of one another's ideas?" (Possible answers: We'll take turns talking. We'll make sure everyone has an equal chance to share their ideas.)

4 Have students form groups of three to five. Signal them to begin sharing their ideas. After a couple minutes, signal to end the sharing.

5 Invite each group to summarize the ideas they came up with for improving their institution.

VARIATION

■ Have the groups discuss global institutions they've been studying, such as the United Nations, the International Monetary Fund, or the World Health Organization.

EXTENDING THE SOCIAL STUDIES LEARNING BEYOND MORNING MEETING

■ Have students invent an institution to fill a need in their community and then write an essay describing the institution's role and how it would do its work.

Economic Effects

Social Studies Content

Consequences of
economic decisions

NCSS Standards Theme

Production, Distribution, and
Consumption

C3 Framework

D2.Eco.2.3–5 Identify
positive and negative
incentives that influence the
decisions people make.

Common Core Standards

SL.5.1 Engage effectively in a
range of collaborative
discussions (one-on-one, in
groups, and teacher-led) with
diverse partners on grade 5
topics and texts, building on
others' ideas and expressing
their own clearly.

Materials Needed

None

Vocabulary

Decision
Economic
Effect

How to do it:

In advance, choose a major economic decision that the class has been studying, one with far-reaching consequences for many people. For example, you might choose Great Britain's decision to leave the European Union. Have students come to Morning Meeting prepared to share what they feel is a positive or negative effect of the decision.

1 Introduce the sharing: "Today, we'll be sharing thoughts around the circle about possible effects of Great Britain's decision to leave the European Union, also known as Brexit."

2 Explain and model the sharing: "Each person will state a positive or negative thing they think might happen because of Brexit. For example, I might say 'I think a positive effect of Brexit is that the British people will have renewed pride in their heritage.' Someone else might say, 'I think a negative effect of Brexit is that trade could be harder between Great Britain and the rest of Europe.'"

3 Let students know that it's fine for consecutive students to share either positive or negative effects, and that they can also say "Pass" if they are having difficulty coming up with an idea.

4 Begin the sharing. You may want to list students' ideas.

5 Reflect on the ideas shared. For example, does the class think the overall effect of the decision was negative or positive?

VARIATION

■ List several economic events the class has studied, and let students choose which one to share about.

**EXTENDING THE SOCIAL STUDIES LEARNING
BEYOND MORNING MEETING**

■ Have students explore the pros and cons of another economic decision or event. A few students at a time can share their findings at future Morning Meetings.

Identity Influencers

Social Studies Content

Elements of personal identity

NCSS Standards Theme

Individual Development and Identity

C3 Framework

D2.Geo.7.3–5 Explain how cultural and environmental characteristics affect the distribution and movement of people, goods, and ideas.

Common Core Standards

W.5.1 Write opinion pieces on topics or texts, supporting a point of view with reasons and information. (Extending the learning)

SL.5.1 Engage effectively in a range of collaborative discussions (one-on-one, in groups, and teacher-led) with diverse partners on grade 5 topics and texts, building on others' ideas and expressing their own clearly.

Materials Needed

Chart paper or whiteboard

Vocabulary

Identity
Influencer

How to do it:

Display a chart like this:

Identity Influencers

Skills

Hobbies

Birthplace

Family

Favorite books, music, movies

---

1 Introduce the sharing: "We've talked about things that influence a person's identity—their sense of who they are and where they fit in the world. As we go around the circle today, we'll each share one thing that we think significantly influences our identity."

2 Explain how to do the sharing: "You can choose an influencer from the chart or something else that's had a big impact on you. For example, I might say 'I love to cook for my family and friends. It's a really important part of my identity.' Or 'I grew up speaking Spanish, and that's a big part of who I am.'"

3 Invite a student volunteer to begin the sharing and continue around the circle until everyone has had a turn.

EXTENDING THE SOCIAL STUDIES LEARNING BEYOND MORNING MEETING

■ Have students write short essays about how their identity might have been different if they had been born in another place or time the class has studied.

Grade Level

5

Sharing

The Common Good

Social Studies Content

Citizen action for the common good

NCSS Standards Theme

Civic Ideals and Practices

C3 Framework

D2.Civ.8.3–5 Identify core civic virtues and democratic principles that guide government, society, and communities.

Common Core Standards

W.5.4 Produce clear and coherent writing in which the development and organization are appropriate to task, purpose, and audience. (Extending the learning)

SL.5.1 Engage effectively in a range of collaborative discussions (one-on-one, in groups, and teacher-led) with diverse partners on grade 5 topics and texts, building on others' ideas and expressing their own clearly.

Materials Needed

None

Vocabulary

Citizen
Common good
Community

How to do it:

1 Introduce the sharing: "We've talked about how 'the common good' means the interests of everyone in our community. Today, we'll share around the circle about actions we can take as citizens to help strengthen the common good. For example, I might say 'If a neighbor who wants to vote can't drive, I could volunteer to drive her to the voting location.'"

2 Ask: "What are some ways we can show one another respect as we share today?" (Possible answers: Listen attentively even if you don't agree with someone's idea; look at the person while they're sharing.)

3 Give students a minute or so to think of an idea. Then begin the sharing around the circle.

VARIATION

■ Have students share specific examples from history in which one person's actions benefitted many people, such as Rosa Parks' refusal to give up her seat on a Montgomery, Alabama, bus.

EXTENDING THE SOCIAL STUDIES LEARNING BEYOND MORNING MEETING

■ Have students write a letter to a community leader expressing thanks for specific actions the leader has taken for the common good.

A Traveler's Guide to World Climates

Social Studies Content

Global climates

NCSS Standards Theme

People, Places, and
Environments

C3 Framework

D2.Geo.2.3–5 Use maps,
satellite images, photographs,
and other representations
to explain relationships
between the locations of
places and regions and their
environmental characteristics.

D2.Geo.10.3–5 Explain why
environmental characteristics
vary among different world
regions.

Common Core Standards

SL.5.1 Engage effectively in a
range of collaborative
discussions (one-on-one, in
groups, and teacher-led)
with diverse partners on grade
5 topics and texts, building on
others' ideas and expressing
their own clearly.

Materials Needed

Small maps of global climate
regions (search the Internet
for "global climate regions
reproducible")

Vocabulary

Climate
Continent

How to do it:

In advance, display the following sentence stem:

> We're going to _____. We'll pack _____, _____,
> and _____ because the climate there is _____.

1 Introduce the activity: "We've been learning about how climate influences people's lives. Today, you'll work in groups to plan what you'd need
to pack if you were traveling to a particular climate zone."

2 Explain how to do the activity: "Each group will get a global climate map,
and I'll tell you which part of a continent you'll be visiting. You'll have to
decide on three things to bring to keep yourselves safe and comfortable
there. A spokesperson from each group will use the sentence stem to
report out what you decided. Here's how it might sound: 'We're going to
northern Australia. We'll pack shorts, bug spray, and sunglasses because
the climate there is tropical.'"

3 Have students form groups of three to five. Give each group their location
and signal to begin. After about two minutes, signal to stop.

4 Ask each group to make their report. Reinforce students' map-reading
skills and growing geographical knowledge: "You all checked your maps
carefully to find out the climate in your part of the continent. That's important, because we've learned that one continent can have several different
climate zones."

EXTENDING THE SOCIAL STUDIES LEARNING
BEYOND MORNING MEETING

■ Have students research cities in their location and list findings about how
climate affects people's lives. For example, they could note what foods
people grow, what kinds of homes they build, how they travel from place
to place, what the seasons are like, and what animals live there.

Give Me an Ideal Clue!

Social Studies Content

Democracy

NCSS Standards Theme

Civic Ideals and Practices

C3 Framework

D2.Civ.8.3–5 Identify core civic virtues and democratic principles that guide government, society, and communities.

Common Core Standards

SL.5.1 Engage effectively in a range of collaborative discussions (one-on-one, in groups, and teacher-led) with diverse partners on grade 5 topics and texts, building on others' ideas and expressing their own clearly.

Materials Needed

Paper with sets of words printed on them

Vocabulary

Civic
Equality
Ideal
Justice
Liberty

How to do it:

In advance, print out several sets of words like the ones below, each set on its own sheet of paper. The first word in each set is the civic ideal to be guessed. The words below it are those that *cannot* be used as clue words.

Liberty	Justice	Equality
pursuit	fair	same
statue	Supreme Court	fair

1 Introduce the activity: "You're going to give clues to help one person guess a word taped to their back. The word will name one of the civic ideals we've been studying."

2 Explain how to do the activity: "The person who's guessing will stand in the center. They can ask for up to three clues and make up to three guesses. Here's the challenge: You can't use any of the words listed below the civic ideal in your clues." You might want to choose a volunteer to keep track of the number of clues and guesses.

3 Say: "It can be challenging to be the guesser. What can we do to support the person who's guessing?" (Possible responses: Be supportive if they make a wrong guess; be quiet while they're thinking.)

4 Ask for a volunteer and tape one set of words to their back. Have the student rotate slowly so everyone in the circle can see the words.

5 Call on three students to provide clues. If the guesser doesn't guess the word after three tries, tell them what it is and invite them to give the first clue for the next word. Repeat as time permits.

VARIATION

- To provide more challenge, add more terms to the words list that students cannot say when providing clues.

EXTENDING THE SOCIAL STUDIES LEARNING BEYOND MORNING MEETING

- Invite pairs of students to work together to create their own sets of words related to civic ideals or other content.

Historical Charades

Social Studies Content

Historical events

NCSS Standards Theme

Time, Continuity, and Change

C3 Framework

D2.His.1.3–5 Create and use a chronological sequence of related events to compare developments that happened at the same time.

Common Core Standards

W.5.4 Produce clear and coherent writing in which the development and organization are appropriate to task, purpose, and audience. (Extending the learning)

SL.5.1 Engage effectively in a range of collaborative discussions (one-on-one, in groups, and teacher-led) with diverse partners on grade 5 topics and texts, building on others' ideas and expressing their own clearly.

Materials Needed

Slips of paper

Vocabulary

Varies, depending on historical content

How to do it:

1 Introduce the activity: "Today, you'll play charades to act out historical events for everyone to guess. First, let's brainstorm some historical events that we've studied." As students brainstorm, write the events on slips of paper.

2 Explain how to do the activity: "You'll divide up into small groups, and each group will get one of the events we brainstormed. You'll have a few minutes to talk about how to act out the event without using any words or sounds." If needed, go over the rules and gestures of charades, such as how to indicate word or syllable count.

3 Have students form groups of three to five. Then randomly hand out one slip of paper to each group. Give students two to three minutes to plan how they will act out their event. Ask: "What are some ways you can make sure everyone in your group contributes?" (Possible answers: Make sure everyone has a chance to share their ideas; let someone have a larger or smaller role in the pantomime if they ask for it.)

4 Have each group act out their event while everyone else guesses what it is. If needed, you can spread this activity over several Morning Meetings or have some groups do their pantomime during the social studies lesson later in the day.

VARIATION

■ Instead of historical events, have students pantomime scientific discoveries or inventions, such as the telegraph or airplane.

EXTENDING THE SOCIAL STUDIES LEARNING BEYOND MORNING MEETING

■ Have students work in small groups to write a summary of their historical event or create an infographic about it. Construct a timeline from everyone's events.

Service Providers Then and Now

Social Studies Content

Services past and present

NCSS Standards Themes

Production, Distribution, and Consumption

Time, Continuity, and Change

C3 Framework

D2.His.2.3–5 Compare life in specific historical time periods to life today.

D4.2.3–5 Construct explanations using reasoning, correct sequence, examples, and details with relevant information and data.

Common Core Standards

SL.5.1 Engage effectively in a range of collaborative discussions (one-on-one, in groups, and teacher-led) with diverse partners on grade 5 topics and texts, building on others' ideas and expressing their own clearly.

Materials Needed

None

Vocabulary

Provider

Service

How to do it:

In advance, list some service providers from modern times who also would have worked in the 19th century, such as farmer, doctor, teacher, barber, librarian, journalist, and mail carrier. Choose service providers you've studied in class or are reasonably sure students are familiar with.

1 Introduce the activity: "You're going to think about various types of service providers and how their jobs today differ from the way they were back in the 19th century."

2 Explain how to do the activity: "I'll ask a question about a service provider and point to the left side of the room to represent the 21st century and the right side to represent the 19th century. You'll make a choice and move to that side of the room. Once there, you'll find a partner and share your reasons for your choice."

3 Ask the first question, indicating a side of the room for each choice: "Would you rather be a farmer today [left] or in the 19th century [right]?" Take a moment to think, and then move to the side of your choice and discuss your reasoning with a partner."

4 Give students a minute or two for discussion. Invite a few volunteers to share their choice and reasoning.

5 Repeat with a new question, such as "Do you think it's more challenging to be a journalist today [left] or in the 19th century [right]? Why?" And so on.

VARIATION

- Challenge students to do this activity in silence, taking turns with their partner to list reasons on sticky notes and then post them on a designated space. Give everyone a few minutes to read the notes silently, and then discuss them as a whole group.

EXTENDING THE SOCIAL STUDIES LEARNING BEYOND MORNING MEETING

- Have students research service providers in two different centuries and present their findings in Venn diagrams or "then and now" charts.

Technology Mind Map

Social Studies Content

Social change

NCSS Standards Theme

Science, Technology, and Society

C3 Framework

D2.His.2.3–5 Compare life in specific historical time periods to life today.

Common Core Standards

SL.5.1 Engage effectively in a range of collaborative discussions (one-on-one, in groups, and teacher-led) with diverse partners on grade 5 topics and texts, building on others' ideas and expressing their own clearly.

Materials Needed

Chart paper and marker (one set per group)

Vocabulary

Society
Technology

How to do it:

1 Introduce the activity: "Today, you're going to make mind maps by brainstorming ways that developments in technology related to transportation have changed society over time. One example might be how the invention of the steam engine led to the Industrial Revolution."

2 Explain how to do the activity: "You'll work in small groups to think of as many ideas as you can. Your group's recorder will write the word 'transportation' in the middle of the chart paper, and then write everyone's ideas all around it."

3 Have students form groups of three or four, and choose one person in each group to be the recorder. Remind students to be respectful when brainstorming: "Remember to listen to every idea and include it even if you disagree with it."

4 Signal students to begin. Give them four to five minutes to brainstorm and record. Signal a one-minute warning before time is up.

5 Invite each group to share one idea they came up with. Other groups can circle items on their own maps that are similar.

VARIATION

- Have students brainstorm the impact of different types of technology within a specific time period they're studying.

EXTENDING THE SOCIAL STUDIES LEARNING BEYOND MORNING MEETING

- Invite students to choose one recent technological advance in transportation and research how it has affected people's lives in the United States or in a different country.

The Extraordinary Ordinary

Social Studies Content

Awareness of the historical contributions of ordinary people

NCSS Standards Theme

Time, Continuity, and Change

C3 Framework

D2.His.3.3–5 Generate questions about individuals and groups who have shaped significant historical changes and continuities.

Common Core Standards

W.5.7 Conduct short research projects that use several sources to build knowledge through investigation of different aspects of a topic. (Extending the learning)

SL.5.1 Engage effectively in a range of collaborative discussions (one-on-one, in groups, and teacher-led) with diverse partners on grade 5 topics and texts, building on others' ideas and expressing their own clearly.

Materials Needed

Paper and marker for each group

Vocabulary

Accomplishment
Extraordinary
Ordinary

How to do it:

1 Introduce the activity: "You've learned that history is not just about heroes. Lots of people doing jobs we may think of as ordinary help make extraordinary things happen."

2 Explain how to do the activity: "I'll call out a historical accomplishment we've studied. You'll work in small groups to brainstorm and write down as many people as you can who helped make the accomplishment possible. For example, if I call out 'First moon landing,' you might first think of astronauts. But dig deeper and think of all the others who played key roles: machinists, nutritionists, mathematicians, scientists, computer programmers, and so on."

3 Have students form groups of three to five. Call out a historical accomplishment and signal students to begin brainstorming and writing examples. Signal again when one minute is up, and have groups take turns stating one example from their lists.

4 Call out additional accomplishments as time allows. Reinforce students' analytical thinking: "Your answers show that you're thinking hard about the different types of work that go into making the extraordinary possible."

VARIATION

■ Have students think about something they've accomplished and describe some ways that people helped them succeed.

**EXTENDING THE SOCIAL STUDIES LEARNING
BEYOND MORNING MEETING**

■ Have students research other historic events and accomplishments and report on the various people who played a role in them.

Civilization Survival Bag

Social Studies Content

Ancient civilizations

NCSS Standards Theme

Time, Continuity, and Change

C3 Framework

D2.Eco.3.3–5 Identify examples of the variety of resources (human capital, physical capital, and natural resources) that are used to produce goods and services.

D2.His.2.3–5 Compare life in specific historical time periods to life today.

Common Core Standards

SL.5.1 Engage effectively in a range of collaborative discussions (one-on-one, in groups, and teacher-led) with diverse partners on grade 5 topics and texts, building on others' ideas and expressing their own clearly.

Materials Needed

Paper bag

Index cards or slips of paper

Vocabulary

Ancient
Civilization
Resource

How to do it:

In advance, label a paper bag "Civilization Survival Bag" and place it near the message with some index cards or slips of paper.

1 Display a message like the one below:

> Dear Civilization Savers,
>
> We have been studying the history of ancient Egypt. If you could travel back in time with one resource that might have helped that civilization survive, what would it be? On an index card, fill in the blanks in the sentence below, and put the card in the Civilization Survival Bag.
>
> "If ancient Egyptians had _____, then they _____."

2 Invite a volunteer to read the message.

3 Have each student pick one note from the Civilization Survival Bag and read it out loud.

4 Categorize the resources suggested (for example, technology, medical care, food or water) and discuss why these might have helped the civilization survive longer.

VARIATION

- If the class has been studying more than one ancient civilization, let students choose which one to focus on in their answer.

EXTENDING THE SOCIAL STUDIES LEARNING BEYOND MORNING MEETING

- Have students write a story about how the ancient civilization might have evolved if its people had had access to a needed or modern resource.

Econo-Me-Too!

Social Studies Content

Basic economic concepts

NCSS Standards Theme

Production, Distribution, and Consumption

C3 Framework

D2.Eco.2.3–5 Identify positive and negative incentives that influence the decisions people make.

Common Core Standards

SL.5.1 Engage effectively in a range of collaborative discussions (one-on-one, in groups, and teacher-led) with diverse partners on grade 5 topics and texts, building on others' ideas and expressing their own clearly.

Materials Needed

None

Vocabulary

Choice
Consumers
Demand
Scarcity
Supply

How to do it:

1 Display a message like the one below:

Dear Conscious Consumers,

I was so frustrated at the grocery store! They had only one cashier to help the long line of customers, and they ran out of the chocolate milk that was on sale. I almost left without buying anything! How does my experience connect to the economic terms listed below that we've been studying? Be ready to share your thoughts.

Scarcity   Supply   Demand   Choice

My demand for
chocolate milk
was not met!

---

2 Have the class read the message aloud together.

3 Call on as many students as time allows to share their connections.

4 Reinforce students' understanding by asking them to define the economic terms in their own words and to use the terms in complete sentences.

VARIATION

■ Substitute an economic scenario that is relevant to the current life of the class. For example, if students are raising money for a class trip through a healthy snack sale, they might think about which types of snacks they ordered (supply), how much of each type customers might buy (demand), and so on.

EXTENDING THE SOCIAL STUDIES LEARNING BEYOND MORNING MEETING

■ Have students analyze and share other economic experiences they've had through a personal narrative or visual display.

Historical Headlines

Social Studies Content

Major historical events

NCSS Standards Theme

Time, Continuity, and Change

C3 Framework

D2.His.1.3–5 Create and use a chronological sequence of related events to compare developments that happened at the same time.

D2.His.14.3–5 Explain probable causes and effects of events and developments.

Common Core Standards

W.5.2 Write informative/ explanatory texts to examine a topic and convey ideas and information clearly. (Extending the learning)

SL.5.1 Engage effectively in a range of collaborative discussions (one-on-one, in groups, and teacher-led) with diverse partners on grade 5 topics and texts, building on others' ideas and expressing their own clearly.

Materials Needed

Sticky notes

Vocabulary

Breaking news
Event
Headline

How to do it:

1 Display a message like the one below:

Good morning!

We've studied many historical events that led up to the Civil War. Choose one event you think was very important. On a sticky note, create a newspaper headline about it. Post your headline below.

Supreme Court Rules in Dred Scott Case

2 Read the message to the class.

3 Invite several students to read their headlines to the class as if they were reporters breaking exciting news.

4 Challenge students to put the events in chronological order and explain their significance.

VARIATION

- Have students write headlines about current events, scientific discoveries, or other notable events.

EXTENDING THE SOCIAL STUDIES LEARNING BEYOND MORNING MEETING

- Have students write a brief news report to go along with the headline they wrote. Assemble the reports into a class newspaper, magazine, or website.

Protecting the Earth

Social Studies Content

Environmental protection

NCSS Standards Theme

Individuals, Groups, and Institutions

C3 Framework

D2.Geo.12.3–5 Explain how natural and human-made catastrophic events in one place affect people living in other places.

Common Core Standards

SL.5.1 Engage effectively in a range of collaborative discussions (one-on-one, in groups, and teacher-led) with diverse partners on grade 5 topics and texts, building on others' ideas and expressing their own clearly.

Materials Needed

None

Vocabulary

Agency
Environment
Issue

How to do it:

1 Display a message like the one below:

> Dear Earth Protectors,
>
> The Environmental Protection Agency (EPA) is a government agency that looks after the health of our nation's waterways, plants, and wild animals. If you worked for the EPA, what environmental issues would you want to address, and why? Write an issue starting with one of the letters below next to that letter.
>
> E
> N
> V
> I
> R
> O—Ocean pollution
> N
> M
> E
> N
> T—Toxic chemicals

2 Invite student volunteers to read each sentence of the message aloud. Ask a few volunteers to share their environmental concern and why they listed it.

3 Invite students to discuss other issues of environmental concern and add these to the message.

VARIATION

■ Adapt the message for another organization relevant to content students have been studying (for example, those helping communities cope with natural disasters, such as the American Red Cross).

EXTENDING THE SOCIAL STUDIES LEARNING BEYOND MORNING MEETING

■ Have students visit the EPA website (*www.epa.gov*) or other reliable websites to learn more about environmental issues and report on their findings.

Texting the President

Social Studies Content

U.S. president and
executive branch

NCSS Standards Theme

Power, Authority, and
Governance

C3 Framework

D2.Civ.1.3–5 Distinguish the
responsibilities and powers
of government officials at
various levels and branches of
government and in different
times and places.

Common Core Standards

SL.5.1 Engage effectively in a
range of collaborative
discussions (one-on-one, in
groups, and teacher-led) with
diverse partners on grade 5
topics and texts, building on
others' ideas and expressing
their own clearly.

Materials Needed

None

Vocabulary

Armed services
Congress
Execute laws
President
Responsibility

How to do it:

1 Display a message like the one below, including an example of a text message as a model for students:

> Dear 21st Century Thinkers,
>
> We've learned that the U.S. president executes the laws passed by Congress, leads the armed services, and represents our nation in the world. That's a lot of responsibility! What's one piece of advice you would text to our current president? Write your text message below.
>
> Pick advisors you trust.
>
> Visit other countries.

2 Ask a volunteer to read the message aloud. Invite several students to read their text messages.

3 Have students discuss what they think is the most important piece of advice the president could receive. Extend students' thinking with open-ended questions: "In what situations might this advice be important? What problems might arise if the president didn't follow this advice?"

VARIATION

■ Have students offer advice from the perspective of foreign leaders they've studied or other people they've learned about.

EXTENDING THE SOCIAL STUDIES LEARNING BEYOND MORNING MEETING

■ Leave the message displayed for the rest of the day or unit of study. Encourage students to add additional text messages as they think of them.

Word Travelers

Social Studies Content
World languages

NCSS Standards Themes
Global Connections
Culture and Cultural Diversity

C3 Framework
D2.Geo.7.3–5 Explain how cultural and environmental characteristics affect the distribution and movement of people, goods, and ideas.

Common Core Standards
SL.5.1 Engage effectively in a range of collaborative discussions (one-on-one, in groups, and teacher-led) with diverse partners on grade 5 topics and texts, building on others' ideas and expressing their own clearly.

Materials Needed
None

Vocabulary
Culture
Language

How to do it:

1 Display a message like the one below:

Dear Vocabulary Explorers,

Many words we use in English come from languages spoken all around the globe. What languages do you think the following words came from? Draw a line from one word to a language.

WORDS	LANGUAGES
pajamas	Swahili
television	Arabic
kindergarten	French
mosquito	German
antibiotic	Inuit
safari	Hindi
kayak	Greek
lime	Spanish

(**Answer key:** safari, Swahili; lime, Arabic; television, French; kindergarten, German; antibiotic, Greek; pajamas, Hindi; kayak, Inuit; mosquito, Spanish)

2 Have students read the message by each saying one word in turn around the circle.

3 Invite students to share their ideas about which language each of the words came from and their reasons for thinking so.

4 Share the correct word-language pairings with students. Extend their thinking with an open-ended question: "What might these words tell us about the cultures they come from?"

EXTENDING THE SOCIAL STUDIES LEARNING BEYOND MORNING MEETING

- Have students research other words that came from these or other languages. Use students' findings to add new information to the Morning Message throughout the week.

Grade Level

6

Greeting

Guess the President

Social Studies Content

U.S. presidents

NCSS Standards Theme

Power, Authority, and Governance

C3 Framework

D2.His.3.6–8 Use questions generated about individuals and groups to analyze why they, and the developments they shaped, are seen as historically significant.

Common Core Standards

SL.6.1 Engage effectively in a range of collaborative discussions (one-on-one, in groups, and teacher-led) with diverse partners on grade 6 topics, texts, and issues, building on others' ideas and expressing their own clearly.

WHST.6–8.2 Write informative/explanatory texts, including the narration of historical events, scientific procedures/experiments, or technical processes. (Extending the learning)

Materials Needed

None

Vocabulary

None

How to do it:

In advance, have students choose one U.S. president and write down three clues about that president's life or time in office. Have students bring these clues to Morning Meeting.

1 Introduce the greeting: "In today's greeting, you'll find a partner and take turns sharing clues and guessing each other's U.S. president."

2 Explain how to do the greeting: "Mix and mingle to greet as many class-mates as you can with a friendly 'Hello' and the person's name. When I signal, you'll stop and find a partner near you. After you greet your part-ner, you'll take turns giving clues about the president you picked and guessing who the other person's president is." You may want to tell stu-dents to wait until all clues are given before guessing.

3 If students have any questions about the facts shared, tell them they'll have a chance later in the day to research the answers with their partner.

4 Ask an open-ended question to prompt further reflection: "What can the lives of the U.S. presidents tell us about our country's history?"

VARIATION

■ Do the same activity using scientists, inventors, or other historical figures students have studied.

EXTENDING THE SOCIAL STUDIES LEARNING BEYOND MORNING MEETING

■ Have students research and write a short narrative about a key event in the life of a president or other historical figure and read their narrative aloud to the class or display it.

Economic Connections

Social Studies Content

Economic factors of
historic events

NCSS Standards Theme

Production, Distribution, and
Consumption

C3 Framework

D2.Eco.6.6–8 Explain how
changes in supply and
demand cause changes
in prices and quantities of
goods and services, labor,
credit, and foreign currencies.

Common Core Standards

SL.6.1 Engage effectively in a
range of collaborative
discussions (one-on-one, in
groups, and teacher-led) with
diverse partners on grade 6
topics, texts, and issues,
building on others' ideas and
expressing their own clearly.

WHST.6–8.2 Write
informative/explanatory texts,
including the narration of
historical events, scientific
procedures/experiments, or
technical processes.
(Extending the learning)

Materials Needed

None

Vocabulary

Varies, depending on
economic content

How to do it:

1 Introduce the greeting/sharing: "Today, you'll use inside-outside circles to greet each other and share connections between economic factors and the Great Depression."

2 Have students form two groups: One group forms an inner circle facing out; the second group forms an outside circle facing in. Students should be facing each other, forming pairs.

3 Explain how to do the greeting/sharing: "I'll call out an economic term. Then you'll greet your partner and take turns sharing ideas about how that term connects to what we've learned about the Great Depression. When I signal, the outside circle will take one step to the right to form new pairs, and I'll call out another term."

4 Call out the first term: "Scarcity." Allow a minute or two for students to greet each other and share their ideas. Then signal for students to change partners, and call out a new term. Repeat so that students greet and talk with three to five partners.

5 Invite students to reflect with an open-ended question: "What connections did you hear that surprised you?"

VARIATION

- Use economic factors related to another historical period being studied.

EXTENDING THE SOCIAL STUDIES LEARNING BEYOND MORNING MEETING

- Have students create a graphic organizer about the Great Depression or another historical period using an economic term as the central focus.

What's the Positive News?

Social Studies Content

Positive world events

NCSS Standards Theme

Global Connections

C3 Framework

D2.Geo.6.6–8 Explain how the physical and human characteristics of places and regions are connected to human identities and cultures.

Common Core Standards

SL.6.1 Engage effectively in a range of collaborative discussions (one-on-one, in groups, and teacher-led) with diverse partners on grade 6 topics, texts, and issues, building on others' ideas and expressing their own clearly.

Materials Needed

None

Vocabulary

Headline
Human interest story

How to do it:

In advance, have students research one positive current event or human interest story from another country and write a headline for the event on a slip of paper. Review with students what types of events would be considered "positive," and show one or two examples of what the headlines should look like. (Possible examples: Panda bear adopts orphaned monkey as own in China; More rainforest land protected in Brazil.)

1 Have students bring their headlines to Morning Meeting and stand in a circle. Introduce the greeting: "Today, we'll go around the circle to greet each other using the current events we researched."

2 Explain how to do the greeting/sharing: "I'll greet the person to my left by name and ask 'What's the positive news?' They'll greet me by name and read their headline. Then I'll sit down, and they'll greet the person on their left and ask, 'What's the positive news?' and so on around the circle.

3 Begin the greeting/sharing. After everyone has been greeted and shared their headline, reinforce students' efforts: "You spoke loudly and clearly so the whole class could hear. You shared positive world events that were fascinating to learn!"

4 To conclude, ask an open-ended question: "What is one headline you connected with, and why?"

VARIATION

■ Have students research and share positive current events from one particular country or region the class is studying.

EXTENDING THE SOCIAL STUDIES LEARNING BEYOND MORNING MEETING

■ Post all the headlines on a bulletin board, organized by country or pinned to a world map. Challenge students to research and write headlines from countries not yet represented.

Words of Wisdom

Social Studies Content

Global cultures

NCSS Standards Theme

Culture and Cultural Diversity

C3 Framework

D2.Geo.5.6–8 Analyze the combinations of cultural and environmental characteristics that make places both similar to and different from other places.

Common Core Standards

W.6.4 Produce clear and coherent writing in which the development, organization, and style are appropriate to task, purpose, and audience. (Extending the learning)

SL.6.2 Interpret information presented in diverse media and formats (e.g., visually, quantitatively, orally) and explain how it contributes to a topic, text, or issue under study.

L.6.5 Demonstrate understanding of figurative language, word relationships, and nuances in word meanings.

Materials Needed

Index cards or slips of paper

Vocabulary

Proverb

How to do it:

In advance, write or print proverbs from cultures around the world on index cards or slips of paper (one for each student). For example:

"We will be known forever by the tracks we leave."
—Dakota Sioux proverb

"A journey of a thousand miles begins with a single step."
—Chinese proverb

"If you think you are too small to make a difference, you haven't spent a night with a mosquito."
—African proverb

1 Introduce the greeting/sharing: "Today, we'll greet each other with proverbs from around the world. A proverb is a saying that offers words of wisdom or general life advice."

2 Hand out one card to each student and explain how to do the greeting/sharing: "Mix and mingle to find a partner. Greet them by saying 'Hello' and the person's name. Then read your proverb and share an idea about how that proverb might apply to you or to the whole class. After you and your partner have both read your proverbs, mix and mingle to find a new partner."

3 After students have greeted and shared with a few classmates, signal for them to return to their circle spots. Ask a few volunteers to share their proverb and idea with the class.

VARIATION

■ Use quotes from American historical figures from a time period the class is studying.

EXTENDING THE SOCIAL STUDIES LEARNING BEYOND MORNING MEETING

■ Have students create their own proverbs, using references and imagery from their everyday lives. They can share these proverbs and their meanings at a future Morning Meeting.

Cause and Effect

Social Studies Content

Cause and effect

NCSS Standards Theme

Time, Continuity, and Change

C3 Framework

D2.His.14.6–8 Explain multiple causes and effects of events and developments in the past.

Common Core Standards

SL.6.1 Engage effectively in a range of collaborative discussions (one-on-one, in groups, and teacher-led) with diverse partners on grade 6 topics, texts, and issues, building on others' ideas and expressing their own clearly.

SL.6.4 Present claims and findings, sequencing ideas logically and using pertinent descriptions, facts, and details to accentuate main ideas or themes; use appropriate eye contact, adequate volume, and clear pronunciation.

WHST.6–8.2 Write informative/explanatory texts, including the narration of historical events, scientific procedures/experiments, or technical processes. (Extending the learning)

Materials Needed

None

Vocabulary

Cause
Effect
Event

How to do it:

1 Introduce the sharing: "Today, we'll share in small groups about causes and effects. I'll state an important historical event that we've been studying, and you'll think of things that happened as a result of that event."

2 Explain how to do the sharing: "I'll name an event, which will be the cause. Then each person in your group will share an effect of that event." Assign students to groups of three to five and have each group gather in a circle.

3 State the first event. "On October 29, 1929, the stock market crashed." Remind students to give themselves some time to think before they respond. Allow several minutes for the sharing. If time allows, name another event for students to discuss.

4 Reinforce students' efforts: "I saw people giving their classmates their full attention and waiting for their turn to speak."

5 Ask an open-ended question to prompt further reflection: "What do you think was the most important result of this event, and why?"

VARIATION

■ Challenge students to think of as many effects as they can in two minutes, have a recorder list them, and then tally the results for the class as a whole (excluding duplicates).

**EXTENDING THE SOCIAL STUDIES LEARNING
BEYOND MORNING MEETING**

■ Have students create a cause-and-effect poster or graphic organizer about a historical event discussed during Morning Meeting, or write a five-paragraph essay on three of the most significant effects.

Fact or Opinion?

Social Studies Content

Ancient cultures

NCSS Standards Theme

People, Places, and
Environments

C3 Framework

D1.5.6–8 Determine the
kinds of sources that will be
helpful in answering
compelling and supporting
questions, taking into
consideration multiple points
of views represented in the
sources.

Common Core Standards

SL.6.3 Delineate a speaker's
argument and specific claims,
distinguishing claims that are
supported by reasons and
evidence from claims that
are not.

RH.6–8.8 Distinguish among
fact, opinion, and reasoned
judgment in a text.
(Extending the learning)

Materials Needed

None

Vocabulary

Fact
Opinion
Reasoned judgment

How to do it:

1 Introduce the sharing: "Today, you'll share your thoughts on what you've learned so far about the Mayan civilization. Each person will share one thought, and you'll have to figure out whether it's a fact or an opinion."

2 Explain how to do the sharing: "Going around the circle, each of you will make one statement about the Mayans. After each statement, I'll ask the rest of the class 'Fact or opinion?' If you think the statement is a fact, point at your head. If you think the statement is an opinion, point at your heart. I'll start: 'The Mayans had really beautiful architecture.'"

3 Give students a moment to think and respond. Say: "Because my statement expresses my personal belief about how Mayan architecture looks, it's an opinion."

4 Continue around the circle, with each student sharing their statement and the class responding. Confirm which responses are accurate ("Sharif's statement is a fact"), or gently clarify any confusion ("Dina's statement may sound like a fact because the Mayans did create a calendar with 365 days, but saying that the calendar was their greatest contribution makes it an opinion"). If needed, spread this sharing over multiple Morning Meetings.

VARIATION

■ Add the option to state a reasoned judgment (an opinion with supporting evidence), with students crossing both arms over their chest to indicate that they think someone's statement is a reasoned judgment.

**EXTENDING THE SOCIAL STUDIES LEARNING
BEYOND MORNING MEETING**

■ Have students write an essay about the Mayans that incorporates at least one fact, one opinion, and one reasoned judgment. Have them pick a color for each type of statement and highlight or underline those statements in their essay.

Government Gab

Social Studies Content

Branches of government

NCSS Standards Theme

Power, Authority, and Governance

C3 Framework

D2.Civ.4.6–8 Explain the powers and limits of the three branches of government, public officials, and bureaucracies at different levels in the United States and in other countries.

Common Core Standards

SL.6.4 Present claims and findings, sequencing ideas logically and using pertinent descriptions, facts, and details to accentuate main ideas or themes; use appropriate eye contact, adequate volume, and clear pronunciation.

RH.6–8.7 Integrate visual information (e.g., in charts, graphs, photographs, videos, or maps) with other information in print and digital texts. (Extending the learning)

Materials Needed

None

Vocabulary

Executive branch
Government
Judicial branch
Legislative branch

How to do it:

1 Introduce the sharing: "Today, you're going to share in groups about the three branches of our government."

2 Explain how to do the sharing: "I'll ask a question, and you'll share ideas about it within your group." Have students count off around the circle by saying "executive," "legislative," or "judicial," and gather into groups according to their branch.

3 Read the first question: "What are some important responsibilities of your branch of government?" Give some think time and then signal groups to begin sharing.

4 Invite a student from each group to share some of the key ideas their group discussed with the whole class. Continue with other questions as time allows:

➤ How would you explain your branch of government to a third grader?

➤ Our three branches function through a system of checks and balances. What are some ways your branch might make sure another branch doesn't get too powerful?

➤ If you could change or improve something about your branch, what would it be?

EXTENDING THE SOCIAL STUDIES LEARNING BEYOND MORNING MEETING

■ Have students create infographics or graphic organizers that help explain one branch of government or how each branch works with the others.

■ Challenge students to generate additional questions about the U.S. government for use at future Morning Meetings.

Vantage Point

Social Studies Content

Historical perspectives

NCSS Standards Theme

Individual Development and Identity

C3 Framework

D2.His.4.6–8 Analyze multiple factors that influenced the perspectives of people during different historical eras.

Common Core Standards

SL.6.1 Engage effectively in a range of collaborative discussions (one-on-one, in groups, and teacher-led) with diverse partners on grade 6 topics, texts, and issues, building on others' ideas and expressing their own clearly.

SL.6.4 Present claims and findings, sequencing ideas logically and using pertinent descriptions, facts, and details to accentuate main ideas or themes; use appropriate eye contact, adequate volume, and clear pronunciation.

Materials Needed

None

Vocabulary

Perspective
Vantage point

How to do it:

1 Introduce the sharing: "In studying different historical events, we've discussed how the people involved had different perspectives, or vantage points, that influenced how they experienced the event. Today, you'll share with a partner how you think different people involved in the French and Indian War/Seven Years War might have felt or reacted based on their vantage point."

2 Explain how to do the sharing: "I'll ask a question about one group of people involved in the French and Indian War. You and a partner will have a moment to think about it, and then you'll take turns sharing ideas about how that group's vantage point might have influenced their view of the war."

3 Have students pair up, and then pose the first question: "If you were a British colonist during the French and Indian War, what might have been your perspective?" Give students one or two minutes to share, and then signal them to wrap up their discussions.

4 Repeat Step 3, asking students to share their thoughts from the perspectives of various indigenous groups who were involved in the conflict, and then the French colonists.

5 Invite volunteers to summarize their discussion of one perspective for the class.

VARIATION

■ Have one person in each pair take on one perspective and the other person take on a different perspective. After a minute or two of discussion, signal partners to swap perspectives.

EXTENDING THE SOCIAL STUDIES LEARNING BEYOND MORNING MEETING

■ Have students choose an event from history, research various perspectives on it, and create a skit or presentation that highlights the different perspectives. For example, perspectives on the California Gold Rush might include miners from the eastern United States and Mexico, and immigrants from around the world.

Whose Expedition?

Social Studies Content

Exploring personal interests

NCSS Standards Theme

Individual Development and
Identity

C3 Framework

D2.His.4.6–8 Analyze
multiple factors that
influenced the perspectives
of people during different
historical eras.

Common Core Standards

SL.6.1 Engage effectively in a
range of collaborative
discussions (one-on-one, in
groups, and teacher-led) with
diverse partners on grade 6
topics, texts, and issues,
building on others' ideas and
expressing their own clearly.

WHST.6–8.4 Produce clear
and coherent writing in
which the development,
organization, and style are
appropriate to task, purpose,
and audience. (Extending
the learning)

Materials Needed

Chart paper or whiteboard
with questions

Vocabulary

Expedition
Exploration

How to do it:

In advance, display a list of questions like the following:

THOUGHT SPARKERS

— What questions do you have about the expedition?

— How does one of your hobbies or interests connect to the expedition?

— What new skill would you like to learn before going on the expedition,
and why?

1 Introduce the sharing: "We've been studying some exciting explorations
and expeditions. Today, you'll get to think about which expedition you
would have joined if you'd had the chance to choose between two
famous ones."

2 Explain how to do the sharing: "You'll choose either the land expedition
of Lewis and Clark or the space expedition of Neil Armstrong. Look at the
Thought Sparkers chart and think about your responses to the questions
before you choose your expedition. Put your thumb up when you've
decided, but keep your choice to yourself."

3 Once everyone has thumbs up, have students pair up and share with their
partner which expedition they chose and why, based on the Thought
Sparkers questions.

4 After a couple of minutes, end the sharing. Prompt reflection: "What's
one interesting thing you learned from your partner? Did anyone change
their mind as a result of listening to their partner? Why?"

VARIATION

■ Choose other topics that enable students to explore aspects of their personal identity, such as future careers, places to visit, and so on.

**EXTENDING THE SOCIAL STUDIES LEARNING
BEYOND MORNING MEETING**

■ Have students write a persuasive advertisement or essay encouraging
others to join them on an expedition of their choosing (such as a mountain climbing trip, deep sea exploration, or Arctic adventure).

Adding to the Answer

Social Studies Content

Impact of inventions
and technology

NCSS Standards Theme

Science, Technology, and
Society

C3 Framework

D2.Geo.7.6–8 Explain how
changes in transportation and
communication technology
influence the spatial
connections among human
settlements and affect
the diffusion of ideas and
cultural practices.

Common Core Standards

SL.6.1 Engage effectively in a
range of collaborative
discussions (one-on-one, in
groups, and teacher-led) with
diverse partners on grade 6
topics, texts, and issues,
building on others' ideas and
expressing their own clearly.

SL.6.4 Present claims and
findings, sequencing ideas
logically and using pertinent
descriptions, facts, and details
to accentuate main ideas or
themes; use appropriate eye
contact, adequate volume,
and clear pronunciation.

Materials Needed

Chart paper or whiteboard

Vocabulary

Influence
Invention
Technology

How to do it:

1 Introduce the activity: "Today, we'll work together to answer a question about the influence of technological inventions."

2 Explain how to do the activity: "I'll pose the question. Then, going around the circle, each of you will say one word to make a complete sentence that answers the question." Give an example, pointing to each student to demonstrate: "If I ask how the smartphone has influenced communication, the first five students might say in turn, 'The,' 'smartphone,' 'has,' 'made,' 'a.' As you share your words, I'll write them on the chart so you can see your response as it forms."

3 Remind students of behavior expectations, as needed: "How can we follow our rule that says 'Treat everyone with respect' if someone forgets and says more than one word?"

4 Pose a question: "How have changes to the automobile influenced transportation over time?" Invite the student to your left to begin the answer, and write the words as students say them.

5 After the last student shares their word, have the class read the complete response chorally. Edit and revise as a class to clarify or improve the response.

VARIATION

■ Add challenge by having each student add at least two words, but no more than five, to the response.

EXTENDING THE SOCIAL STUDIES LEARNING BEYOND MORNING MEETING

■ Invite students to write their own questions about the impact of technology in the past or present. Use the questions that students generate for future group activities.

Document Drill

Social Studies Content

Important historical documents

NCSS Standards Theme

Civic Ideals and Practices

C3 Framework

D2.Civ.3.6–8 Examine the origins, purposes, and impact of constitutions, laws, treaties, and international agreements.

Common Core Standards

SL.6.1 Engage effectively in a range of collaborative discussions (one-on-one, in groups, and teacher-led) with diverse partners on grade 6 topics, texts, and issues, building on others' ideas and expressing their own clearly.

WHST.6–8.7 Conduct short research projects to answer a question (including a self-generated question), drawing on several sources and generating additional related, focused questions that allow for multiple avenues of exploration. (Extending the learning)

Materials Needed

Chart paper or whiteboard

Paper

Pens or pencils

Vocabulary

Articles of Confederation
Bill of Rights
Declaration of Independence
Historical document
U.S. Constitution

How to do it:

In advance, display a list of the following historical documents:

➤ Declaration of Independence

➤ Articles of Confederation

➤ United States Constitution

➤ Bill of Rights

1 Introduce the activity: "Today, we'll work in pairs to learn more about the important historical documents listed here."

2 Explain how to do the activity: "With your partner, you'll write one fact about one of these documents, along with the name of the document."

3 Have students form pairs and begin writing. When everyone is finished, say: "Now crumple your paper into a snowball and gently toss it into the center of the circle." When all have tossed their snowballs, invite each pair to pick up a snowball.

4 Signal for pairs to join another pair nearby. One student in each pair will read the statement on their snowball and one student in the other pair will guess the name of the document. Then the other two students will do the reading and guessing.

5 Signal for pairs to join a different pair, repeating Step 4. End after pairs have interacted with two to three other pairs.

EXTENDING THE SOCIAL STUDIES LEARNING BEYOND MORNING MEETING

■ Invite students to research one of these historical documents (or another of their choice) and generate a "Top Ten Facts" list or write a summary of the document's significance.

Economic Brainstorm

Social Studies Content

Economic concepts
and terms

NCSS Standards Theme

Production, Distribution, and
Consumption

C3 Framework

D2.Eco.1.6–8 Explain how
economic decisions affect the
well-being of individuals,
businesses, and society.

Common Core Standards

SL.6.1 Engage effectively in
a range of collaborative
discussions (one-on-one, in
groups, and teacher-led) with
diverse partners on grade 6
topics, texts, and issues,
building on others' ideas and
expressing their own clearly.

Materials Needed

Chart paper

Markers

Vocabulary

Imports
Interdependence
Productivity
Scarcity

How to do it:

1 Introduce the activity: "For today's activity, you'll brainstorm examples of economic terms and concepts we've studied."

2 Explain how to do the activity: "You'll work in small groups to brainstorm examples of the terms or concepts I name. You can use examples from history or from the world today. For example, if I ask for examples of the term 'imports,' your group might say that in ancient times, Italy imported silk and spices from China. You might also say that in the modern world, the United States imports olive oil and motor vehicles from Italy."

3 Have students count off by fours and gather into groups. Give each group a piece of chart paper and a marker, and designate a recorder for each group. Remind students about brainstorming respectfully: "Remember to listen to and record everyone's ideas."

4 Pose the first question: "What are examples of scarcity?" As students brainstorm, reinforce their efforts: "I see people giving all the members of their group a chance to give ideas without being interrupted."

5 After two minutes, signal for students to wrap up their brainstorming. Then invite recorders to share one or two ideas from their lists. As time allows, have students brainstorm examples of other terms, such as "productivity" and "interdependence." Post the charts for future reference.

VARIATION

■ Have students work with key political terms.

**EXTENDING THE SOCIAL STUDIES LEARNING
BEYOND MORNING MEETING**

■ Choose one of the terms used in Morning Meeting and have students make an acrostic, using examples from everyone's charts.

Human Timeline

Social Studies Content

American Revolution

NCSS Standards Theme

Time, Continuity, and Change

C3 Framework

D2.His.1.6–8 Analyze connections among events and developments in broader historical contexts.

Common Core Standards

SL.6.1 Engage effectively in a range of collaborative discussions (one-on-one, in groups, and teacher-led) with diverse partners on grade 6 topics, texts, and issues, building on others' ideas and expressing their own clearly.

Materials Needed

Date strips on index cards/ slips of paper

Event strips on index cards/slips of paper

Vocabulary

American Revolution

Timeline

How to do it:

In advance, prepare strips of paper with important events of the American Revolution on them, and separate strips with the dates of those events. (A sample set is available to download; see page 12.)

1 Introduce the activity: "You're going to construct a human timeline of key events from the American Revolution."

2 Explain how to do the activity: "I'll give each of you a strip of paper, with either a month and year or an event from the war. Your first goal is to match the events with the corresponding dates."

3 Hand out the strips and tell students: "When I say 'Go,' move carefully around the room looking for the person whose information goes with yours. When you find your match, stand together and wait until everyone's ready." Reinforce students' efforts: "You're having thoughtful discussions about whether your information matches or not."

4 Once all students have found their matches, say: "Now line up in order from the earliest event to the latest. Dates are first; events go to the right of the date."

5 When everyone is lined up, go down the line and have students read their date and event aloud. If anyone is incorrectly paired or out of order, have them rearrange themselves until the timeline is correct.

VARIATIONS

■ Use dates related to a different event students are studying.

■ After students have found their match, collect the date cards and challenge students to put the events in the proper sequence.

EXTENDING THE SOCIAL STUDIES LEARNING
BEYOND MORNING MEETING

■ Display the timeline and add to it as students learn about other historical events before, during, or after the American Revolution.

Pop-Up Countries

Social Studies Content

Continents and countries

NCSS Standards Theme

People, Places, and
Environments

C3 Framework

D2.Geo.2.6–8 Use maps,
satellite images, photographs,
and other representations to
explain relationships between
the locations of places and
regions, and changes in their
environmental characteristics.

Common Core Standards

SL.6.1 Engage effectively in
a range of collaborative
discussions (one-on-one, in
groups, and teacher-led) with
diverse partners on grade 6
topics, texts, and issues,
building on others' ideas and
expressing their own clearly.

Materials Needed

Optional: Globe or world map

Vocabulary

Varies, depending on
geographical content

How to do it:

1 Introduce the activity: "Today, we're going to do a country pop-up. I'll name a continent, and you'll name as many countries as you can from that continent."

2 Explain how to do the activity: "Everyone will begin seated. Then, after I name a continent and say 'Go,' anyone can pop up and name a country. Here's the catch: Only one person at a time can stand up, and no country can be repeated. If two people pop up at the same time, or if you name a country that's already been named, you'll sit down and try again. When you successfully name a country, sit down, put your thumb up, and stay seated."

3 Name a continent, give students a few seconds of think time, and begin the activity.

4 End the activity after everyone has their thumb up.

Note: During the activity, change the continent if students have named most of its countries or are having trouble coming up with countries.

VARIATION

■ Use U.S. states and capitals, languages and other elements of a particular culture, or geographical features of a particular region.

**EXTENDING THE SOCIAL STUDIES LEARNING
BEYOND MORNING MEETING**

■ Have students research the countries they named and create brief "pop-up" reports to share during future Morning Meetings.

Back in Time

Social Studies Content

Impact of science and technology

NCSS Standards Themes

Time, Continuity, and Change

Science, Technology, and Society

C3 Framework

D2.His.1.6–8 Analyze connections among events and developments in broader historical contexts.

Common Core Standards

W.6.3 Write narratives to develop real or imagined experiences or events using effective techniques, relevant descriptive details, and well-structured event sequences. (Extending the learning)

SL.6.1 Engage effectively in a range of collaborative discussions (one-on-one, in groups, and teacher-led) with diverse partners on grade 6 topics, texts, and issues, building on others' ideas and expressing their own clearly.

Materials Needed

None

Vocabulary

Hydroelectricity
Industrial Revolution
Invention

How to do it:

1 Display a message like the one below:

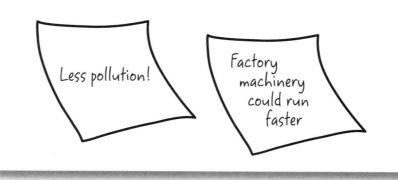

Dear Time Travelers,

We've seen how inventions can change history! Imagine this: You travel back to the start of the Industrial Revolution in Great Britain and introduce hydroelectricity. How might that have changed people's lives? Write one idea on a sticky note and put it below.

Less pollution!

Factory machinery could run faster

2 Have students read the message to themselves, and then invite a volunteer to paraphrase it. Invite other students to read two or three responses aloud.

3 Guide students in creating categories for the ways technology can affect people's lives. Sort the sticky notes into the categories. (Possible categories: Environment, education, health, economy, transportation)

4 Challenge students to think of a few more ideas to list under each category.

EXTENDING THE SOCIAL STUDIES LEARNING
BEYOND MORNING MEETING

■ Have students extend their thoughts about their own or a classmate's idea by writing a narrative essay or creating an illustration showing how life might have been different.

By the People

Social Studies Content

Responsible government

NCSS Standards Theme

Civic Ideals and Practices

C3 Framework

D2.Civ.14.6–8 Compare historical and contemporary means of changing societies, and promoting the common good.

Common Core Standards

SL.6.1 Engage effectively in a range of collaborative discussions (one-on-one, in groups, and teacher-led) with diverse partners on grade 6 topics, texts, and issues, building on others' ideas and expressing their own clearly.

Materials Needed

None

Vocabulary

Gettysburg Address

Ideals

How to do it:

1 Display a message like the one below:

> Dear Thoughtful Citizens,
>
> In his Gettysburg Address, President Lincoln said the government should be "of the people, by the people, and for the people." What are some ways this ideal is at work in our government today? Be ready to share your ideas with a partner.

2 Have students read the message silently and then pair up and share their responses with their partner.

3 Invite a few pairs to summarize their discussion for the class. Reinforce students' efforts: "Your responses show your understanding of the connections between our present government and our country's past."

4 Extend students' thinking: "If our government isn't living up to our ideals, what can we the people do to change that?"

VARIATION

■ Invite students to explore another ideal that is central to our form of government, such as the separation of powers or the primacy of the Constitution.

EXTENDING THE SOCIAL STUDIES LEARNING BEYOND MORNING MEETING

■ Invite students to read or review another historical document, such as the Declaration of Independence, and note connections between it and the Gettysburg Address. In your next morning message, invite students to share their connections.

Cultural Intrigue

Social Studies Content

Interpreting artifacts

NCSS Standards Theme

Culture and Cultural Diversity

C3 Framework

D2.Geo.10.6–8 Analyze the ways in which cultural and environmental characteristics vary among various regions of the world.

Common Core Standards

SL.6.1 Engage effectively in a range of collaborative discussions (one-on-one, in groups, and teacher-led) with diverse partners on grade 6 topics, texts, and issues, building on others' ideas and expressing their own clearly.

WHST.6–8.2 Write informative/explanatory texts, including the narration of historical events, scientific procedures/experiments, or technical processes. (Extending the learning)

Materials Needed

Artifact (pottery, jewelry, clothing, etc.) or photo of artifact

Sticky notes

Vocabulary

Artifact

Culture

Yield

How to do it:

1 Display a message like the one below:

2 Ask for a volunteer to read the message aloud.

3 Invite a few volunteers to read their own sticky note and briefly share their ideas about what the artifact can help them learn about the culture.

4 Extend students' reflection with open-ended questions: "Did anyone have an idea similar to one that was shared? Did anyone have a very different or opposite idea?"

EXTENDING THE SOCIAL STUDIES LEARNING BEYOND MORNING MEETING

■ Have students use their ideas to write an essay about the artifact or create a visual display highlighting its significance.

#LearningAboutLaws

Social Studies Content

Laws

NCSS Standards Theme

Civic Ideals and Practices

C3 Framework

D2.Civ.12.6–8 Assess specific rules and laws (both actual and proposed) as means of addressing public problems.

Common Core Standards

W.6.2 Write informative/ explanatory texts to examine a topic and convey ideas, concepts, and information through the selection, organization, and analysis of relevant content.

SL.6.1 Engage effectively in a range of collaborative discussions (one-on-one, in groups, and teacher-led) with diverse partners on grade 6 topics, texts, and issues, building on others' ideas and expressing their own clearly.

Materials Needed

None

Vocabulary

Bill
Law

How to do it:

1 Display a message like the one below:

#GoodMorningClass,

We have been learning how laws are made in our country. Think about the steps needed for a bill to become a law. Then choose a hashtag below to show how you would like to learn more about law-making. Write your "handle" (real or made-up) below your choice.

#lawstudent	**#lawmaker**	**#lawprofessor**
(I would like to read about the lawmaking process.)	(I would like to do a project about the lawmaking process.)	(I would like to have a group discussion about the lawmaking process.)
@ArthurLawDawg	@Toby_law_is_cool	@JamiFutureLawyer

---

2 Have a student volunteer read the message aloud.

3 Summarize students' responses: "I see that a number of you are interested in each of these activities! I'm excited to hear your questions and wonderings as we continue our learning."

VARIATION

■ Have students create their own hashtag to express different steps in the lawmaking process.

EXTENDING THE SOCIAL STUDIES LEARNING BEYOND MORNING MEETING

■ Divide students into small groups. Assign each group one or two of the steps needed to make a bill a law and have them create a 140-character summary of their step(s).

Making Connections

Social Studies Content

Louisiana Purchase

NCSS Standards Theme

Time, Continuity, and Change

C3 Framework

D2.His.1.6–8 Analyze connections among events and developments in broader historical contexts.

Common Core Standards

SL.6.1 Engage effectively in a range of collaborative discussions (one-on-one, in groups, and teacher-led) with diverse partners on grade 6 topics, texts, and issues, building on others' ideas and expressing their own clearly.

SL.6.4 Present claims and findings, sequencing ideas logically and using pertinent descriptions, facts, and details to accentuate main ideas or themes; use appropriate eye contact, adequate volume, and clear pronunciation.

Materials Needed

None

Vocabulary

Associations
Connections
Louisiana Purchase

How to do it:

1 Display a message like the one below:

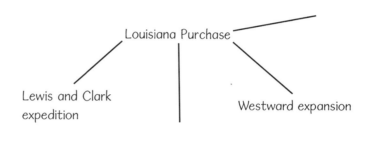

Dear Historians,

Later today, we'll learn more about the Louisiana Purchase. But right now, think about what you already know. Who was involved in the purchase? Who was affected by it? What other events happened as a result of this huge expansion of U.S. territory? Write a word or phrase, and then draw a line that connects it to the term "Louisiana Purchase" below.

Louisiana Purchase

Lewis and Clark expedition

Westward expansion

2 Have two students read the message aloud together.

3 Invite students to read and briefly explain a connection they wrote.

4 Prompt students to think more deeply about the significance of the Louisiana Purchase: "What do you think our country might be like today if we had not purchased the Louisiana territory?" Discuss as a group.

VARIATION

- Choose a concept currently being studied, such as immigration, and have students list people, events, places, or terms associated with it.

EXTENDING THE SOCIAL STUDIES LEARNING BEYOND MORNING MEETING

- Have students use the concept map to write a summary paragraph about the Louisiana Purchase.

Writing History

Social Studies Content

World events; literary
responses to historical events

NCSS Standards Themes

Global Connections
Time, Continuity, and Change

C3 Framework

D2.His.4.6–8 Analyze
multiple factors that
influenced the perspectives
of people during different
historical eras.

Common Core Standards

W.6.3 Write narratives to
develop real or imagined
experiences or events using
effective technique, relevant
descriptive details, and well-
structured event sequences.
(Extending the learning)

SL.6.4 Present claims and
findings, sequencing ideas
logically and using pertinent
descriptions, facts, and details
to accentuate main ideas or
themes; use appropriate eye
contact, adequate volume,
and clear pronunciation.

Materials Needed

None

Vocabulary

Novel
World War II

How to do it:

1 Display a message like the one below:

> Dear Culture Analyzers,
>
> We've been talking about works of fiction that explore historical
> events. Think back on our learning about World War II. If you were
> writing a novel about that war, whose story would you tell? Why?
> Be ready to share your thoughts during Morning Meeting.

2 Invite volunteers to alternate reading sentences of the message.

3 Prompt students to discuss several different perspectives, such as young
children, teens, and older adults in various countries around the world.
Reinforce students' respectful listening: "I notice group members giving
everyone a chance to speak and listening with full attention."

4 Extend students' thinking: "Who are some of the minor characters you'd
want to include in your story, and why?"

VARIATION

- If the class has read a work of children's fiction about World War II, such
as *The War That Saved My Life* by Kimberly Brubaker Bradley or *Under
the Blood-Red Sun* by Graham Salisbury, invite them to share their
responses to this question: "What new perspectives about World War II
did you learn from this book?"

**EXTENDING THE SOCIAL STUDIES LEARNING
BEYOND MORNING MEETING**

- Invite students to complete a story map and use it to draft their story about
World War II.

10 Complete Meeting Ideas

Focusing an entire Morning Meeting on a particular social studies theme can build extra excitement for this learning. It can also allow you to build even more social studies learning into your students' day—without having to cut anything out or shorten any other content you teach.

In this section, you'll find ten social studies themed Morning Meetings, in which all four components (greeting, sharing, group activity, and morning message) cover the same social studies theme. Here are some tips for using them:

Adapt as needed ■ All ten of these meetings can be adapted to fit grades beyond the ones indicated. If your students have a deeper knowledge about any of these topics, you may need to add complexity. Conversely, if a topic is unfamiliar to students, you may need to simplify. And you will want to tailor the morning messages to your students' reading levels.

Create your own themed meetings ■ Use the ideas included in this book to come up with combinations of social studies themed greetings, sharings, group activities, and morning messages that fit your students and curriculum.

Consider the overall flow of the meeting ■ When you start creating your own themed meetings, balance the energy level of the components. In general, these meetings should have an ebb and flow to them. An active greeting should generally be followed by a relatively calm sharing. If the meeting has a complicated group activity, keep the reading and use of the message fairly simple and straightforward.

Let students help ■ Students love coming up with a variation for a greeting, sharing, group activity, or morning message. If you want to plan a meeting on a given topic, consider asking for students' ideas several days beforehand.

Remember to focus on community ■ A primary purpose of Morning Meeting is for students to begin the day on a positive note and build community. Reinforce friendly words and tone of voice, inclusiveness, and cooperation rather than competition.

Grade Level

K–2

Themed Meeting

Social Studies Content

United States Constitution

NCSS Standards Theme

Power, Authority, and Governance

C3 Framework

D2.Civ.7.K–2 Apply civic virtues when participating in school settings.

D2.Civ.8. K–2 Describe democratic principles such as equality, fairness, and respect for legitimate authority and rules.

Common Core Standards

SL.K.6
SL.1.4
SL.2.1

Materials Needed

List of classroom or school rules

Optional: Pen with a feather attached to resemble a quill pen; chart paper or whiteboard; gavel (real or makeshift)

Vocabulary

Document
Founders
Preamble
United States Constitution

Constitution Convention

How to do it:

Display a message like the one below:

> Good Morning, Constitution Students!
>
> What do you want to learn about the Constitution? Use the quill pen to print your name under your choice below. (Our Founders signed the Constitution with a quill pen!)
>
> | Who | What does | Why was it | Why is it |
> | wrote it? | it say? | written? | important today? |

Greeting: "We the Students . . ."

➤ Introduce the greeting: "In 1787, our Founders signed the United States Constitution. This document set the rules for how our government would work. The beginning of the Constitution is called the preamble. It starts with the words 'We the people of the United States.' Today, we're going to use similar words in our greeting."

➤ Display a preamble like the following and read it aloud together:

"We, the students of Ms. Carson's class, greet each other today in order to create a friendly classroom!"

➤ Have all students mingle in the center of the circle, greeting each other by name with a "Good Morning" and shaking hands. Bang the gavel or use a similar signal to end the greeting.

Sharing: Classroom Constitution

➤ Introduce the sharing: "The people who wrote the U.S. Constitution wanted to make sure our government followed rules, just like we follow rules. They had lots of different ideas. Today we're going to share ideas about different ways we can follow our rules to make our classroom a happier place." (Optional: Display the classroom or school rules.)

➤ Model the sharing: "For my idea, I might say 'Our classroom is a happier place when we speak kindly to each other.'" Then give students some time to think of an idea.

➤ Have students share one idea in an around-the-circle format. (Optional: List student ideas on chart paper or a whiteboard.)

Group Activity: Four Corners Freedom of Speech

➤ Remind students about the Bill of Rights: "The U.S. Constitution has a very important part called the Bill of Rights. The Bill of Rights is a list of ten additional rights called amendments that were added to the Constitution after it was signed. These amendments make sure that people in our country have certain freedoms, like the freedom of religion, freedom of the press, and freedom of speech."

➤ Introduce the activity: "We're going to do Four Corners to practice the First Amendment, which is about the freedom of speech. I'll call out a topic and give you four options. You'll choose one and go to the corner of your choice. Then you'll discuss in small groups why you made that choice."

➤ Read the following topics and options one at a time, designating a corner of the room for each option. Give students some think time before signaling them to move to their choice.

　✳ Your favorite weekend activity: Reading books (corner one); Playing games (corner two); Spending time outdoors (corner three); Going on a trip (corner four)

　✳ Which do you like better: Math (corner one); Art (corner two); Either (corner three); Neither (corner four)

　✳ Which classroom task do you enjoy most: Handout manager (corner one); Line leader (corner two); Materials collector (corner three); Other (corner four)

➤ Ask an open-ended question to help students connect their discussions to the First Amendment: "How does having the freedom to say what we think help us learn?"

Morning Message: Sign Right Here

➤ Have the class read the message aloud chorally.

➤ Invite three to four volunteers to share out what they want to learn about the U.S. Constitution, and why.

➤ Encourage student reflection: "Why is it important for a country to have a constitution (a set of rules)?"

Social Studies Content

Peace

NCSS Standards Theme

Culture and Cultural Diversity

C3 Framework

D2.Civ.7.K–2 Apply civic virtues when participating in school settings.

Common Core Standards

SL.K.6

SL.1.3

SL.2.1

Materials Needed

Chart paper or whiteboard

Picture of a leader who advocated for peaceful conflict resolution (for example, Dr. Martin Luther King, Jr., Mother Teresa, Mahatma Gandhi, or Nelson Mandela)

Optional: Image of a dove

Vocabulary

Dove

Leader

Peace

Symbol

Practicing Peace

How to do it:

Display a message like the one below:

> Greetings, Peacemakers,
>
> Many world leaders have helped people solve problems peacefully. Do you know who Mahatma Gandhi was? Draw a peace sign to show your answer.
>
> Yes   Not Yet
>
>

Tip: Add a photo of the person to your message.

Greeting: Pass the Dove of Peace

> ➤ Introduce the greeting: "There are different symbols that show peace. One symbol is a dove. Today, we're going to send the dove of peace around the circle for our greeting."

> ➤ With students standing in a circle, walk across the circle and choose a student to greet. Both of you hold up your right hands, interlock thumbs, and wave your fingers, making the "wings" of a dove. Then say: "Mara, have a peaceful day!" The student responds: "Thanks, Mr. Tuller. Have a peaceful day, too!"

> ➤ Walk back to your spot in the circle and sit. The student who was greeted walks across the circle to greet another classmate, and so on.

> ➤ After everyone has been greeted, ask: "What might it look and sound like to have a peaceful day?"

Sharing: Peaceful Partner Shares

➤ Introduce the sharing: "Today, you're going to share your thoughts about this question with a partner: 'What makes you feel peaceful?' Perhaps it's a place or something you like to do. Remember to listen carefully to your partner so you can tell the rest of the class what they said."

➤ Have students pair up and share their ideas. Then go around the circle and have students share out their partner's peaceful place or activity.

Group Activity: Peaceful Problem-Solvers

➤ Introduce the activity: "Solving problems peacefully means solving them in ways that are kind and respectful. I'm going to describe a problem that could happen at school. We'll brainstorm peaceful ways to solve that problem and then act out one of those ways."

➤ Present a scenario: "Hailey is looking at countries on the globe, but Lucas needs the globe for a project he's working on. What can Lucas do to solve this problem peacefully?" Give a possible solution as an example: "Lucas can look at the wall map while he's waiting for a turn with the globe."

➤ Guide students to ensure that their brainstorming includes appropriate solutions. Record students' ideas.

➤ Invite volunteers to act out a few of the ideas.

Morning Message: Peaceful People

➤ Ask: "What would it sound like if we read the message in a peaceful way?" Take a few suggestions, such as reading in a quiet, calm voice.

➤ Lead students in reading the message as suggested one or two times. Point to each word as you read.

➤ Read the message again and have students do peaceful motions as they read along. For example, each time you point to a "peace" word, students make the peace sign with their fingers. Each time you point to the word "leader," students make a "Follow me" motion by extending their arm and scooping it toward themselves.

➤ As a class, discuss how everyone can use peaceful words and gestures throughout the day.

Here, There, and Everywhere

Social Studies Content

Transportation

NCSS Standards Theme

Science, Technology, and Society

C3 Framework

D2.Geo.5.K–2 Describe how human activities affect the cultural and environmental characteristics of places or regions.

D3.1.K–2 Gather relevant information from one or two sources while using the origin and structure to guide the selection.

Common Core Standards

SL.K.1
SL.K.6
SL.1.1

Materials Needed

Students' premade drawings

Vocabulary

Transportation
Vehicles

How to do it:

Display a message like the one below:

> Hello, Traveling Students!
>
> Transportation helps us move from place to place. Long ago, people walked or rode horses. Now we have cars, trucks, buses, and airplanes. How did you get to school today? Put a tally mark below:
>
> Bus ✔ ✔ ✔
>
> Car ✔ ✔
>
> Walk ✔
>
> Bike ✔
>
> Other

Tip: Customize the morning message for the types of transportation used by your students.

Greeting: Vehicle Greeting

➤ In a circle, brainstorm and practice different vehicle sounds (for example, "honk" for car, "vroom" for truck, "toot" for train).

➤ Introduce the greeting: "First, I'll name a vehicle and say 'Go.' You'll 'drive' into the circle, making the sound. Then, when I say 'Stop,' greet several people near you. Next, I'll say 'Freeze,' and you'll freeze where you are."

➤ Name a vehicle. As students mingle, reinforce positive behaviors: "I notice that you're driving carefully into the circle so you don't bump into others." Repeat with other vehicles.

Sharing: Vehicle of the Future

In advance, have students draw pictures of an idea they have for a future form of transportation. Have students name their creations.

➤ Pair students up and then introduce the sharing: "Today, you'll share about your 'vehicle of the future' with your partner. Take a moment now to decide who will go first." Give a few seconds for pairs to decide. "When I ring the chime, the first student will share. When I ring it again, you'll switch and your partner will share. I'll signal again when time is up."

➤ Allow one or two minutes for each student to share, and then signal everyone to stop. Call on a few volunteers to reflect: "What's one thing that interested you most about your partner's vehicle of the future?"

Group Activity: Traveling Song

➤ Introduce the activity: "Today we're going to sing a song about different forms of transportation. We'll do this by adding verses to the song 'Row, Row, Row Your Boat.'"

➤ Lead students in singing one verse of "Row, Row, Row Your Boat" and then teach the following variations:

Drive, drive, drive your car,
Carefully down the street
Happily, happily, happily, happily
Smiling in your seat.

Ride, ride, ride your train,
Safely down the track
Clickety, clackety, clickety, clackety
All the way there and back.

Fly, fly, fly your plane
High up in the air
Quickly, quickly, quickly, quickly
Travel anywhere!

Morning Message: How Did You Get to School?

➤ As a class, decide on transportation noises for each of the punctuation marks in the message (for example, "whoosh" for commas, "beep" for periods). Then read the message aloud, tracking your reading with a pointer so students can make the sound effects.

➤ As a class, count up the tally marks. Then list the total for each type. Ask a reflective question: "What was the most common way that we got to school today? What does that information tell us about our class?"

Money, Money, Money

Social Studies Content

Economics

NCSS Standards Theme

Production, Distribution, and Consumption

C3 Framework

D2.Eco.2.K–2 Identify the benefits and costs of making various personal decisions.

D2.Eco.10.K–2 Explain why people save.

Common Core Standards

SL.2.1

SL.3.1

Materials Needed

1 coin for each student (or pictures of coins)—equal numbers of pennies, nickels, dimes and quarters

Play paper five-dollar bills (find printable images online), enough so each student has at least 3 bills

3 bags labeled "Spend," "Save," and "Donate"

Vocabulary

Donate
Needs
Save
Spend
Wants

How to do it:

Display a message like the one below:

> Good Morning, Wise Consumers,
>
> Making smart choices about money can be hard. But it's a skill we all can learn! Read the Thinking Challenge below. Be ready to share your ideas at Morning Meeting.
>
> Thinking Challenge: Tyler has $20. Should Tyler spend it on movie tickets this weekend or save it for a bike? What advice would you give Tyler?

Greeting: Coin Meet and Greet

➤ Pass out coins to students and introduce the greeting: "Today, you're going to use coins to find your greeting partners. When I say 'Go,' find the other people who have the same coin as you. When you find them, create a standing group and say good morning to each other."

➤ After students have greeted one another, say: "You may have noticed that all your coins have faces of people on them. Take a look at your coins and talk with your group about who you think is on your coin."

➤ Invite volunteers to share their guesses. Then say: "Throughout this week, we'll investigate coins further and learn more about the people who are on them." (If possible, show students Susan B. Anthony and/or Sacagawea dollar coins.)

Sharing: If I Had the Money

In advance, print play money so that each student has three five-dollar bills. Place the three labeled bags (see Materials Needed) in the circle center.

➤ Introduce the sharing: "I'm going to give each of you some play money. As I'm handing it out, think about what you might do with this money if it were real. Would you spend it, save it, or donate it?" Model putting three bills in two or three of the bags.

➤ Have students take turns putting their bills in the bags and then return to their seats. Then explain the sharing: "Now, you'll have a chance to explain what you did with your money, and why." Model a simple explanation: "I put two bills in the 'save' bag and one in the 'donate' bag. I like to save money for something I'll need later. And I like to donate money as a way to help others."

➤ Have as many students share as time allows. (You can do this sharing over a few days.) Prompt student reflection: "What would happen if we only spent [saved, donated] our money?"

Group Activity: Earn It

➤ Introduce the activity: "In order to spend money, we first have to earn it. Today, you'll get to decide ways you'd like to earn money. When I call out two options, walk to the side of the room that best represents your choice. Then discuss with a partner why you chose that way to earn money."

➤ Call out the following options, one at a time:

   ✳ Walk a neighbor's dog (left side of the room). Sell cookies you made (right side of the room).

   ✳ Sweep the sidewalk (left). Wash the floor (right).

   ✳ Sing songs (left). Tell stories (right).

   ✳ Make jewelry [birdhouses, clothing] (left). Provide a service like cutting hair or delivering mail (right).

Morning Message: Financial Advice

➤ Read the message chorally with students. Then have them turn to a partner and discuss their advice for Tyler.

➤ Lead a whole-class discussion about the thinking challenge by asking:

   ✳ What's challenging about this decision?

   ✳ Why might Tyler choose to spend the money on a movie?

   ✳ Why might Tyler choose to save it for a bike?

➤ Conclude the discussion by reminding students that everyone has "needs" and "wants." Say: "Each time you're faced with a decision like Tyler's, you need to consider all your options so you can make the best choice for yourself."

Me in the World

Social Studies Content

Relating places to
personal identity

NCSS Standards Themes

Individual Development and
Identity

People, Places, and Environments

C3 Framework

D2.Geo.2.3–5 Use maps, satellite
images, photographs, and other
representations to explain
relationships between the
locations of places and regions
and their environmental
characteristics.

D2.Geo.10.3–5 Explain why
environmental characteristics vary
among different world regions.

Common Core Standards

SL.3.1
SL.4.1

Materials Needed

Sticky notes or sheets of paper

Vocabulary

Climate
Continent
Landform
Location

How to do it:

Display a message like the one below:

> Dear World Travelers,
>
> There are so many unique places in the world! Some places, like Antarctica, are very cold and have glaciers. Some places, like the Sahara Desert, can get very hot and have sand dunes. Which landforms or waterways would influence your decision to visit another continent? Be prepared to share your thoughts.

Greeting: Where I Am

➤ Introduce the greeting: "First, you'll all mix and mingle. When I call someone's name, everyone will stop. That student will greet the class and state which continent they'd like to visit and give one reason why. For example: 'I'd like to visit Australia because it has beautiful waterfalls.' Then the class will greet that student back."

➤ When all students have been greeted, conclude by saying in unison: "Hello, World!"

Sharing: My Ideal Place

➤ Introduce the sharing: "We've studied three different categories of climate—tropical, mild, and polar. As we go around the circle, each of you will share which category or sub-category of climate you'd like to live in, and why. For example: 'I'd like to live in a Mediterranean climate because the temperature is warm in the summer and mild in the winter.'"

➤ Give students some time to think of a place, and then start the sharing.

Group Activity: Choose Your Location

➤ With sticky notes, designate areas around the room as the continents (North America, South America, Africa, Europe, Asia, Australia, and Antarctica).

➤ Tell students that as you call out different statements, they will move to the continent that best matches their answer. For example, you might call out:

  ✻ Where a lot of my family is from

  ✻ A place I'd like to visit

  ✻ A place with a mountain or river I'd like to explore

  ✻ A place with a famous building or historic site I'd like to research

➤ Remind students to move safely: "Lots of people will be moving at once, so you'll need to move slowly and be aware of who's around you."

➤ Prompt students' reflection: "What's one thing you noticed about Antarctica?"

Morning Message: Connections to Me

➤ Invite a few students to each read one sentence of the message. Then have them share their responses with a partner.

➤ Encourage reflection with open-ended questions: "What landform on the North American continent do you think would most amaze a person from a different continent? Why?"

Celebrating Women's History

Social Studies Content

Women's History Month

NCSS Standards Theme

Time, Continuity, and Change

C3 Framework

D2.His.3.3–5 Generate questions about individuals and groups who have shaped significant historical changes and continuities.

D2.His.3.6–8 Use questions generated about individuals and groups to analyze why they, and the developments they shaped, are seen as historically significant.

Common Core Standards

SL.3.6
SL.4.4
SL.5.1
SL.6.1

Materials Needed

Blank name tag labels

Index cards with names of significant women students are studying

Vocabulary

Fact
Significant
Woman
Women's History Month
(Names of significant women in history students are studying)

How to do it:

Display a message like the one below:

> Hello, History Buffs,
>
> March is Women's History Month! One way to honor important people in history is to create a landmark, such as Mount Rushmore, which honors four U.S. presidents. If you could choose one important woman in U.S. history to honor with a landmark, who would it be? Write the name of a woman you think should be honored below.

Greeting: "Hello, My Name Is _____"

In advance, have students research a significant woman of their choice and write one fact about her. Have students write their person on a nametag (for example, "Sally Ride") and wear it to Morning Meeting.

➤ Introduce the greeting: "Today, you're going to mix and mingle, greeting as many classmates as you can in two minutes. When you greet someone, introduce yourself as the person you chose and share your one fact. For example: 'Hi, I'm Sally Ride. I'm the first American woman to go into space.'"

➤ After two or three minutes, signal for everyone to return to their seats. Invite a few volunteers to share out one fact they heard that was new to them or that surprised them.

Sharing: Significant Woman in Your Life

➤ Introduce the sharing: "Today, you're going to talk with a partner about one woman who is important to you, and why. This woman could be a relative, neighbor, coach, or any other woman who's important in your life. For example, one woman who's important in my life is my cousin Charlotte because she's always there for me when I need someone to talk to."

➤ Give students some think time. Then have them stand up, put their hand up, and pair up with someone nearby. Remind students of the expectations for respectful listening: "What will you do to be a respectful listener?"

➤ Allow about two minutes for the sharing.

Group Activity: Mystery Woman

➤ Introduce the activity: "Today, you're going to do an activity called 'Mystery Woman.' One student will be the guesser. Taped to the guesser's back will be the name of one significant woman in history whom we've been studying. The guesser will call on three to five people for clues."

➤ Ask for a volunteer to be the first guesser. Tape a Mystery Woman card to their back and have them stand in the middle of the circle and turn around slowly so that everyone can read the name. The guesser then calls on three to five students for clues. For example, some clues for Wilma Rudolph might be:

❋ She had polio as a child and struggled to walk.

❋ She made the Olympic team when she was just a teenager.

❋ She was the first American woman to win three gold medals in a single Olympics in track and field.

➤ If the guesser still doesn't know the answer after hearing three to five clues, the class reveals it.

Morning Message: The Next U.S. Landmark

➤ Read the message aloud with your students, and then read their answers.

➤ Ask for a few volunteers to share whom they chose to honor and why.

Constitution Day

How to do it:

Before the meeting, print or write four of the following quotes (or others of your choice) on slips of paper or index cards. Make enough so that each student will have a quote.

"The Constitution is the guide, which I will never abandon."
—George Washington

"Don't interfere with anything in the Constitution. That must be maintained, for it is the only safeguard of our liberties."
—Abraham Lincoln

"In framing a system which we wish to last for ages, we should not lose sight of the changes which ages will produce."
—James Madison

"The principle of the Constitution is that of a separation of legislative, executive and judiciary functions."
—Thomas Jefferson

"The strength of the Constitution lies entirely in the determination of each citizen to defend it."
—Albert Einstein

Display a message like the one below:

Dear Constitutional Class:

We are learning about the Founders of this country who proposed ideas for the U.S. Constitution. The Constitution established many of our rights as citizens.

Which of the Founders below do you find most inspiring as a leader? Shade a section on one of the bars in the graph below. Be ready to share your thinking during Morning Meeting.

John Adams	Benjamin Franklin	Alexander Hamilton	Thomas Jefferson	James Madison

---

Social Studies Content

U.S. Constitution

NCSS Standards Theme

Power, Authority, and Governance

C3 Framework

D2.Civ.3.3–5 Examine the origins and purposes of rules, laws, and key U.S. constitutional provisions.

D2.Civ.8.6–8 Analyze ideas and principles contained in the founding documents of the United States, and explain how they influence the social and political system.

Common Core Standards

RI.4.3
RI.5.3
SL.4.1
SL.5.1
SL.6.1
RH.6–8.2

Materials Needed

Slips of paper/index cards with quotes

Music

Vocabulary

Constitution
Founder
Leadership

Greeting: Quote Match

➤ Hand each student a quote and explain the greeting: "When I say 'Go,' mix and mingle. When you greet a classmate, say 'Good morning,' and take turns reading your quotes and who said them. If the quotes *don't* match, give each other a handshake and say 'Nice quote!' If your quotes *do* match, give each other a gentle high-five and say 'Quote match!' Then move on to greet someone else."

➤ Remind students to greet each other respectfully: "Greeting each person with respect matters more than how many people you greet. What are some ways we show respect when we're greeting each other?" Take a few suggestions, then begin the greeting.

➤ End the greeting after students have greeted three or four classmates. Have students hold on to their quotes.

Sharing: Which Founder?

➤ Introduce the sharing: "For today's sharing, going around the circle, you'll each share the Founder you chose and give one reason why."

➤ Give students a moment to plan their responses, and then begin the sharing.

Group Activity: Here's What I Think!

➤ Have students form inside-outside circles by counting off by twos. Ones form the inside circle and face out; twos form the outside circle and face in. Everyone should have a partner (one pairing can have three students).

➤ Explain the activity: "You'll take turns reading your quote and discussing with your partner what it means to you or some connections you have to it. I'll signal you to end your discussion, and then the outside circle will move one person to the left to discuss your ideas with a new partner."

➤ Each round, give students one or two minutes for discussion. Repeat for three or four rounds.

Morning Message: Shadowing a Founder

➤ Have a student volunteer read the message.

➤ Ask students to analyze the graph: "Which of the Founders was voted the most inspiring? Why do you think the class chose that Founder?"

➤ Prompt students to explore leadership in more depth: "What qualities do you think it takes to be an inspiring leader? Does an effective leader have to be someone who everyone admires? Why, or why not?"

169

Economics Everywhere

Social Studies Content

Scarcity and choice

NCSS Standards Theme

Production, Distribution, and Consumption

C3 Framework

D2.Eco.1.3–5 Compare the benefits and costs of individual choices.

D2.Eco.2.3–5 Identify positive and negative incentives that influence the decisions people make.

D2.Eco.1.6–8 Explain how economic decisions affect the well-being of individuals, businesses, and society.

Common Core Standards

SL.3.1
SL.4.1
SL.5.1
SL.6.1

Materials Needed

Index cards/slips of paper with economic terms

Vocabulary

Decision
Needs
Scarcity
Wants

How to do it:

Display a message like the one below:

Dear Decision Makers,

We make decisions every day! We may think about what we *want* or what we *need*. Sometimes, scarcity affects our decisions.

If the school day were only 3 hours long, which three subjects do you think would be most important to learn? List your first, second, and third choices below.

<u>First</u>   <u>Second</u>   <u>Third</u>

Greeting: Economic Connections

In advance, write or print out cards with economic terms students have studied and cards with their matching definitions. Make enough so that each student has a card.

> Pass out the cards and introduce the greeting: "You'll mix and mingle to find someone with a card that matches your economic term or definition. For example, the card with the term 'scarcity' matches the card with the definition 'in short supply.' You'll greet that person, return to the circle, and sit next to each other. This person will be your partner throughout today's Morning Meeting."

> After everyone is seated, call on a few pairs to read their economic term and definition.

Sharing: Scarcity of Time

> Introduce the sharing: "With your partner, you'll share an experience you had when time was scarce and you had to make a decision about how best to use the time. For example: 'On Monday, I had 30 minutes before school started. I had to decide whether to review students' homework or create a new lesson plan. I decided to review students' homework because I knew we'd be talking about it right after Morning Meeting.'"

➤ Give students some think time, and then signal to begin the sharing.

➤ After two or three minutes, invite a few volunteers to summarize what their partner said for the whole class.

Group Activity: 10 Economic Questions

➤ As a class, brainstorm and list economic words being studied.

➤ Silently choose one word from the generated list. Invite students to ask you up to ten "yes or no" questions to help them guess the word.

➤ Reinforce students' efforts: "You listened closely and built on each other's guesses. That strategy helped you figure out my word!"

➤ Repeat with student volunteers choosing words and taking questions, as time allows.

Morning Message: A Teaching Decision

➤ Echo-read the message (one student reads a sentence, and then the rest of the class reads the same sentence).

➤ Invite students to share their responses to the message prompt with their partner and explain why they chose those three subjects.

➤ Prompt students' deeper thinking: "How do you think needs and wants factored into people's decisions?" "What do you notice about our priorities as a class?"

The Olympic Games

Social Studies Content

Continents
Shared cultural events
Personal skills and interests

NCSS Standards Themes

People, Places, and Environments

Individual Development and
Identity

C3 Framework

D2.Geo.7.3–5 Explain how
cultural and environmental
characteristics affect the
distribution and movement of
people, goods, and ideas.

Common Core Standards

SL.4.1
SL.5.1

Materials Needed

Cards or slips of paper with
continents listed

Vocabulary

Continent
Olympics

How to do it:

Display a message like the one below:

> Dear Olympic Observers,
>
> The Olympic Games has been a world event since 1896. Many places around the world have hosted it. Place one check under all the continents you think have hosted the Olympic Games.
>
> | Africa | Asia | Europe | Australia | Antarctica | North America | South America |
> | --- | --- | --- | --- | --- | --- | --- |
> | | | | | | | |

Greeting: International Greeting

In advance, write the names of continents on cards or slips of paper, one continent per card. Make enough for each student to have one.

➤ Pass out the cards and introduce the greeting: "You'll mix and mingle around the world and greet classmates using the name of your continent. For example: 'Good morning, Yagil! Greetings from Australia!' Shake hands with people from other continents. High-five classmates from your continent. When you have greeted someone from all seven continents, return to your circle spot and sit."

➤ After everyone has been greeted, tell students to keep their cards for the rest of today's Morning Meeting.

Sharing: My Olympic Specialty

Consider posting the following sentence stem for students' reference:

I think [_____] should be included in
name of a sport or activity

the Olympics because _____ .

➤ Introduce the sharing: "In small groups, you'll each share an activity you love to do that you think should be part of the Olympics. This could be an activity you do by yourself or with other people. It doesn't have to be a sport. For example: 'I think knitting should be included in the Olympics because it's fun to do and you can create lots of useful things.'"

➤ Have students gather in continent groups based on their cards. Give them a minute to think of activities, and then signal them to start sharing.

➤ After two minutes or so, end the sharing. Have students stay in their continent groups.

Group Activity: Olympic Charades

➤ Explain the activity: "In your continent groups, brainstorm the winter and summer Olympic sports that you've seen. Then choose one and plan how you'll act it out. Everyone in your group needs to be part of the planning and the acting."

➤ Give students three or four minutes to brainstorm, plan, and practice acting out their sport.

➤ Invite one group to go first. After they've acted out their sport, they call on another group to make a guess (allow up to three guesses, one per group). Repeat as time allows.

Morning Message: Olympic Locations

➤ Going around the circle, have each student read one word of the message.

➤ Ask students which continents they think have *not* yet hosted the Olympics (Africa and Antarctica).

➤ Invite students' reflection: "In what ways do you think the Olympics brings together people from all over the world? Think about how doing today's activity brought everyone together before you answer."

The Right to Vote

Social Studies Content

Voting rights and responsibilities

NCSS Standards Theme

Civic Ideals and Practices

C3 Framework

D2.Civ.2.3–5 Explain how a democracy relies on people's responsible participation, and draw implications for how individuals should participate.

D2.Civ.1.6–8 Distinguish the powers and responsibilities of citizens, political parties, interest groups, and the media in a variety of governmental and nongovernmental contexts.

D2.Civ.2.6–8 Explain specific roles played by citizens (such as voters, jurors, taxpayers, members of the armed forces, petitioners, protesters, and office-holders).

Common Core Standards

SL.5.1
SL.6.1
SL.6.4

Materials Needed

List of 4–5 topics students have learned about recently

Vocabulary

Citizen
Election
Voting

How to do it:

Display a message like the one below:

> Dear Future Voters,
>
> Voting is a right for citizens of the United States. Voting is also a responsibility. When we vote, we help elect government officials and make our thoughts known.
>
> To vote, you must be at least 18 years old. Do you think the voting age should be higher, be lower, or stay the same? Place a check mark under your choice.
>
> | Lower | Higher | Stay the same |
> |-------|--------|---------------|
> | ✔ ✔ | ✔ ✔ | ✔ ✔ ✔ |

Greeting: It's a Fact

➤ Introduce the greeting: "You're going to greet the person to your right, with an important fact you've learned about voting or a question or wondering you still have about voting. For example, I might say 'Good morning, Emily. Women got the right to vote in Great Britain in 1918—but only *some* women.'"

➤ Invite a student volunteer to begin the greeting, and continue around the circle.

➤ Reinforce students' thinking: "I heard so many facts and questions about voting! You're really thinking deeply about this topic."

Sharing: Vote Your Thoughts

In advance, post an anchor chart with four or five social studies topics students have recently studied. (Number each topic; you'll need these numbers for the group activity.)

➤ Introduce the sharing: "Read this list of social studies topics you've recently learned about. Then, going around the circle, you'll share your response to this question: 'If you were to vote for one of these topics to learn more about, which topic would you vote for, and why?' Give a thumbs-up when you're ready to share."

➤ Ask a volunteer to start the sharing and continue around the circle. As students share, tally the topics they vote for on the list.

Group Activity: Convince Me

➢ Explain the activity: "Hold up your fingers to show which topic you voted for. For example, if you voted for number three, hold up three fingers. When I say 'Go,' mix and mingle and pair up with a classmate who voted for a topic different than yours. Decide who will go first. That person will try to convince the other person to change their vote. When I say 'Switch,' the other person gets their turn to speak. You'll each have about 30 seconds."

➢ Remind students about positive behavior expectations: "What will this activity look and sound like if everyone is following our rule about taking care of each other?" (Possible answer: We'll be polite even if we can't convince the other person to switch.)

➢ Signal students to begin. Do as many rounds as you have time for. To conclude, ask if anyone's vote changed, and why.

Morning Message: Voting Age

➢ Have students silently read the message.

➢ Invite one student to summarize the message and another to summarize the posted responses.

➢ Deepen student thinking with open-ended questions: "What kinds of things are you looking forward to voting on when you turn eighteen?" "How can you learn about the issues and people running for election before you vote?"

Activities Listed by NCSS Theme

Theme	Grade	Component	Title and Page
Culture and Cultural Diversity	K	Greeting Greeting Sharing Sharing	Kind Kids Greeting, p. 15 Red, White, and Blue . . . , p. 16 Artifacts Around the World, p. 17 Family Foods, p. 19
	1	Greeting	Musical Meet and Greet, p. 36
	3	Group Activity Morning Message	History Wordsmiths, p. 87 ABCs of History, p. 91
	4	Sharing Sharing	Compare and Contrast, p. 99 Culture Brainstorm, p. 100
	5	Morning Message	Word Travelers, p. 134
	6	Greeting/Sharing Morning Message	Words of Wisdom, p. 138 Cultural Intrigue, p. 151
	K–2	Themed Meeting	Practicing Peace, pp. 158–159

Theme	Grade	Component	Title and Page
Time, Continuity, and Change	K	Morning Message	The First Thanksgiving, p. 31
	1	Group Activity Morning Message	Human Calendar, p. 44 Picture History, p. 52
	2	Greeting/Sharing Group Activity Group Activity Morning Message Morning Message	People of Interest, p. 58 Black History Month, p. 63 Fidget Family Back Then, pp. 66–67 History by the Numbers, p. 73 School Tools Long Ago, p. 74
	3	Group Activity Morning Message	Ellis Island Timeline, p. 85 Tell Me More, p. 93
	4	Greeting/Sharing Group Activity Group Activity Group Activity Morning Message	Musical Questions, p. 98 History Mystery, p. 104 Loyalist and Patriot Song, p. 106 Two Facts and a Falsehood, p. 108 Time Travel, p. 114
	5	Group Activity Group Activity Group Activity Morning Message Morning Message	Historical Charades, p. 125 Service Providers . . . , p. 126 The Extraordinary Ordinary, p. 128 Civilization Survival Bag, p. 129 Historical Headlines, p. 131
	6	Sharing Group Activity Morning Message Morning Message Morning Message	Cause and Effect, p. 139 Human Timeline, p. 147 Back in Time, p. 149 Making Connections, p. 153 Writing History, p. 154
	3–6	Themed Meeting	Celebrating Women's . . . , pp. 166–167

Theme	Grade	Component	Title and Page
People, Places, and Environments	K	Greeting Group Activity Group Activity Morning Message	Address Match, p. 13 Follow the Directions!, p. 23 Learning All Around, pp. 26–27 Where Do You Like to Work?, p. 33
	1	Greeting Sharing Group Activity Group Activity Morning Message Morning Message	Block Party Greeting, p. 34 Whose Favorite Place?, p. 42 Landform Match, p. 45 North, East, South, West, p. 46 Attention, Mapmakers!, p. 49 Our Favorite Places, p. 51
	2	Greeting Greeting Greeting Sharing Group Activity Group Activity Morning Message Morning Message Morning Message	Body of Water Greeting, p. 54 Global Good Mornings, p. 55 State Postcard Puzzles, p. 56 Explore Galore, p. 59 Eyes-Closed True or False, p. 65 We Wonder . . . , p. 69 Classroom Grid, p. 70 Climate Conversation, p. 71 Country Commonalities, p. 72
	3	Greeting Greeting Greeting Group Activity Group Activity Group Activity Group Activity Morning Message	Are You My Capital?, p. 75 Around the World, p. 76 Latitude and Longitude, p. 78 Continent Chant, p. 84 Guess My State!, p. 86 History Wordsmiths, p. 87 Pin the Capital, p. 89 Use the Map, p. 94
	4	Greeting Greeting Sharing/Group Activity Group Activity Morning Message	Cardinal Directions, p. 95 Landform Greeting, p. 97 Landform Chatter, p. 102 Human Compass, p. 105 Exploring Our Natural Resources, p. 111
	5	Greeting Group Activity	Geographical Connections, p. 116 A Traveler's Guide to World Climates, p. 123
	6	Sharing Group Activity	Fact or Opinion?, p. 140 Pop-Up Countries, p. 148
	3–4	Themed Meeting	Me in the World, pp. 164–165
	4–5	Themed Meeting	The Olympic Games, pp. 172–173

CONTINUED ▶

Theme	Grade	Component	Title and Page
Individual Development and Identity	K	Greeting Sharing Group Activity	Greeting Now and Long Ago, p. 14 Time Capsule, p. 20 Just Like My Family!, p. 25
	1	Greeting Greeting/Sharing Sharing Sharing	Jobs of the Future, p. 35 Super Citizen Sharing, p. 37 Fairness First, p. 38 Family Flags, p. 39
	2	Sharing	What's Your Animal?, p. 61
	3	Group Activity	Personal Hero . . . , p. 88
	5	Sharing	Identity Influencers, p. 121
	6	Sharing Sharing	Vantage Point, p. 142 Whose Expedition?, p. 143
	3–4	Themed Meeting	Me in the World, pp. 164–165
	4–5	Themed Meeting	The Olympic Games, pp. 172–173

Theme	Grade	Component	Title and Page
Individuals, Groups, and Institutions	K	Sharing Morning Message	Classroom Citizens, p. 18 Community Places, p. 29
	3	Sharing Morning Message	What's Your Perspective?, p. 82 Express Your Thoughts, p. 92
	4	Greeting	Institutional Greeting, p. 96
	5	Sharing Morning Message	Build a Better Institution, p. 119 Protecting the Earth, p. 132

Theme	Grade	Component	Title and Page
Power, Authority, and Governance	2	Sharing	If I Were Mayor, p. 60
	5	Greeting Greeting/Sharing Greeting/Sharing Morning Message	Branching Out, p. 115 The Justices Speak, p. 117 They Should Pass a Law!, p. 118 Texting the President, p. 133
	6	Greeting Sharing	Guess the President, p. 135 Government Gab, p. 141
	K–2	Themed Meeting	Constitution Convention, pp. 156–157
	4–6	Themed Meeting	Constitution Day, pp. 168–169

Theme	Grade	Component	Title and Page
Production, Distribution, and Consumption	K	Group Activity Group Activity	Choose Your Natural Resource, p. 22 Let's Plant a Garden!, p. 28
	1	Sharing Group Activity	Shop Around, p. 41 Everyone Has Needs . . . , p. 43
	2	Greeting/Sharing Group Activity	Bread, Meet Baker!, p. 57 Community Worker Riddles, p. 64
	3	Greeting Group Activity	Needs and Wants, p. 79 Spend It or Save It?, p. 90
	4	Group Activity Group Activity Group Activity Morning Message	Economic Minds, p. 103 Made in Our State!, p. 107 We're All in This Together, p. 109 At Your Service, p. 110
	5	Sharing Group Activity Morning Message	Economic Effects, p. 120 Service Providers . . . , p. 126 Econo-Me-Too!, p. 130
	6	Greeting/Sharing Group Activity	Economic Connections, p. 136 Economic Brainstorm, p. 146
	2–3	Themed Meeting	Money, Money, Money, pp. 162–163
	3–6	Themed Meeting	Economics Everywhere, pp. 170–171

Theme	Grade	Component	Title and Page
Science, Technology, and Society	K	Morning Message	Tools From the Past, p. 32
	1	Morning Message	Invention Convention, p. 50
	4	Sharing Morning Message	Scientifically Speaking, p. 101 My Favorite Scientist, p. 112
	5	Group Activity	Technology Mind Map, p. 127
	6	Group Activity Morning Message	Adding to the Answer, p. 144 Back in Time, p. 149
	K–1	Themed Meeting	Here, There, and . . . , pp. 160–161

Theme	Grade	Component	Title and Page
Global Connections	3	Greeting	Around the World, p. 76
	4	Morning Message	One Big World, p. 113
	5	Morning Message	Word Travelers, p. 134
	6	Greeting/Sharing Morning Message	What's the Positive News?, p. 137 Writing History, p. 154

Theme	Grade	Component	Title and Page
Civic Ideals and Practices	K	Sharing/Group Activity Group Activity Morning Message	Taking Care Everywhere, p. 21 It's Our Job!, p. 24 Put It to a Vote!, p. 30
	1	Sharing Group Activity Group Activity Morning Message	Rules in the Round, p. 40 Our Leaders Song, p. 47 U.S. Symbol Refrain, p. 48 We've Got a Job to Do!, p. 53
	2	Sharing/Group Activity Group Activity	Cooperation Call-Out, p. 62 National Symbols Loop Cards, p. 68
	3	Sharing Sharing Group Activity Group Activity	Community News Desk, p. 80 Get Out the Vote, p. 81 Citizen Chant, p. 83 Personal Hero . . . , p. 88
	5	Sharing Group Activity	The Common Good, p. 122 Give Me an Ideal Clue!, p. 124
	6	Group Activity Morning Message Morning Message	Document Drill, p. 145 By the People, p. 150 #LearningAboutLaws, p. 152
	5–6	Themed Meeting	The Right to Vote, pp. 174–175

Activities Listed by C3 Framework Standard

Standard	Grade	Component	Title
D2.Civ.1.K–2 Describe roles and responsibilities of people in authority.	1 2	Group Activity Sharing	Our Leaders Song, p. 47 If I Were Mayor, p. 60
D2.Civ.2.K–2 Explain how all people, not just official leaders, play important roles in a community.	1 1 1 2	Greeting Greeting/Sharing Morning Message Group Activity	Jobs of the Future, p. 35 Super Citizen Sharing, p. 37 We've Got a Job to Do!, p. 53 Community Worker Riddles, p. 64
D2.Civ.3.K–2 Explain the need for and purposes of rules in various settings inside and outside of school.	1	Sharing	Rules in the Round, p. 40
D2.Civ.6.K–2 Describe how communities work to accomplish common tasks, establish responsibilities, and fulfill roles of authority.	K K 1	Group Activity Morning Message Morning Message	It's Our Job!, p. 24 Community Places, p. 29 We've Got a Job to Do!, p. 53
D2.Civ.7.K–2 Apply civic virtues when participating in school settings.	K K K 1 2 K–2 K–2	Greeting Sharing Sharing/Group Activity Sharing Sharing/Group Activity Themed Meeting Themed Meeting	Kind Kids Greeting, p. 15 Classroom Citizens, p. 18 Taking Care Everywhere, p. 21 Fairness First, p. 38 Cooperation Call-Out, p. 62 Constitution Convention, pp. 156–157 Practicing Peace, pp. 158–159
D2.Civ.8.K–2 Describe democratic principles such as equality, fairness, and respect for legitimate authority and rules.	K 1 1 2 K–2	Greeting Sharing Group Activity Group Activity Themed Meeting	Kind Kids Greeting, p. 15 Fairness First, p. 38 U.S. Symbol Refrain, p. 48 National Symbols Loop Cards, p. 68 Constitution Convention, pp. 156–157
D2.Civ.10.K–2 Compare their own point of view with others' perspectives.	K K 1 2	Sharing Group Activity Sharing Sharing	Time Capsule, p. 20 Just Like My Family!, p. 25 Family Flags, p. 39 What's Your Animal?, p. 61
D2.Civ.11.K–2 Explain how people can work together to make decisions in the classroom.	K K	Greeting Morning Message	Red, White, and Blue . . . , p. 16 Put It to a Vote, p. 30
D2.Civ.14.K–2 Describe how people have tried to improve their communities over time.	1	Greeting	Block Party Greeting, p. 34

CONTINUED ▶

Standard	Grade	Component	Title
D2.Eco.2.K–2 Identify the benefits and costs of making various personal decisions.	1 1 2–3	Sharing Group Activity Themed Meeting	Shop Around, p. 41 Everyone Has Needs and Wants, p. 43 Money, Money, Money, pp. 162–163
D2.Eco.4.K–2 Describe the goods and services that people in the local community produce and those that are produced in other communities.	2	Greeting/Sharing	Bread, Meet Baker! , p. 57
D2.Eco.10.K–2 Explain why people save.	2–3	Themed Meeting	Money, Money, Money , pp. 162–163
D2.Eco.14.K–2 Describe why people in one country trade goods and services with people in other countries.	K	Group Activity	Let's Plant a Garden!, p. 28
D2.Geo.1.K–2 Construct maps, graphs, and other representations of familiar places.	K 1	Morning Message Morning Message	Where Do You Like to Work?,* p. 33 Attention, Mapmakers!, p. 49
D2.Geo.2.K–2 Use maps, graphs, photographs and other representations to describe places and the relationships and interactions that shape them.	K K K K 1 2 2	Greeting Group Activity Group Activity Morning Message Group Activity Greeting Morning Message	Address Match, p. 13 Follow the Directions!, p. 23 Learning All Around, pp. 26–27 Where Do You Like to Work?, p. 33 North, East, South, West, p. 46 Global Good Mornings, p. 55 Classroom Grid, p. 70
D2.Geo.3.K–2 Use maps, globes, and other simple geographic models to identify cultural and environmental characteristics of places.	2	Morning Message	Climate Conversation, p. 71
D2.Geo.4.K–2 Explain how weather, climate, and other environmental characteristics affect people's lives in a place or region.	2	Morning Message	Climate Conversation, p. 71
D2.Geo.5.K–2 Describe how human activities affect the cultural and environmental characteristics of places or regions.	K–1	Themed Meeting	Here, There, and Everywhere, pp. 160–161

* Standard applies only to the "Extending the Social Studies Learning . . ." portion of the activity.

Activities Listed by C3 Framework Standard

Standard	Grade	Component	Title
D2.Geo.6.K–2 Identify some cultural and environmental characteristics of specific places.	K K 1 1 1 1 2 2 2 2 2 2	Sharing Sharing Greeting Sharing Group Activity Morning Message Greeting Greeting Sharing Group Activity Group Activity Morning Message	Artifacts Around the World, p. 17 Family Foods, p. 19 Musical Meet and Greet, p. 36 Whose Favorite Place?, p. 42 Landform Match, p. 45 Our Favorite Places, p. 51 Body of Water Greeting, p. 54 State Postcard Puzzles, p. 56 Explore Galore, p. 59 Eyes-Closed True or False, p. 65 We Wonder . . . , p. 69 Country Commonalities, p. 72
D2.Geo.8.K–2 Compare how people in different types of communities use local and distant environments to meet their daily needs.	K 2	Group Activity Morning Message	Choose Your Natural Resource, p. 22 Country Commonalities, p. 72
D2.His.1.K–2 Create a chronological sequence of multiple events.	1	Group Activity	Human Calendar, p. 44
D2.His.2.K–2 Compare life in the past to life today.	K K K 1 2 2	Greeting Morning Message Morning Message Morning Message Group Activity Morning Message	Greeting Now and Long Ago, p. 14 The First Thanksgiving, p. 31 Tools From the Past, p. 32 Invention Convention, p. 50 Fidget Family Back Then, pp. 66–67 School Tools Long Ago, p. 74
D2.His.3.K–2 Generate questions about individuals and groups who have shaped a significant historical change.	1 2 2	Morning Message Greeting/Sharing Group Activity	Picture History, p. 52 People of Interest,* p. 58 Black History Month, p. 63
D2.His.14.K–2 Generate possible reasons for an event or development in the past.	2	Morning Message	History by the Numbers, p. 73
D3.1.K–2 Gather relevant information from one or two sources while using the origin and structure to guide the selection.	K–1	Themed Meeting	Here, There, and Everywhere, pp. 160–161
D4.3.K–2 Present a summary of an argument using print, oral, and digital technologies.	K	Sharing/Group Activity	Taking Care Everywhere,* p. 21

* Standard applies only to the "Extending the Social Studies Learning . . ." portion of the activity.

Activities Listed by C3 Framework Standard

Standard	Grade	Component	Title
D1.4.3–5 Explain how supporting questions help answer compelling questions in an inquiry.	3	Group Activity	Guess My State!, p. 86
D2.Civ.1.3–5 Distinguish the responsibilities and powers of government officials at various levels and branches of government and in different times and places.	5 5	Greeting Morning Message	Branching Out, p. 115 Texting the President, p. 133
D2.Civ.2.3–5 Explain how a democracy relies on people's responsible participation, and draw implications for how individuals should participate.	3 3 5–6	Sharing Morning Message Themed Meeting	Get Out the Vote, p. 81 Express Your Thoughts, p. 92 The Right to Vote, pp. 174–175
D2.Civ.3.3–5 Examine the origins and purposes of rules, laws, and key U.S. constitutional provisions.	4–6	Themed Meeting	Constitution Day, pp. 168–169
D2.Civ.4.3–5 Explain how groups of people make rules to create responsibilities and protect freedoms.	5	Greeting/Sharing	They Should Pass a Law!, p. 118
D2.Civ.6.3–5 Describe ways in which people benefit from and are challenged by working together, including through government, workplaces, voluntary organizations, and families.	3 4 5	Sharing Greeting Sharing	Community News Desk, p. 80 Institutional Greeting, p. 96 Build a Better Institution, p. 119
D2.Civ.7.3–5 Apply civic virtues and democratic principles in school settings.	3	Greeting	Beach Ball Review, p. 77
D2.Civ.8.3–5 Identify core civic virtues and democratic principles that guide government, society, and communities.	3 5 5	Group Activity Sharing Group Activity	Citizen Chant, p. 83 The Common Good, p. 122 Give Me an Ideal Clue!, p. 124
D2.Civ.10.3–5 Identify the beliefs, experiences, perspectives, and values that underlie their own and others' points of view about civic issues.	3 5	Sharing Greeting/Sharing	What's Your Perspective?, p. 82 The Justices Speak, p. 117
D2.Civ.12.3–5 Explain how rules and laws change society and how people change rules and laws.	5	Greeting/Sharing	They Should Pass a Law!, p. 118
D2.Eco.1.3–5 Compare the benefits and costs of individual choices.	3 3 3–6	Greeting Group Activity Themed Meeting	Needs and Wants, p. 79 Spend It or Save It?, p. 90 Economics Everywhere, pp. 170–171

Activities Listed by C3 Framework Standard

Standard	Grade	Component	Title
D2.Eco.2.3–5 Identify positive and negative incentives that influence the decisions people make.	3 3 5 5 3–6	Greeting Group Activity Sharing Morning Message Themed Meeting	Needs and Wants, p. 79 Spend It or Save It?, p. 90 Economic Effects, p. 120 Econo-Me-Too!, p. 130 Economics Everywhere, pp. 170–171
D2.Eco.3.3–5 Identify examples of the variety of resources (human capital, physical capital, and natural resources) that are used to produce goods and services.	4 4 4 4 5	Group Activity Group Activity Morning Message Morning Message Morning Message	Economic Minds, p. 103 Made in Our State!, p. 107 At Your Service, p. 110 Exploring Our Natural Resources, p. 111 Civilization Survival Bag, p. 129
D2.Eco.11.3–5 Explain the meaning of inflation, deflation, and unemployment	4	Group Activity	Economic Minds, p. 103
D2.Eco.15.3–5 Explain the effects of increasing economic interdependence on different groups within participating nations.	4	Group Activity	We're All in This Together, p. 109
D2.Geo.1.3–5 Construct maps and other graphic representations of both familiar and unfamiliar places.	3 4 4	Greeting Greeting Group Activity	Latitude and Longitude, p. 78 Cardinal Directions, p. 95 Human Compass, p. 105
D2.Geo.2.3–5 Use maps, satellite images, photographs, and other representations to explain relationships between the locations of places and regions and their environmental characteristics.	3 3 3 3 3 4 4 5 5 3–4	Greeting Group Activity Group Activity Group Activity Morning Message Greeting Group Activity Greeting Group Activity Themed Meeting	Are You My Capital?, p. 75 Continent Chant, p. 84 Guess My State!, p. 86 Pin the Capital, p. 89 Use the Map, p. 94 Landform Greeting, p. 97 Human Compass, p. 105 Geographical Connections, p. 116 A Traveler's Guide . . . , p. 123 Me in the World, pp. 164–165
D2.Geo.3.3–5 Use maps of different scales to describe the locations of cultural and environmental characteristics.	3	Greeting	Around the World, p. 76
D2.Geo.4.3–5 Explain how culture influences the way people modify and adapt to their environments.	3	Greeting	Around the World, p. 76
D2.Geo.7.3–5 Explain how cultural and environmental characteristics affect the distribution and movement of people, goods, and ideas.	4 4 5 5 4–5	Sharing Morning Message Sharing Morning Message Themed Meeting	Culture Brainstorm, p. 100 One Big World, p. 113 Identity Influencers, p. 121 Word Travelers, p. 134 The Olympic Games, pp. 172–173

CONTINUED ▶

Standard	Grade	Component	Title
D2.Geo.10.3–5 Explain why environmental characteristics vary among different world regions.	4 5 3–4	Sharing/Group Activity Group Activity Themed Meeting	Landform Chatter, p. 102 A Traveler's Guide . . . , p. 123 Me in the World, pp. 164–165
D2.Geo.12.3–5 Explain how natural and human-made catastrophic events in one place affect people living in other places.	5	Morning Message	Protecting the Earth, p. 132
D2.His.1.3–5 Create and use a chronological sequence of related events to compare developments that happened at the same time.	3 4 5 5	Group Activity Morning Message Group Activity Morning Message	Ellis Island Timeline, p. 85 Time Travel, p. 114 Historical Charades, p. 125 Historical Headlines, p. 131
D2.His.2.3–5 Compare life in specific historical time periods to life today.	3 3 5 5 5	Group Activity Morning Message Group Activity Group Activity Morning Message	History Wordsmiths, p. 87 ABCs of History, p. 91 Service Providers Then and Now, p. 126 Technology Mind Map, p. 127 Civilization Survival Bag, p. 129
D2.His.3.3–5 Generate questions about individuals and groups who have shaped significant historical changes and continuities.	3 3 4 4 4 4 4 5 3–6	Group Activity Morning Message Greeting/Sharing Group Activity Group Activity Group Activity Morning Message Group Activity Themed Meeting	Personal Hero Postage Stamps, p. 88 Tell Me More, p. 93 Musical Questions, p. 98 History Mystery, p. 104 Loyalist and Patriot Song, p. 106 Two Facts and a Falsehood, p. 108 My Favorite Scientist, p. 112 The Extraordinary Ordinary, p. 128 Celebrating Women's History, pp. 166–167
D2.His.4.3–5 Explain why individuals and groups during the same historical period differed in their perspectives.	4	Sharing	Compare and Contrast, p. 99
D2.His.14.3–5 Explain probable causes and effects of events and developments.	5	Morning Message	Historical Headlines, p. 131
D4.2.3–5 Construct explanations using reasoning, correct sequence, examples, and details with relevant information and data.	4 5	Sharing Group Activity	Scientifically Speaking, p. 101 Service Providers Then and Now, p. 126
D4.6.3–5 Draw on disciplinary concepts to explain the challenges people have faced and opportunities they have created, in addressing local, regional, and global problems at various times and places.	5	Sharing	Build a Better Institution, p. 119

Standard	Grade	Component	Title
D1.5.6–8 Determine the kinds of sources that will be helpful in answering compelling and supporting questions, taking into consideration multiple points of views represented in the sources.	6	Sharing	Fact or Opinion?, p. 140
D2.Civ.1.6–8 Distinguish the powers and responsibilities of citizens, political parties, interest groups, and the media in a variety of governmental and nongovernmental contexts.	5–6	Themed Meeting	The Right to Vote, pp. 174–175
D2.Civ.2.6–8 Explain specific roles played by citizens (such as voters, jurors, taxpayers, members of the armed forces, petitioners, protesters, and office-holders).	5–6	Themed Meeting	The Right to Vote, pp. 174–175
D2.Civ.3.6–8 Examine the origins, purposes, and impact of constitutions, laws, treaties, and international agreements.	6	Group Activity	Document Drill, p. 145
D2.Civ.4.6–8 Explain the powers and limits of the three branches of government, public officials, and bureaucracies at different levels in the United States and in other countries.	6	Sharing	Government Gab, p. 141
D2.Civ.8.6–8 Analyze ideas and principles contained in the founding documents of the United States, and explain how they influence the social and political system.	4–6	Themed Meeting	Constitution Day, pp. 168–169
D2.Civ.12.6–8 Assess specific rules and laws (both actual and proposed) as means of addressing public problems.	6	Morning Message	#LearningAboutLaws, p. 152
D2.Civ.14.6–8 Compare historical and contemporary means of changing societies, and promoting the common good.	6	Morning Message	By the People, p. 150
D2.Eco.1.6–8 Explain how economic decisions affect the well-being of individuals, businesses, and society.	6 3–6	Group Activity Themed Meeting	Economic Brainstorm, p. 146 Economics Everywhere, pp. 170–171
D2.Eco.6.6–8 Explain how changes in supply and demand cause changes in prices and quantities of goods and services, labor, credit, and foreign currencies.	6	Greeting/Sharing	Economic Connections, p. 136

CONTINUED ▶

Standard	Grade	Component	Title
D2.Geo.2.6–8 Use maps, satellite images, photographs, and other representations to explain relationships between the locations of places and regions, and changes in their environmental characteristics.	6	Group Activity	Pop-Up Countries, p. 148
D2.Geo.5.6–8 Analyze the combinations of cultural and environmental characteristics that make places both similar to and different from other places.	6	Greeting/Sharing	Words of Wisdom, p. 138
D2.Geo.6.6–8 Explain how the physical and human characteristics of places and regions are connected to human identities and cultures.	6	Greeting/Sharing	What's the Positive News?, p. 137
D2.Geo.7.6–8 Explain how changes in transportation and communication technology influence the spatial connections among human settlements and affect the diffusion of ideas and cultural practices.	6	Group Activity	Adding to the Answer, p. 144
D2.Geo.10.6–8 Analyze the ways in which cultural and environmental characteristics vary among various regions of the world.	6	Morning Message	Cultural Intrigue, p. 151
D2.His.1.6–8 Analyze connections among events and developments in broader historical contexts.	6 6 6	Group Activity Morning Message Morning Message	Human Timeline, p. 147 Back in Time, p. 149 Making Connections, p. 153
D2.His.3.6–8 Use questions generated about individuals and groups to analyze why they, and the developments they shaped, are seen as historically significant.	6 3–6	Greeting Themed Meeting	Guess the President, p. 135 Celebrating Women's History, pp. 166–167
D2.His.4.6–8 Analyze multiple factors that influenced the perspectives of people during different historical eras.	6 6 6	Sharing Sharing Morning Message	Vantage Point, p. 142 Whose Expedition?, p. 143 Writing History, p. 154
D2.His.14.6–8 Explain multiple causes and effects of events and developments in the past.	6	Sharing	Cause and Effect, p. 139

K Activities Listed by Common Core Standards

Standard	Component	Title
RI.K.10 Actively engage in group reading activities with purpose and understanding.	Greeting Sharing Sharing Group Activity Group Activity Morning Message	Greeting Now and Long Ago,* p. 14 Family Foods,* p. 19 Time Capsule,* p. 20 Just Like My Family!,* p. 25 Let's Plant a Garden!,* p. 28 The First Thanksgiving,* p. 31
W.K.2 Use a combination of drawing, dictating, and writing to compose informative/explanatory texts in which they name what they are writing about and supply some information about the topic.	Sharing Sharing Group Activity Morning Message	Classroom Citizens,* p. 18 Family Foods,* p. 19 Learning All Around,* pp. 26–27 The First Thanksgiving,* p. 31
W.K.8 With guidance and support from adults, recall information from experiences or gather information from provided sources to answer a question.	Group Activity Morning Message Morning Message	Choose Your Natural Resource,* p. 22 Community Places, p. 29 Tools From the Past, p. 32
SL.K.1 Participate in collaborative conversations with diverse partners about kindergarten topics and texts with peers and adults in small and larger groups.	Greeting Greeting Greeting Sharing Sharing/Group Activity Group Activity Group Activity Group Activity Morning Message Morning Message Themed Meeting	Address Match, p. 13 Greeting Now and Long Ago, p. 14 Red, White, and Blue . . . , p. 16 Time Capsule, p. 20 Taking Care Everywhere, p. 21 Choose Your Natural Resource, p. 22 It's Our Job!, p. 24 Let's Plant a Garden!, p. 28 Put It to a Vote, p. 30 Where Do You Like to Work?, p. 33 Here, There, and Everywhere, pp. 160–161
SL.K.2 Confirm understanding of a text read aloud or information presented orally or through other media by asking and answering questions about key details and requesting clarification if something is not understood.	Group Activity	Just Like My Family!, p. 25
SL.K.3 Ask and answer questions in order to seek help, get information, or clarify something that is not understood.	Group Activity	Choose Your Natural Resource, p. 22
SL.K.4 Describe familiar people, places, things, and events and, with prompting and support, provide additional detail.	Sharing Sharing	Classroom Citizens, p. 18 Family Foods, p. 19

* Standard applies only to the "Extending the Social Studies Learning . . ." portion of the activity.

CONTINUED ▶

K Activities Listed by Common Core Standards

Standard	Component	Title
SL.K.5 Add drawings or other visual displays to descriptions as desired to provide additional detail.	Morning Message	The First Thanksgiving, p. 31
SL.K.6 Speak audibly and express thoughts, feelings, and ideas clearly.	Greeting Greeting Greeting Sharing Sharing Sharing Sharing Sharing/Group Activity Morning Message Themed Meeting Themed Meeting Themed Meeting	Address Match, p. 13 Greeting Now and Long Ago, p. 14 Red, White, and Blue . . . , p. 16 Artifacts Around the World, p. 17 Classroom Citizens, p. 18 Family Foods, p. 19 Time Capsule, p. 20 Taking Care Everywhere, p. 21 Tools From the Past, p. 32 Constitution Convention, pp. 156–157 Here, There, and Everywhere, pp. 160–161 Practicing Peace, pp. 158–159
L.K.4 Determine or clarify the meaning of unknown and multiple-meaning words and phrases based on kindergarten reading and content.	Group Activity	Learning All Around, pp. 26–27
L.K.5 With guidance and support from adults, explore word relationships and nuances in word meanings.	Greeting Group Activity Group Activity	Kind Kids Greeting, p. 15 Follow the Directions!, p. 23 It's Our Job!, p. 24
L.K.6 Use words and phrases acquired through conversations, reading and being read to, and responding to texts.	Group Activity	Let's Plant a Garden!, p. 28

Activities Listed by Common Core Standards

Standard	Component	Title
RI.1.7 Use the illustrations and details in a text to describe its key ideas.	Morning Message	Invention Convention, p. 50
RI.1.10 With prompting and support, read informational texts appropriately complex for grade 1.	Greeting	Musical Meet and Greet,* p. 36
RF.1.4 Read with sufficient accuracy and fluency to support comprehension.	Group Activity Morning Message	U.S. Symbol Refrain, p. 48 Attention, Mapmakers!, p. 49
W.1.2 Write informative/explanatory texts in which they name a topic, supply some facts about the topic, and provide some sense of closure.	Sharing Morning Message	Shop Around,* p. 41 Our Favorite Places,* p. 51
W.1.7 Participate in shared research and writing projects (e.g., explore a number of "how-to" books on a given topic and use them to write a sequence of instructions).	Morning Message	Picture History,* p. 52
W.1.8 With guidance and support from adults, recall information from experiences or gather information from provided sources to answer a question.	Greeting Greeting/Sharing Sharing Sharing	Jobs of the Future, p. 35 Super Citizen Sharing, p. 37 Fairness First,* p. 38 Whose Favorite Place?, p. 42
SL.1.1 Participate in collaborative conversations with diverse partners about grade 1 topics and texts with peers and adults in small and larger groups.	Greeting Sharing Sharing Sharing Group Activity Morning Message Morning Message Themed Meeting	Block Party Greeting, p. 34 Rules in the Round, p. 40 Shop Around, p. 41 Whose Favorite Place?, p. 42 Landform Match, p. 45 Our Favorite Places, p. 51 We've Got a Job to Do!, p. 53 Here, There, and Everywhere, pp. 160–161
SL.1.2 Ask and answer questions about key details in a text read aloud or information presented orally or through other media.	Sharing	Rules in the Round, p. 40
SL.1.3 Ask and answer questions about what a speaker says in order to gather additional information or clarify something that is not understood.	Themed Meeting	Practicing Peace, pp. 158–159

* Standard applies only to the "Extending the Social Studies Learning . . ." portion of the activity.

CONTINUED ▶

Activities Listed by Common Core Standards

Standard	Component	Title
SL.1.4 Describe people, places, things, and events with relevant details, expressing ideas and feelings clearly.	Greeting/Sharing Sharing Sharing Sharing Group Activity Morning Message Themed Meeting	Super Citizen Sharing, p. 37 Fairness First, p. 38 Family Flags, p. 39 Whose Favorite Place?, p. 42 Human Calendar, p. 44 Picture History, p. 52 Constitution Convention, pp. 156–157
SL.1.5 Add drawings or other visual displays to descriptions when appropriate to clarify ideas, thoughts, and feelings.	Greeting Sharing Sharing Group Activity Group Activity Morning Message Morning Message	Musical Meet and Greet,* p. 36 Family Flags, p. 39 Whose Favorite Place?,* p. 42 Everyone Has Needs and Wants, p. 43 U.S. Symbol Refrain, p. 48 Attention, Mapmakers!, p. 49 Invention Convention,* p. 50
SL.1.6 Produce complete sentences when appropriate to task and situation.	Greeting Greeting	Jobs of the Future, p. 35 Musical Meet and Greet, p. 36
L.1.5 With guidance and support from adults, demonstrate understanding of word relationships and nuances in word meanings.	Group Activity Group Activity Group Activity Group Activity	Everyone Has Needs and Wants, p. 43 Landform Match, p. 45 North, East, South, West, p. 46 Our Leaders Song, p. 47

* Standard applies only to the "Extending the Social Studies Learning . . ." portion of the activity.

Activities Listed by Common Core Standards

Standard	Component	Title
W.2.1 Write opinion pieces in which they introduce the topic or book they are writing about, state an opinion, supply reasons that support the opinion, use linking words (e.g., because, and, also), and provide a concluding statement or section.	Sharing	If I Were Mayor,* p. 60
W.2.2 Write informative/explanatory texts in which they introduce a topic, use facts and definitions to develop points, and provide a concluding statement or section.	Greeting/Sharing Greeting/Sharing Group Activity Morning Message	Bread, Meet Baker!,* p. 57 People of Interest,* p. 58 Black History Month,* p. 63 School Tools Long Ago, p. 74
W.2.6 With guidance and support from adults, use a variety of digital tools to produce and publish writing, including in collaboration with peers.	Sharing Sharing Morning Message	Explore Galore,* p. 59 What's Your Animal?,* p. 61 Country Commonalities,* p. 72
W.2.8 Recall information from experiences or gather information from provided sources to answer a question.	Group Activity	We Wonder . . . , p. 69
SL.2.1 Participate in collaborative conversations with diverse partners about grade 2 topics and texts with peers and adults in small and larger groups.	Greeting Greeting Greeting Greeting/Sharing Sharing Sharing Sharing/Group Activity Group Activity Group Activity Group Activity Morning Message Morning Message Morning Message Themed Meeting Themed Meeting Themed Meeting	Body of Water Greeting, p. 54 Global Good Mornings, p. 55 State Postcard Puzzles, p. 56 Bread, Meet Baker!, p. 57 Explore Galore, p. 59 What's Your Animal?, p. 61 Cooperation Call-Out, p. 62 Black History Month, p. 63 National Symbols Loop Cards, p. 68 We Wonder . . . , p. 69 Classroom Grid, p. 70 History by the Numbers, p. 73 School Tools Long Ago, p. 74 Constitution Convention, pp. 156–157 Money, Money, Money, pp. 162–163 Practicing Peace, pp. 158–159
SL.2.2 Recount or describe key ideas or details from a text read aloud or information presented orally or through other media.	Greeting/Sharing Group Activity Morning Message Morning Message	People of Interest, p. 58 Eyes-Closed True or False, p. 65 Climate Conversation, p. 71 Country Commonalities, p. 72

* Standard applies only to the "Extending the Social Studies Learning . . ." portion of the activity.

CONTINUED ▶

Standard	Component	Title
SL.2.3 Ask and answer questions about what a speaker says in order to clarify comprehension, gather additional information, or deepen understanding of a topic or issue.	Group Activity Group Activity Group Activity	Community Worker Riddles, p. 64 Fidget Family Back Then, pp. 66–67 National Symbols Loop Cards, p. 68
SL.2.6 Produce complete sentences when appropriate to task and situation in order to provide requested detail or clarification.	Sharing	If I Were Mayor, p. 60

Activities Listed by Common Core Standards

Standard	Component	Title
RI.3.2 Determine the main idea of a text; recount the key details and explain how they support the main idea.	Sharing	Community News Desk, p. 80
RI.3.3 Describe the relationship between a series of historical events, scientific ideas or concepts, or steps in technical procedures in a text, using language that pertains to time, sequence, and cause/effect.	Group Activity	Ellis Island Timeline, p. 85
RI.3.7 Use information gained from illustrations (e.g., maps, photographs) and the words in a text to demonstrate understanding of the text (e.g., where, when, why, and how key events occur).	Morning Message	Use the Map, p. 94
W.3.2 Write informative/explanatory texts to examine a topic and convey ideas and information clearly.	Greeting Greeting Sharing	Around the World,* p. 76 Beach Ball Review,* p. 77 Community News Desk,* p. 80
W.3.3 Write narratives to develop real or imagined experiences or events using effective technique, descriptive details, and clear event sequences.	Group Activity	Ellis Island Timeline,* p. 85
W.3.6 With guidance and support from adults, use technology to produce and publish writing (using keyboarding skills) as well as to interact and collaborate with others.	Group Activity	History Wordsmiths,* p. 87
W.3.8 Recall information from experiences or gather information from print and digital sources; take brief notes on sources and sort evidence into provided categories.	Morning Message	ABCs of History, p. 91

* Standard applies only to the "Extending the Social Studies Learning . . ." portion of the activity.

CONTINUED ▶

Standard	Component	Title
SL.3.1 Engage effectively in a range of collaborative discussions (one-one-one, in groups, and teacher-led) with diverse partners on grade 3 topics and texts, building on others' ideas and expressing their own clearly.	Greeting Greeting Greeting Sharing Sharing Group Activity Group Activity Group Activity Group Activity Morning Message Morning Message Themed Meeting Themed Meeting Themed Meeting	Are You My Capital?, p. 75 Beach Ball Review, p. 77 Needs and Wants, p. 79 Get Out the Vote, p. 81 What's Your Perspective?, p. 82 Citizen Chant, p. 83 Continent Chant, p. 84 Personal Hero Postage Stamps, p. 88 Spend It or Save It?, p. 90 Express Your Thoughts, p. 92 Use the Map, p. 94 Economics Everywhere, pp. 170–171 Me in the World, pp. 164–165 Money, Money, Money, pp. 162–163
SL.3.3 Ask and answer questions about information from a speaker, offering appropriate elaboration and detail.	Group Activity Group Activity	Guess My State!, p. 86 Spend It or Save It?, p. 90
SL.3.4 Report on a topic or text, tell a story, or recount an experience with appropriate facts and relevant, descriptive details, speaking clearly at an understandable pace.	Greeting Sharing Group Activity	Around the World, p. 76 Community News Desk, p. 80 Guess My State!,* p. 86
SL.3.6 Speak in complete sentences when appropriate to task and situation in order to provide requested detail or clarification.	Sharing Sharing Group Activity Morning Message Themed Meeting	Get Out the Vote, p. 81 What's Your Perspective?, p. 82 Pin the Capital, p. 89 Tell Me More, p. 93 Celebrating Women's History, pp. 166–167
L.3.6 Acquire and use accurately grade-appropriate conversational, general academic, and domain-specific words and phrases, including those that signal spatial and temporal relationships (e.g., After dinner that night we went looking for them).	Greeting Greeting Group Activity Group Activity	Beach Ball Review, p. 77 Latitude and Longitude, p. 78 History Wordsmiths, p. 87 Pin the Capital, p. 89

* Standard applies only to the "Extending the Social Studies Learning . . ." portion of the activity.

4 Activities Listed by Common Core Standards

Standard	Component	Title
RI.4.3 Explain events, procedures, ideas, or concepts in a historical, scientific, or technical text, including what happened and why, based on specific information in the text.	Themed Meeting	Constitution Day, pp. 168–169
RI.4.10 By the end of year, read and comprehend informational texts, including history/social studies, science, and technical texts, in the grades 4–5 text complexity band proficiently, with scaffolding as needed at the high end of the range.	Group Activity	Loyalist and Patriot Song, p. 106
W.4.2 Write informative/explanatory texts to examine a topic and convey ideas and information clearly.	Sharing	Scientifically Speaking,* p. 101
W.4.7 Conduct short research projects that build knowledge through investigation of different aspects of a topic.	Sharing	Compare and Contrast,* p. 99
SL.4.1 Engage effectively in a range of collaborative discussions (one-on-one, in groups, and teacher-led) with diverse partners on grade 4 topics and texts, building on others' ideas and expressing their own clearly.	Greeting Greeting Greeting Greeting/Sharing Sharing Sharing Sharing Sharing/Group Activity Group Activity Group Activity Group Activity Group Activity Group Activity Group Activity Morning Message Morning Message Morning Message Morning Message Morning Message Themed Meeting Themed Meeting Themed Meeting Themed Meeting	Cardinal Directions, p. 95 Institutional Greeting, p. 96 Landform Greeting, p. 97 Musical Questions, p. 98 Compare and Contrast, p. 99 Culture Brainstorm, p. 100 Scientifically Speaking, p. 101 Landform Chatter, p. 102 Economic Minds, p. 103 History Mystery, p. 104 Human Compass, p. 105 Made in Our State!, p. 107 Two Facts and a Falsehood, p. 108 We're All in This Together, p. 109 At Your Service, p. 110 Exploring Our Natural Resources, p. 111 My Favorite Scientist, p. 112 One Big World, p. 113 Time Travel, p. 114 Constitution Day, pp. 168–169 Economics Everywhere, pp. 170–171 Me in the World, pp. 164–165 The Olympic Games, p. 172–173

* Standard applies only to the "Extending the Social Studies Learning . . ." portion of the activity.

CONTINUED ▶

Standard	Component	Title
SL.4.4 Report on a topic or text, tell a story, or recount an experience in an organized manner, using appropriate facts and relevant, descriptive details to support main ideas or themes; speak clearly at an understandable pace.	Sharing/Group Activity Themed Meeting	Landform Chatter,* p. 102 Celebrating Women's History, pp. 166–167

* Standard applies only to the "Extending the Social Studies Learning . . ." portion of the activity.

Activities Listed by Common Core Standards

Standard	Component	Title
RI.5.3 Explain the relationships or interactions between two or more individuals, events, ideas, or concepts in a historical, scientific, or technical text based on specific information in the text.	Themed Meeting	Constitution Day, pp. 168–169
W.5.1 Write opinion pieces on topics or texts, supporting a point of view with reasons and information.	Greeting/Sharing Sharing	The Justices Speak,* p. 117 Identity Influencers,* p. 121
W.5.2 Write informative/explanatory texts to examine a topic and convey ideas and information clearly.	Morning Message	Historical Headlines,* p. 131
W.5.4 Produce clear and coherent writing in which the development and organization are appropriate to task, purpose, and audience.	Greeting/Sharing Sharing Group Activity	They Should Pass a Law!,* p. 118 The Common Good,* p. 122 Historical Charades,* p. 125
W.5.7 Conduct short research projects that use several sources to build knowledge through investigation of different aspects of a topic.	Group Activity	The Extraordinary Ordinary,* p. 128
SL.5.1 Engage effectively in a range of collaborative discussions (one-on-one, in groups, and teacher-led) with diverse partners on grade 5 topics and texts, building on others' ideas and expressing their own clearly.	Greeting Greeting Greeting/Sharing Greeting/Sharing Sharing Sharing Sharing Sharing Group Activity Group Activity Group Activity Group Activity Group Activity Group Activity Morning Message Morning Message Morning Message Morning Message Morning Message Morning Message Themed Meeting	Branching Out, p. 115 Geographical Connections, p. 116 The Justices Speak, p. 117 They Should Pass a Law!, p. 118 Build a Better Institution, p. 119 Economic Effects, p. 120 Identity Influencers, p. 121 The Common Good, p. 122 A Traveler's Guide to World Climates, p. 123 Give Me an Ideal Clue!, p. 124 Historical Charades, p. 125 Service Providers Then and Now, p. 126 Technology Mind Map, p. 127 The Extraordinary Ordinary, p. 128 Civilization Survival Bag, p. 129 Econo-Me-Too!, p. 130 Historical Headlines, p. 131 Protecting the Earth, p. 132 Texting the President, p. 133 Word Travelers, p. 134 Celebrating Women's History, pp. 166–167

* Standard applies only to the "Extending the Social Studies Learning . . ." portion of the activity.

CONTINUED ▶

Standard	Component	Title
SL.5.1 (continued)	Themed Meeting Themed Meeting Themed Meeting Themed Meeting	Constitution Day, pp. 168–169 Economics Everywhere, pp. 170–171 The Olympic Games, pp. 172–173 The Right to Vote, pp. 174–175
SL.5.5 Include multimedia components (e.g., graphics, sound) and visual displays in presentations when appropriate to enhance the development of main ideas or themes.	Greeting	Branching Out,* p. 115

* Standard applies only to the "Extending the Social Studies Learning . . ." portion of the activity.

Standard	Component	Title
W.6.2 Write informative/explanatory texts to examine a topic and convey ideas, concepts, and information through the selection, organization, and analysis of relevant content.	Morning Message	#LearningAboutLaws, p. 152
W.6.3 Write narratives to develop real or imagined experiences or events using effective technique, relevant descriptive details, and well-structured event sequences.	Morning Message Morning Message	Back in Time,* p. 149 Writing History,* p. 154
W.6.4 Produce clear and coherent writing in which the development, organization, and style are appropriate to task, purpose, and audience.	Greeting/Sharing	Words of Wisdom,* p. 138
SL.6.1 Engage effectively in a range of collaborative discussions (one-on-one, in groups, and teacher-led) with diverse partners on grade 6 topics, texts, and issues, building on others' ideas and expressing their own clearly.	Greeting Greeting/Sharing Greeting/Sharing Sharing Sharing Sharing Group Activity Group Activity Group Activity Group Activity Group Activity Morning Message Morning Message Morning Message Morning Message Morning Message Themed Meeting Themed Meeting Themed Meeting Themed Meeting	Guess the President, p. 135 Economic Connections, p. 136 What's the Positive News?, p. 137 Cause and Effect, p. 139 Vantage Point, p. 142 Whose Expedition?, p. 143 Adding to the Answer, p. 144 Document Drill, p. 145 Economic Brainstorm, p. 146 Human Timeline, p. 147 Pop-Up Countries, p. 148 Back in Time, p. 149 By the People, p. 150 Cultural Intrigue, p. 151 #LearningAboutLaws, p. 152 Making Connections, p. 153 Celebrating Women's History, pp. 166–167 Constitution Day, pp. 168–169 Economics Everywhere, pp. 170–171 The Right to Vote, pp. 174–175
SL.6.2 Interpret information presented in diverse media and formats (e.g., visually, quantitatively, orally) and explain how it contributes to a topic, text, or issue under study.	Greeting/Sharing	Words of Wisdom, p. 138
SL.6.3 Delineate a speaker's argument and specific claims, distinguishing claims that are supported by reasons and evidence from claims that are not.	Sharing	Fact or Opinion?, p. 140

* Standard applies only to the "Extending the Social Studies Learning . . ." portion of the activity.

CONTINUED ▶

6 Activities Listed by Common Core Standards

Standard	Component	Title
SL.6.4 Present claims and findings, sequencing ideas logically and using pertinent descriptions, facts, and details to accentuate main ideas or themes; use appropriate eye contact, adequate volume, and clear pronunciation.	Sharing Sharing Sharing Group Activity Morning Message Morning Message Themed Meeting	Cause and Effect, p. 139 Government Gab, p. 141 Vantage Point, p. 142 Adding to the Answer, p. 144 Making Connections, p. 153 Writing History, p. 154 The Right to Vote, pp. 174–175
L.6.5 Demonstrate understanding of figurative language, word relationships, and nuances in word meanings.	Greeting/Sharing	Words of Wisdom, p. 138
RH.6–8.2 Determine the central ideas or information of a primary or secondary source; provide an accurate summary of the source distinct from prior knowledge or opinions.	Themed Meeting	Constitution Day, pp. 168–169
RH.6–8.7 Integrate visual information (e.g., in charts, graphs, photographs, videos, or maps) with other information in print and digital texts.	Sharing	Government Gab,* p. 141
RH.6–8.8 Distinguish among fact, opinion, and reasoned judgment in a text.	Sharing	Fact or Opinion?,* p. 140
WHST.6–8.2 Write informative/explanatory texts, including the narration of historical events, scientific procedures/experiments, or technical processes.	Greeting Greeting/Sharing Sharing Morning Message	Guess the President,* p. 135 Economic Connections,* p. 136 Cause and Effect,* p. 139 Cultural Intrigue,* p. 151
WHST.6–8.4 Produce clear and coherent writing in which the development, organization, and style are appropriate to task, purpose, and audience.	Sharing	Whose Expedition?,* p. 143
WHST.6–8.7 Conduct short research projects to answer a question (including a self-generated question), drawing on several sources and generating additional related, focused questions that allow for multiple avenues of exploration.	Group Activity	Document Drill,* p. 145

* Standard applies only to the "Extending the Social Studies Learning . . ." portion of the activity.

Index of Activities

Selected Children's Books
That Support Social Studies Learning

Grades K–1

Civics

Clothesline Clues to Jobs People Do by Kathryn Heling and Deborah Hembrook, illustrated by Andy Robert Davies

F Is for Flag by Wendy Cheyette Lewison, illustrated by Barbara Duke

Last Stop on Market Street by Matt de la Peña, illustrated by Christian Robinson

On the Town: A Community Adventure by Judith Caseley

We the Kids: The Preamble to the Constitution of the United States of America by David Catrow

What if Everybody Did That? by Ellen Javernick, illustrated by Colleen M. Madden

Economics

Alexander, Who Used to Be Rich Last Sunday by Judith Viorst, illustrated by Ray Cruz

One Cent, Two Cents, Old Cent, New Cent: All About Money by Bonnie Worth, illustrated by Aristides Ruiz and Joe Mathieu

Geography

A Day in India by Jonathan and Angela Scott

Mapping Penny's World by Loreen Leedy

Me on the Map by Joan Sweeney, illustrated by Annette Cable

My Map Book by Sara Fanelli

History

Amelia Earhart (Little People, Big Dreams) by Ma Isabel Sánchez Vegara, illustrated by Mariadiamantes

Martin's Big Words: The Life of Dr. Martin Luther King, Jr. by Doreen Rappaport, illustrated by Bryan Collier

Off to Plymouth Rock! by Dandi Daley Mackall, illustrated by Gene Barretta

You Forgot Your Skirt, Amelia Bloomer! by Shana Corey, illustrated by Chesley McLaren

Grades 2–3

Civics

Be My Neighbor by Maya Ajmera and John D. Ivanko

Chang's Paper Pony by Eleanor Coerr, illustrated by Deborah Kogan Ray

City Green by DyAnne DiSalvo-Ryan

Grace for President by Kelly DiPucchio, illustrated by LeUyen Pham

How Full is Your Bucket? For Kids by Tom Rath and Mary Reckmeyer, illustrated by Maurie J. Manning

If I Ran for President by Catherine Stier, illustrated by Lynne Avril

Officer Buckle and Gloria by Peggy Rathmann

O, Say Can You See: America's Symbols, Landmarks, and Inspiring Words by Sheila Keenan, illustrated by Ann Boyajian

The Flag We Love by Pam Muñoz Ryan, illustrated by Ralph Masiello

Economics

A Chair for My Mother by Vera B. Williams

Erandi's Braids by Antonio Hernández Madrigal, illustrated by Tomie dePaola

How to Make an Apple Pie and See the World by Marjorie Priceman

Lily Learns About Wants and Needs by Lisa Bullard, illustrated by Christine M. Schneider

Pigs Will Be Pigs: Fun With Math and Money by Amy Axelrod, illustrated by Sharon McGinley-Nally

The Runaway Wok by Ying Chang Compestine, illustrated by Sebastià Serra

Geography

Everybody Cooks Rice by Norah Dooley, illustrated by Peter J. Thornton

If You Lived Here: Houses of the World by Giles Laroche

On the Same Day in March: A Tour of the World's Weather by Marilyn Singer, illustrated by Frane Lessac

Somewhere in the World Right Now by Stacey Schuett

This is New York by Miroslav Sasek

Weslandia by Paul Fleischman, illustrated by Kevin Hawkes

History

Abe Lincoln: The Boy Who Loved Books by Kay Winters, illustrated by Nancy Carpenter

Coming to America: The Story of Immigration by Betsy Maestro, illustrated by Susannah Ryan

Elizabeth Leads the Way: Elizabeth Cady Stanton and the Right to Vote by Tanya Lee Stone, illustrated by Rebecca Gibbon

Henry's Freedom Box: A True Story From the Underground Railroad by Ellen Levine, illustrated by Kadir Nelson

A Taste of Freedom: Gandhi and the Great Salt March by Elizabeth Cody Kimmel, illustrated by Giuliano Ferri

The U.S. Constitution (American Symbols) by Norman Pearl, illustrated by Matthew Skeens

Grades 4–6

Civics

If I Were President by Catherine Stier, illustrated by DyAnne DiSalvo-Ryan

Economics

The Story of Salt by Mark Kurlansky, illustrated by S. D. Schindler

Uncle Jed's Barbershop by Margaree King Mitchell, illustrated by James Ransome

Geography

If the World Were a Village: A Book About the World's People by David J. Smith, illustrated by Shelagh Armstrong

The Scrambled States of America by Laurie Keller

History

Blood on the River: James Town 1607 by Elisa Carbone

Encounter by Jane Yolen, illustrated by David Shannon

Motel of the Mysteries by David Macaulay

Roanoke, The Lost Colony: An Unsolved Mystery From History by Jane Yolen and Heidi Elisabet Yolen Stemple, illustrated by Roger Roth

Shades of Gray by Carolyn Reeder

Unspoken: A Story From the Underground Railroad by Henry Cole

All the activities in this book are consistent with the *Responsive Classroom* approach to education, in which Morning Meeting is a key practice. To learn more about Morning Meeting and other key *Responsive Classroom* practices, see the following selected resources published by Center for Responsive Schools and available at www.responsiveclassroom.org.

The Morning Meeting Book, 3rd ed., by Roxann Kriete and Carol Davis. 2014.

Doing Math in Morning Meeting: 150 Quick Activities That Connect to Your Curriculum by Andy Dousis and Margaret Berry Wilson. 2010.

Doing Science in Morning Meeting: 150 Quick Activities That Connect to Your Curriculum by Lara Webb and Margaret Berry Wilson. 2013.

Doing Language Arts in Morning Meeting: 150 Quick Activities That Connect to Your Curriculum by Jodie Luongo, Joan Riordan, and Kate Umstatter. 2015.

80 Morning Meeting Ideas for Grades K–2 by Susan Lattanzi Roser. 2012.

80 Morning Meeting Ideas for Grades 3–6 by Carol Davis. 2012.

99 Activities and Greetings: Great for Morning Meeting . . . and Other Meetings, Too! by Melissa Correa-Connolly. 2004.

The Joyful Classroom: Practical Ways to Engage and Challenge Elementary Students. From *Responsive Classroom* with Lynn Bechtel and Kristen Vincent. 2016.

Energizers! 88 Quick Movement Activities That Refresh and Refocus by Susan Lattanzi Roser. 2009.

The Power of Our Words: Teacher Language That Helps Children Learn, 2nd ed., by Paula Denton, EdD. 2014.

The Language of Learning: Teaching Students Core Thinking, Listening, and Speaking Skills by Margaret Berry Wilson. 2014.

Interactive Modeling: A Powerful Technique for Teaching Children by Margaret Berry Wilson. 2012.

Closing Circles: 50 Activities for Ending the Day in a Positive Way by Dana Januszka and Kristen Vincent. 2012.

Acknowledgments

The inspiration for this book comes from the incredible children of Greenbrook Elementary School. As a teacher, I have delivered many lessons over the years, but the most important lessons have come from my students. They have taught me that the greatest rewards come from perseverance, collaboration, and hard work. Much gratitude goes to my co-author, Jane. Her knowledge of children and social studies continually impresses me. Thank you to my family and friends for your time, support, and patience as you listened to my endless talk of Morning Meeting and social studies! Finally, thank you to Dan and Ella for bringing me laughter and happiness every day.

—Leah Carson

A sincere thank you to all my students past and present who have helped me grow as a teacher and have inspired me to keep on growing, learning, and teaching. Thanks to my colleagues at Garfield Elementary who helped cultivate my love for social studies and my passion for *Responsive Classroom*, and who are always willing to share their ideas and their expertise. A special thank you to my co-author, Leah, who was supportive and encouraging throughout the entire project. A big thank you to my family: my parents, Josey, Jeraldine, Joann, Charles, and Donnett who continually encourage me to keep on growing.

—Jane Cofie

The authors would also like to thank manuscript readers Grace Halsey, Becky Hutto, Andy Moral, and Carolyn Rottman for their valuable suggestions and feedback. Thanks to the team at Center for Responsive Schools—Lynn Bechtel, Jim Brissette, Cathy Hess, Heather Kamins, Helen Merena, Elizabeth Nash, and Sera Rivers—for their patience and support through the whole process.

About the Authors

Leah Carson started her career as a second-grade public school teacher sixteen years ago. Since then, she has taught students in kindergarten through fourth grade as both a classroom teacher and a special educator. Leah has been a proud *Responsive Classroom* consulting teacher for over ten years. Currently, Leah lives and works in South Brunswick, New Jersey. When she is not in the classroom, you can find her walking in the park, cooking, or reading.

Jane Cofie began her journey as an educator working with preschool children over twenty years ago, and since then she has taught pre-K through fifth grade. She is currently a curriculum and instructional designer at Center for Responsive Schools. Jane enjoys spending time reading, doing make-overs, and dancing with her daughter, Sierra Rose.

About the Publisher

Center for Responsive Schools, Inc., a not-for-profit educational organization, offers professional development, curriculum, and books and resources to support academic, social, and emotional learning.

Center for Responsive Schools (CRS) is the developer of *Responsive Classroom®*, a research-based education approach associated with greater teacher effectiveness, higher student achievement, and improved school climate, and of Fly Five, a comprehensive social-emotional learning curriculum for kindergarten through eighth grade.

CRS Publishing, the independent publishing arm of Center for Responsive Schools, creates inspiring yet practical books for educators and students to support growth, learning, and success in and out of school.

Center for Responsive Schools' vision is to influence and inspire a world-class education for every student in every school, every day, and to bring hope and joy to educators and students alike. Visit us at crslearn.org to learn more:

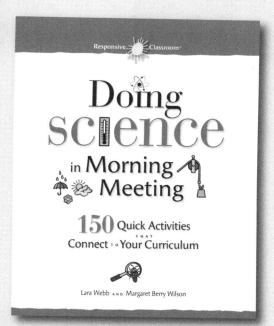

The Complete Series

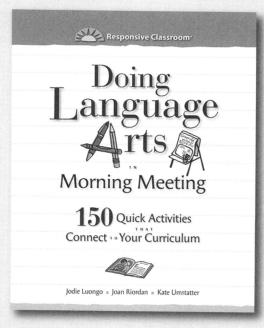

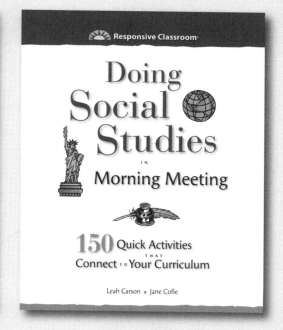